Black for a Day

Black for a Day

White Fantasies of Race and Empathy

Alisha Gaines

The University of North Carolina Press CHAPEL HILL

This book was published with the assistance of the John Hope Franklin Fund of the University of North Carolina Press.

The University of North Carolina Press has been a member of the Green Press Initiative since 2003.

Library of Congress Cataloging-in-Publication Data
Names: Gaines, Alisha, author.
Title: Black for a day : white fantasies of race and empathy / Alisha Gaines.
Description: Chapel Hill : University of North Carolina Press, [2017] |
    Includes bibliographical references and index.
Identifiers: LCCN 2016046558 | ISBN 9781469632827 (cloth : alk. paper) |
ISBN 9781469632834 (pbk : alk. paper) | ISBN 9781469632841 (ebook)
Subjects: LCSH: United States—Race relations—History—20th century. |
    Passing (Identity)—United States—History—20th century. |
    Impersonation. | Empathy—Political aspects. | African Americans—Social
    conditions—20th century.
Classification: LCC E185.625 .G35 2017 | DDC 305.800973—dc23
    LC record available at https://lccn.loc.gov/2016046558

Cover illustration: © iStockphoto.com/Abel Mitja Varela

Portions of chapter 3 were originally published as "A Secondhand Kind of Terror," in *From Uncle Tom's Cabin to The Help: Critical Perspectives on White-Authored Narratives of Black Life*, edited by Claire Oberon Garcia, Vershawn Ashanti Young, and Charise Pimentel (Palgrave Macmillan, 2014). Reproduced with permission of Palgrave Macmillan.

In Memory of
Gail Booker Peterson and Jurina Vincent-Lee

Contents

Illustrations

Acknowledgments

Beyond family, my first love was Michael Jackson. My love for his artistry, and more important, his compelling and complicated performances of identity are the most nascent ideas for this book.

Before attending Spelman College, I never had a teacher of color. My undergraduate teachers and mentors, Shirley Toland, Cynthia Spence, and Donna Akiba Sullivan Harper, embodied the kinds of teachers I never had but still aspire to be. I will never lose the urge to call them Dr. Toland, Dean Spence, and Dr. Harper.

My research has been sustained by funding from a number of institutions, including the Mellon Foundation, Duke University, the Social Science Research Council, the Carter G. Woodson Institute at the University of Virginia, the Florida State University Council on Research and Creativity, the Florida Education Fund, and the Florida State University College of Arts and Sciences. I would be remiss if I did not mention the helpful librarians and staff who curate the Grace Halsell Papers at Texas Christian University and the John Howard Griffin Papers at the Rare Book and Manuscript Library at Columbia University.

During my first year as a graduate student at Duke University, then visiting professor Leigh Raiford encouraged my work even as I suffered impostor syndrome. Sean Metzger always asked the right and most productive questions. Wahneema Lubiano, academia's most insightful reader, modeled what compassionate, constructive criticism looks like and assuaged my anxiety days before my preliminary exams. To this day, Mark Anthony Neal encourages my work, introduces me to the wealth of his extensive professional network, and reminds me to write from my gut. Maurice Wallace taught me the most about how to be a good academic, mentor, and teacher. Maurice's work is the model for my own, and I often write with him in mind.

The 2009–2011 Woodson Fellowship leaders, Deborah E. McDowell and Marlon Ross, made my work infinitely better with their encouraging and rigorous workshops. The communities enabled by the Mellon Mays Undergraduate Fellowship, the Institute for the Recruitment of Teachers, Duke University, and the Woodson Institute brought an amazing group of people into my life. Ultimately, I would not have become the scholar I am without the friendship, support, and scholarly examples of Fiona Barnett, andré carrington, Ashon Crawley, Jonathan Fenderson, Alexis Pauline Gumbs, Cassie Hays, Nicole Ivy, Birgitta Johnson, Jessica Marie Johnson, Alwin Jones, Treva Lindsey, Courtney Marshall, Anoop Mirpuri, Vin Nardizzi, Kinohi Nishikawa, LaKisha Simmons, Elizabeth Todd-Breland, and John Thabiti Willis. Uri McMillan demonstrated generosity when that is not often valued in our profession. I navigated graduate school by first living with and then being inspired by the brilliance of Britt Rusert. In Dennis Tyler, I found a writing accountability buddy, dance instructor, and favorite co-producer.

In many ways, this midwestern girl, born and raised in the LeBron James corridor of northeast Ohio, grew up during her years as a graduate student in Durham, North Carolina. There I learned how to suture teaching and research to activism. I also learned that family is not just biological but also chosen. In Durham, I met my chosen sisters: Naomi Jean-Baptiste and TaShonda Vincent-Lee.

My colleagues at Florida State University and the larger community of Tallahassee have been largely welcoming and supportive. Although I cannot name them all, and some have moved on to other universities, I would like to acknowledge those who have mentored me and commented on or read portions of this manuscript. They include Ralph Berry, Jennine Capó Crucet, Leigh H. Edwards, Andrew Epstein, Barry Faulk, Robin Goodman, Tarez Graban, David Ikard, John Mac Kilgore, Jimmy Kimbrell, Trinyan Paulsen Mariano, Jerrilyn McGregory, Richard Mizelle, Maxine Montgomery, James O'Rourke, Laura Osteen, Timothy Parrish, John Ribo, Robert Stilling, Ned Stuckey-French, Candace Ward, and Nia Witherspoon. I owe particular gratitude to Eric Walker, who has continuously supported my research and teaching. When I first came to FSU, Dennis Moore greeted me with a bottle of tupelo honey, introduced me to (arguably) the best pizza in Tallahassee, and has since been a devout champion of my work and a wonderful mentor. As Rhea Estelle Lathan met her tenure track benchmarks, she always reminded me: "Don't worry, *I'll* be there when you get to this stage." And, before she left for an even sunnier Florida, Jenn Wells was my consummate cruise director; I am thankful to still be able to count on her friendship.

The students in my "Race and Empathy" courses and the U.S. Literature Discussion Group helped further my thinking on race, empathy, and performance. Likewise, graduate students, including Janelle Jennings Alexander, Joshua Burnett, Jessica Cohen, Amber Cresgy, Yolanda J. Franklin,

CJ Hauser, Sakinah Hofler, Jenise Hudson, Kenneth Johnson, Lakey, Ramsey Mathews, Kendra Mitchell, Janeen Price, Jodi Price, Esther Spencer, and Cocoa Williams, pushed my research in productive ways.

This book has been shepherded by the guidance of the University of North Carolina Press. I owe many thanks to the anonymous readers who took my ideas seriously and made them so much better. Mark Simpson-Vos first saw this manuscript's value. Ultimately, my editor, Lucas Church, crafted my ideas into an actual book while also patiently answering my questions.

I would be remiss without recognizing the stability and support of Tracey Morse, who patiently taught me what self-care means.

I am blessed to have family who successfully manage academic life. My aunt, Penny Von Eschen, models how to lovingly balance family and career. My uncle, Kevin Gaines, first demonstrated what being a blackademic meant. He wrote aspirational scholarship, introduced me to his colleagues, read and graciously critiqued my work, and answered all my questions about the professoriate. I hope he is proud of this book.

The rest of my family deserves many thanks in making this book possible. Nicole Bishop, Ashley Gaines, Bradley Gaines, Terence Gaines, Adam and Breyan Haizlip, Acacia Hendricks, Jack and Donna Milhollan, Noah Peterson, Phillip Sales, and Jason Thoms all loved and encouraged me. My sister, Allison Johnson, cheered me on, and always, in the most needed moments, told me: "Lee, you got this." My mother, Karen Sales, is the heart and soul of this project. She never doubts me—even when I doubt me. My grandmother has always been my biggest cheerleader; she is the one who inspires me to teach and write at all. Together, "Mootie" and "Grammie" make impossible things possible.

While writing this book, two important people in my family transitioned from this life to the next. Facing their too-close-together deaths made me want to quit; however, their collective spirit told me to keep going. So, to Jurina and Auntie Gail—thank you for refusing to accept my resignation.

And finally, to Erika Thoms, thank you for knowing the right things to say and when to say them. Thank you for knowing how to love me. Thank you for always wanting to see and change the world with me. You are my best thing.

Black for a Day

Introduction
Once You Go Black

"Am I black yet?" I didn't answer. I wasn't finished smearing the paint on Joe's face. Onstage, the rest of the cast stalled. Their ad-libs were well rehearsed. We had learned that turning someone black takes time. "Alisha, hurry up!" the stage manager frantically whispered, "and don't forget his ears this time!"

We only had a few moments to change Joe from white Senator Billboard Rawkins to his black, cursed alter ego during my high school's 1996 revival of the musical *Finian's Rainbow*. Our director chose three of us to engineer Joe's blackness. One of us darkened Joe's right hand, another his left, and I was in charge of his face. We had practiced the timing of this pivotal scene for weeks; I understood the grave magnitude of this responsibility. Joe's new black face had to be even, and most important, I couldn't forget his ears again.

The black paint covered my hands, mixing with the anxious sweat on my palms. I gave Joe one more pass with the cosmetic sponge to assure even coverage. The paint stained across the roots of his blond hair, but I knew no one would be able to see that from the audience. "I'm done!" I whispered. Right on cue, Joe reentered the stage. I listened for what I knew would come next: the shocked and delighted laughter of the audience.

I was a ninth-grader at a private, Christian school in northeast Ohio, and one of only a few black students among the 700-plus kids milling in its hallways. Attending that too white junior high and high school was an educational gift on one hand and a burdensome tokenism on the other. As both my parents worked multiple jobs so I could avoid the struggling Cleveland public schools they attended, I desperately tried to fit in among the white kids whose parents easily afforded the tuition.

All I wanted was to be in the spring musical, and my parents encouraged me. I worked backstage in the fall play to prove my commitment to the drama department after being told that working backstage would be the catalyst to getting onstage. I was cast in *Finian's Rainbow* in the very brief role of "Gospeleer #2," so I again volunteered to work behind the curtain. Instead of painting sets as I had the semester before, this time I painted Joe.

In " 'I Was a Teenage Negro!': Blackface as a Vehicle of White Liberalism in *Finian's Rainbow*," Russell Peterson details his Sioux Falls junior high school's adaptation of the musical in 1974. However, unlike our production, Peterson's version was mounted without any actual black actors, so the program included a caveat: "Obviously we hope you will enjoy your evening with us, but before the curtain goes up we would like to forewarn you about what you will see."[1] Our program had no such warning, and I was completely unaware of the irony of this blackface moment—even as I stood in the bathroom washing away the much-darker-than-me paint from my streaked hands that had just turned Joe "black." My parents worked to keep me in this private school, and although none of us had the vocabulary of "respectability politics" in 1996, those politics were at work. As a token black family, success meant not making waves and seizing any and all, often problematic, opportunities. Although back then I did not yet understand the meaning of my skin color, I now know that my black hands were the school's alibi against complaints by anyone who might have accused it of racial insensitivity. There were no complaints.

Black for a Day examines narratives, like *Finian's Rainbow*, of temporary, empathetic racial experiments in blackness. My project attempts, in part, to understand my own adolescent culpability in this unsettling spectacle of racial impersonation. That no one, including my own parents, questioned the appropriateness of Joe's "racechange"[2] is telling: evidence of my desire to be a good token black girl, my parents' encouragement of my success in this white space, and our investment in respectability politics. More important, my high school's drama department and governing administration were seduced by the appeal of racial impersonation as theatrically staged, cross-racial empathy. In their logics, Joe's shiny blackness was not racist. It was, puzzlingly, an edgy, instructive, and spectacular critique of the racism and classism routinely and strategically ignored at my conservative high school. At school, we rarely talked about race. When we did, it was clumsy, insensitive, and often constricted to the formulaic dictates of Black History Month. For example, one February, my seventh-grade history teacher called on thirteen-year-old me to explain to my classmates what slavery was really like.

In sum, staging *Finian's Rainbow*, complete with the racist character of Senator Rawkins, allowed our audiences to demonize overt racism at the expense of addressing the daily racial microaggressions students of color like me actually experienced. However awkwardly wrong *Finian's Rainbow* came to be on my high school stage, it exposed racism in ways I could use as a counterpoint to my school's usual silence. "Remember *Finian's Rainbow*?"

White Senator Rawkins, played by actor Keenan Wynn, before being turned black by Sharon McLonergan, played by Petula Clark, in the 1968 film version of *Finian's Rainbow*. Directed by Francis Ford Coppola.

I could later challenge. Like the other empathetic racial impersonations considered in this project, my high school's production of *Finian's Rainbow* reveals profound, uncomfortable, and often contradictory assumptions about the bodies we inhabit and speaks to larger issues of identity—from blackness to authenticity and from affect to performance.

Black Rainbow

Finian's Rainbow opened on January 10, 1947, at Broadway's 46th Street Theater. Written by E. Y. "Yip" Harburg[3] and Fred Saidy, with music by Burton Lane, its libretto takes on the taboos of postwar race and class with absurd satire. *Finian's Rainbow* ran for an impressive 725 performances and would go on to win newly established Tony awards for Best Choreography and Best Performance by a Featured Actor in a Musical in 1947, and Best Conductor and Musical Director in 1948. In 1968, *Finian's Rainbow* became a long-awaited film, directed by Francis Ford Coppola and starring an aging but still lithe Fred Astaire.[4] The musical has been revived on both Broadway and school stages with varying degrees of success; most recently it received a "joyous" and "unexpectedly fresh"[5] 92-show run at Broadway's St. James Theatre in 2009.

The plot of *Finian's Rainbow* is almost impossible to summarize; it is a dizzying combination of didactic satire, fantasy, and political commentary.

The play opens with the title character, Finian McLonergan, and his daughter, Sharon, arriving in Rainbow Valley, Missitucky. As a lovably superstitious Irish immigrant, Finian totes a pot of gold stolen from the leprechaun Og, believing that burying gold in American soil will guarantee wealth. For Finian, America is a new global superpower not because of its postwar industrial boom, spirit of global competition, or commitment to empire building but because Americans bury their money in Fort Knox. In *Finian's Rainbow*, this fertile soil is not in Kentucky but rather in the imaginary southern state of "Missitucky."

The subplots of *Finian's Rainbow* are even more convoluted. Sharon finds immediate love with the other male lead, the guitar-carrying Valley landowner Woody Mahoney;[6] lustful Og becomes increasingly more mortal the longer he is separated from his gold; a black research botanist, Howard, attempts to grow a blend of tobacco and mint that will bankroll the Valley; and Woody's mute and deaf sister, "Susan the Silent," ultimately finds hearing, speech, and love in Og's rapidly disappearing magic. Subplots aside, Rainbow Valley is uniquely notable because of the residents of its racial utopia, an interracial band of sharecroppers who live, dance, and sing together while seeming blissfully unaware of the consequences of Jim Crow segregation.

The sharecroppers in *Finian's Rainbow* only stop singing and dancing when racist Senator Billboard Rawkins finds out McLonergan's gold is buried somewhere in the hills of Rainbow Valley and attempts to seize the land. When the working-class cooperative fights back, Rawkins tries to punish them by evicting the black tenants with a hastily composed writ of seizure. Offended by the senator's racism (and unknowingly standing over the buried pot of gold, which grants mortals three wishes), Sharon angrily curses Rawkins: "There's something wrong with the world he and his kind have made for people like Henry [a young black Rainbow Valley resident]. I wish he could know what that world is like. I wish to God he was black so—!" Sharon's anger is drowned out by the ensuing stage directions, which describe a fantastical provocation: "(*Suddenly there is darkness—a crash of thunder—a streak of lightning. When the lights go up* RAWKINS *is disclosed as a trembling heap on the ground. The people are drawn back, aghast. From their faces it is evident that* SHARON'S *wish has materialized and that the* SENATOR *is now, indeed, a black man.*)"[7]

After shamefully running away, the newly black, now ostracized Rawkins happens on Og in the overgrown foliage of Rainbow Valley and steals an apple from the leprechaun. Between bites, Rawkins confesses to Og that he's been in hiding:

Senator Rawkins, played by Keenan Wynn, catches the first glimpse of his new black face in the 1968 film *Finian's Rainbow*.

OG: What were you hiding from?

RAWKINS: My wife, my people, my friends. You think I want 'em to see me this way?

OG: I see nothing wrong with you.

RAWKINS: You don't? You must be blind. Can't you see I'm black?

OG: Yes, and I think it's very becoming.

RAWKINS: But I'm a white man, dammit, a white man! At least, I was a few weeks ago . . .

OG: You needn't get so excited, mister. I think it's just ridiculous making such a fuss about a person's color.

RAWKINS: You moron! Don't you realize what it means to be black?[8]

Not surprisingly, Og, a mythical creature of the Old World with green skin and vanishing magic, does not know "what it means to be black." But the importance of Rawkins's question was essential to a nation trying to solve the "Negro problem." Although Black History Month celebrates 1947 as the year Jackie Robinson integrated the Brooklyn Dodgers, the previous year witnessed overwhelming examples of racism including the Columbia, Tennessee, race riot and the brutal beating and blinding of World War II veteran Isaac Woodard. The reality of blackness in fictional Missitucky, as in the actual South, was the dehumanizing, oppressive regime of Jim Crow. Rawkins complains: "You can't get into a restaurant. You can't get on a streetcar. You can't buy yourself a cold beer on a hot day. (*With disgust*) You can't even go into a church and pray." When Og rightly asks, "Who says you can't?" Rawkins reminds the naive leprechaun of the law: "Of course [Jim Crow legislation] is legal. I wrote it myself."[9] Politically astute audiences would recognize Rawkins as a satire of the white supremacist politician Theodore G. Bilbo. Bilbo was a two-time Mississippi governor and U.S. senator (1935–1947) famous for denouncing Richard Wright's *Black Boy* on the Senate floor in 1945, virulently opposing desegregation, and advocating the return of black America "back" to Africa. The historical Bilbo is translated onstage through the caricature of Rawkins, a man who ironically has become disenfranchised by his own discriminatory legislation. Importantly, however, while audiences visually witness Rawkins's physical transformation and the sobering truth of his racial testimony, they never actually see him encounter any of the discrimination he so intimately describes.[10]

When Rawkins rebuffs the leprechaun's friendship, Og realizes Sharon's accidental wish has failed to change Rawkins's heart. Worried that the newly black Rawkins is just *"too* unfriendly,"[11] Og supplements Rawkins's black skin with a *Macbeth*-style spell: "Magic vapors, make this person a better person—not a worse 'un," he chants.[12] Under the spell, "RAWKINS *rises and stretches, a smile on his face, like a man emerging from a long sleep. Then he starts to sing a joyous song.*"[13] The "joyous song" is the nineteenth-century blackface minstrel tune "Oh, Dem Golden Slippers,"[14] and it is the first time the audience hears Rawkins sing. With the contrived luck of musical comedy (and the assumed innate musicality of blackness), Rawkins's newly found, resonant baritone is not lost on three black men who are serendipitously having car trouble nearby. They are the Passion Pilgrim Gospeleers, a prize-winning gospel quartet searching for a new member.

After only moments of convincing from the Gospeleers, Billboard nicknames himself "Bill," completes the quartet, and travels with them to their next gig—conveniently, the wedding of the principal romantic characters, Sharon and Woody. Arriving at what should have been a celebration, Rawkins finds that the district attorney has accused Sharon of witchcraft for "demotin' a member of the white race . . . to a member of the Negro race"[15] and has sentenced her to be burned like a Salem witch if she refuses to produce the white-again senator. As death looms over an imprisoned Sharon, elsewhere Finian's desperate plea and Susan the Silent's kiss convince Og that he should use the pot of gold's last wish to turn Rawkins white. (He already used the second wish to grant Susan speech.) "Rawkins you blackguard—I wish you white!"[16] Og declares. As the stage direction indicates, Rawkins "*is now restored to his pristine whiteness.*"[17]

The last few scenes of *Finian's Rainbow* are neatly and unsurprisingly triumphant. The rest of the Valley finds out that Susan the Silent can finally talk after twenty years; Og finds love and human mortality; Howard's tobacco blend proves potentially profitable; and Sharon and Woody get married, thereby making Sharon a U.S. citizen. Only two of Harburg's characters are left unresolved. Finian takes his dashed hopes of soil-grown riches and leaves both Sharon and Rainbow Valley to chase mythical pots of gold at the end of every rainbow. Lastly then, we are left to speculate about how Rawkins's brief blackness might impact Missitucky's future. "I'm with the people," the senator cryptically declares, "and incidentally I'm running for re-election."[18]

In the final scene, the "pristine," rewhitened Rawkins announces his reelection platform: "anti-poll tax, a dam in every valley, and a rainbow in every pot."[19] Such political platitudes are no real assurance to his black constituency that anything will change. They remain as vulnerable to the whims of white supremacy as they did before Rawkins's tar brush with blackness. Ultimately, in order for *Finian's Rainbow* to ignore how race really played out in southern spaces, Missitucky had to be created. This fantastic southern landscape was the only backdrop where Rawkins's transformation could make any sense. Missitucky is a quaintly pastoral, palatable South where the encroachments of Jim Crow can be remedied through a sprite's magic rather than legislation. This rather ambiguous racial future is the climax of *Finian's Rainbow*'s critique of mid-twentieth-century U.S. race relations. Its absurd attempt at a racial critique is the first of our many reminders of how difficult it is for these sincere efforts to achieve cross-racial understanding.

Painted Empathy

The senator's temporary blackness is the very type of empathetic racial impersonation President John F. Kennedy imagines in his landmark 1963 address on civil rights: "If an American, because his skin is dark, cannot eat lunch in a restaurant open to the public, if he cannot send his children to the best public school available, if he cannot vote for the public officials who represent him, if, in short, he cannot enjoy the full and free life which all of us want, then who among us would be content to have the color of his skin changed and stand in his place?"[20] We don't know whether Kennedy was aware of Billboard's forced blackness or, indeed, of Billboard's kin—a small, strange band of blackened impersonators who had already changed their skin to stand in the place of disenfranchisement he describes.

Although Kennedy imagines such individuals as implausible, we, however, will take them seriously. *Black for a Day* constructs a genealogy of temporary black individuals operating under the alibi of racial empathy. Feminist race theorist and cultural critic bell hooks defines empathy as "eating the other." In her essay "Eating the Other: Desire and Resistance," hooks details the relished pleasure in encounters with "the Other." It is an exploitative pleasure she describes as erotic. She writes, "Certainly from the standpoint of white supremacist capitalist patriarchy, the hope is that desires for the 'primitive' or fantasies about the Other can be continually exploited, and that such exploitation will occur in a manner that reinscribes the *status quo*. Whether or not desire for contact with the Other, for connection rooted in the longing for pleasure, can act as a critical intervention challenging and subverting racist domination, inviting and enabling critical resistance, is an unrealized political possibility."[21] She helpfully continues, "To make one's self vulnerable to the seduction of difference, to seek an encounter with the Other, does not require that one relinquish forever one's mainstream positionality."[22] Her definition of empathy and appropriation highlights how empathy fails to bring about systemic or institutional racial change.

In *The Empathy Exams*, Leslie Jamison bolsters hooks when she writes how empathy "comes from the Greek *empatheia*—*em* (into) and *pathos* (feeling)—a penetration, a kind of travel. It suggests you enter another person's pain as you'd enter another country, through immigration and customs, border crossing by way of query: *What grows where you are? What are the laws? What animals graze there?*"[23] She continues, "Empathy is always perched precariously between gift and invasion."[24] Both hooks and Jamison prompt some pertinent questions about empathy and impersonation: How do we know what is gift and what is violence? Are they ever truly separate in the messiness that is race and its consequences? Is the vicarious curiosity of empathetic racial impersonation always only a representational violence? What does true empathy look like? Is empathy ever enough? Ultimately, how can we uncover models of cross-racial empathy in this largely troubling critique of empathetic racial impersonation? For the white impersonators in this genealogy, standing in and for blackness is simultaneously and paradoxically a confounding space of discomfort, pleasure, desire, anxiety, anticipated violence, fame, and care.

President Kennedy explicitly raises the stakes of empathetic racial impersonation by suturing it to the nation's failure to remedy racial inequality. Kennedy's June 11 appeal followed the forced desegregation of the University of Alabama and, in a terrible coincidence, preceded the shocking assassination of Medgar Evers in the early hours of June 12th. Kennedy's bold and emotional rhetoric can be traced to Gunnar Myrdal's overwhelmingly influential sociological text *An American Dilemma: The Negro Problem and Modern Democracy*, published in 1944. Commissioned by the Carnegie Foundation, the research proposal that eventually became *An American Dilemma* called for an ambitious effort, rigorously supported by the most "impeccable" and "objective" social science. The foundation sought an "exceptional man"[25] to head the research team, and after a lengthy search, University of Stockholm professor of Political Economy and Public Finance, member of the Swedish Senate, and eventual Nobel Prize–winning economist Gunnar Myrdal was chosen. Not unlike the racial impersonators we will explore, Myrdal, in accepting the foundation's post, declared that he was eager to "think and dream of the Negro 24 hours a day,"[26] subsequently compiling a massive, two-volume tome complete with 10 appendices and hundreds of pages of footnotes. In it, Myrdal addressed the inconsistencies between the promises of the "American Creed," or U.S. "humanistic liberalism,"[27] and black second-class citizenship. Myrdal writes, "From the point of view of the American Creed the status accorded the Negro in America represents nothing more and nothing less than a century-long lag of public morals. . . . The Negro in America has not yet been given the elemental civil and political rights of formal democracy, including a fair opportunity to earn his living, upon which a general accord was already won when the American Creed was first taking form. And this anachronism constitutes the contemporary 'problem' both to Negroes and to whites."[28] Before Myrdal's intervention, President Franklin Delano Roosevelt's New Deal put relief and recovery nearly exclusively in economic terms.

In the years leading up to World War II, relief policies and programs, from Social Security initiatives and welfare assistance to public-works jobs, spotlighted national attention on class inequities and offered a bit of backhanded help to some African American communities. William H. Chafe reminds us how, during the 1930s, "The system of Jim Crow remained deeply entrenched. Lynchings continued to occur, gruesomely testifying to the degree that physical terrorism reinforced the customs of segregated jobs, schools, and social spaces. More than 75 percent of black Americans lived in the South. Fewer than 5 percent had the right to vote."[29] When the country began the march to war, biological racism, seen as the egregious ideological underpinning of Nazi anti-Semitism, came under both national and international criticism. Coupled with the growing number of African

Americans agitating for equal civil rights and access to eventual wartime prosperity, this criticism forced a shift in cultural understandings of race and racism. Since racial discrimination in the United States made fighting fascism more than awkward, changing America's perceptions on race became a matter of national importance and international public relations. Myrdal continues, "To the great majority of white Americans, the Negro problem has distinctly negative connotations. It suggests something difficult to settle and equally difficult to leave alone. It is embarrassing."[30] After years of research, Myrdal concluded in the introduction to *An American Dilemma* that the solution to the "embarrassing" inconsistency between the country's espoused democratic egalitarianism and the reality of its violent racial past and present, also known as the "Negro problem," was a decidedly "moral issue"[31] resting in the *"heart of the [white] American."* He continues, *"It is there that the interracial tension has its focus. It is there that the decisive struggle goes on. This is the central viewpoint of this treatise."*[32]

Consequently, Myrdal momentously insists that the remedy for the "Negro problem" is both individual and interpersonal,[33] and his conclusion established a new framework for thinking about race relations. Named "the study to end all studies,"[34] *An American Dilemma* was hailed by critics at the *New York Times* and *Life* magazine, along with a number of black intellectuals, including W. E. B. Du Bois, George Schuyler, E. Franklin Frazier, and Horace Cayton. Eventually quoted in the Supreme Court's documents for the 1954 *Brown v. Board of Education* decision as well as providing the concluding line of the introduction to the now infamous 1965 report by Daniel Patrick Moynihan, *An American Dilemma*'s impact cannot be overstated. Even Richard Wright privately admitted he wanted to write "a project that would do for the inner personality, the subjective landscape of the Negro, what Gunnar Myrdal's *An American Dilemma* did for the external, social relations."[35] Ultimately, Myrdal proclaimed that the nation's paradoxical gap between ideal and reality was an issue best solved not through economics and legislation but through conscience, morality, and cross-racial empathy. However, while Myrdal claimed racial equality as the goal, he remained strategically blind to the structural complexities of race and difference. Concluding that the Negro problem was mainly a matter of conscience has been Myrdal's most lasting historical, rhetorical, and discursive legacy—a legacy clearly evident in Kennedy's 1963 speech. This overemphasis on interpersonal, cross-racial empathy inspires the genealogy of racial impersonators considered in this project—to walk in someone else's *skin* rather than in their shoes.

This notion of empathy-enabled equality aided a spate of postwar tolerance narratives like Lillian Smith's 1949 memoir, *Killers of the Dream*, and Laura Z. Hobson's 1947 *New York Times* bestselling novel turned film, *Gentleman's Agreement*.[36] Harburg himself explicitly situates *Finian's Rainbow* in this moment of empathy and tolerance. "Here's a show that was written in 1946," he reflects,

> There had been no such song as "We Shall Overcome." There was no Martin Luther King. There was just a downright lack of civil rights for a minority of people whose skins were black. There were no movements and there were people who felt we should despair about life. Why should there be a thing like racism? It's so idiotic. Volumes and books and lectures and God knows what were written about it; nothing seemed to help. We thought of one way—how could we prick the bubble of this idiocy? How could we reduce all this thing to absurdity? Now you see how one thing usually leads to another—in order to show this folly, I used a dramatic form that will help us laugh this prejudice out of existence—the musical play.[37]

One can assume that at least one of the "volumes . . . written about" racism implicitly references *An American Dilemma*. Despite Harburg's noble effort, *Finian's Rainbow* fails to laugh away prejudice. Rather, it naively sidesteps the real consequences of racism and segregation by portraying the protective cocoon of the improbably integrated Rainbow Valley. Despite this naivety, Miles Jefferson, theater critic for *Phylon*, praised the musical as "an object lesson in race goodwill,"[38] *Finian's* definitive takeaway. *Finian's Rainbow* assumes racism can be undone and outdone by satirical theatrics but fails to provide any meaningful remedies to discrimination. Following the example of *Finian's Rainbow*, the empathetic racial impersonators comprising the following chapters believe racism and segregation can be remedied via good-faith transformations from white to black. However, such racial goodwill has insidious consequences, refusing to admit how race and racism are both structural and institutionalized. As we will see, it is a superficial sentiment undergirding many postwar strategies of cross-racial understanding. Although that conclusion is often an empty and sentimental promise—echoing Rawkins—of "rainbows in every pot," *Black for a Day* critiques that emptiness while still attempting to balance the obvious problems with these experiments with their sometimes surprising potential. The figures and texts under consideration are mostly, but not exclusively, geared toward liberal, white audiences. For example, John Howard Griffin and the reality television show *Black.White.* reveal how empathy can be primed for both white and black audiences.

An Awful Shuffling

Rawkins describes his new black body as an "awful shuffling,"[39] a deeply unsettling racial transformation. Rawkins "shuffles" from a laughable caricature of southern racism to a despondent, newly black man. This shuffling was likely familiar to at least some of the men and women who came to the 46th Street Theater, since postwar audiences already had a visual logic to understand a white man in black makeup—blackface minstrelsy. Knowing that these empathetic racial impersonators learn performative logics about blackness from the long and complicated history of blackface minstrelsy, beginning this genealogy with *Finian's Rainbow* provides the most literal bridge between blackface minstrelsy and empathetic racial experimentation. Both are linked, despite their very different motivations, by a gleeful theatricality. It is no coincidence that Billboard Rawkins would have his racial transformation on a Broadway stage since, as a musical, *Finian's Rainbow* is immediately and intimately tied to the blackface minstrel tradition. It is also no coincidence that Rawkins would join a barbershop quartet after becoming black. Like his minstrel predecessors, Rawkins found his "authentically" black face through song and dance. Rawkins's transformation from a white, racist Missitucky senator to a crooning new black man sutures his temporary blackness to the bizarreness of minstrelsy. However, *Black for a Day* is not just a story about blackface minstrelsy and its legacies. Instead, it is an intervention into those legacies, demonstrating how the visual rhetoric of blackface morphed from the lowest common denominator of American popular culture to a vehicle for cross-racial understanding.

Black for a Day continues with "I Was a Negro in the South for 30 Days," journalist Ray Sprigle's description of the four weeks he traveled throughout the South as a black man named James. His twenty-one–part series was published in the *Pittsburgh Post-Gazette* in 1948. The project then moves to a consideration of John Howard Griffin's experiment as a black man in 1959 for *Sepia* magazine. He then turned those articles into the bestselling 1961 memoir *Black Like Me*, and a film in 1964. *Black for a Day* then turns to Griffin's protégé Grace Halsell and her 1969 memoir, *Soul Sister*. *Black Like Me* inspired Halsell to live as a black woman in Harlem and Mississippi for six months. The fourth chapter of *Black for a Day* takes on the televisual re-scripting of Rawkins, Sprigle, Griffin, and Halsell with a reading of the FX cable series *Black.White.*, a 2006 reality television show where two middle-class families—one black and one white—"switch" races to experience racial difference. Set in Los Angeles, *Black.White.* expands the exploration of racial experimentation beyond the U.S. South. Finally, the epilogue turns to the 2015 viral media story about the former Spokane, Washington, NAACP chapter president Rachel Dolezal and her public "outing" as a white woman. Dolezal troubles the genealogy by complicating the idea of the temporariness of empathetic racial impersonation.

These narratives are seemingly exclusively stories of failure—the failure to acknowledge structural inequalities; the failure to find anticipated racism; the failure to take black women at their word; the failure to "get" twenty-first-century racism; and the failure to admit how blackness can be performed. However, I insist how these overlooked archives comprise "low theory" and deserve sustained scholarly inquiry.[40] As we interrogate all these failures, we will also see how these oft-dismissed narratives of black embodiment and performance offer alternative ways to rethink identity, empathy, and politics, building on Judith Halberstam's definition in *The Queer Art of Failure*. Halberstam writes "low theory . . . makes its peace with the possibility that alternatives dwell in the murky waters of a counterintuitive, often impossibly dark and negative realm of critique and refusal."[41] With texts plumbing "murky waters," *Black for a Day* interrogates the troublingly persistent assumption that becoming black—even temporarily— can cure racism with an interdisciplinary methodology. Bringing together many fields, including literary studies, visual culture, critical race theory, ethnography, memoir, cultural studies, history, southern studies, undercover journalism, cultural tourism, performance studies, and queer theory, it closely reads various types of texts and media from memoir and fiction to film, photography, musical theater, advertising, and television.

During my audition for *Finian's Rainbow*, our director made it clear that he had long wanted to revive the musical but lacked the requisite number of black bodies to complete the cast. The year 1996 proved a good one in my school's blackness, and finally, *Finian* was possible. Our three sold-out shows received standing ovations—and we congratulated ourselves on our theatrical triumphs during the cast party. As the musical's soundtrack bounced off the girl who played Susan's basement walls, we reenacted memorable moments and quoted our favorite lines from the script. I was refilling my punch when Joe, comfortably white again, loudly joked: "Hey, Alisha! Once you go black . . . you *do* go back!"

CHAPTER ONE

Good Niggerhood

Ray Sprigle's Dixie Terror

A decade after winning the 1938 Pulitzer Prize for uncovering the links between Supreme Court Justice Hugo Black and the Ku Klux Klan, Ray Sprigle, a nationally renowned journalist for the *Pittsburgh Post-Gazette*, pitched a new story to his editor. He was confident that the idea would place him back in contention for that coveted prize. Unlike previous assignments—going undercover as a butcher to expose the black market in meat, or posing as an attendant to investigate Pennsylvania's mental health institutions—this time Sprigle wanted to impersonate not just another person but also another race. For what would be his last undercover story, Sprigle wanted to become a black man. However, he was no bleeding heart liberal: "I might as well be honest about this expedition of mine," he later wrote. "I wasn't bent upon any crusade. All I saw at first was the possibility of a darned good newspaper story."[1] Regardless of his motivations, for four "endless, crawling weeks" in May 1948, Sprigle "ate, slept, traveled, [and] lived Black."[2]

On August 9, 1948, the *Post-Gazette* began publishing a twenty-one–part series of highly anticipated front-page articles, what the paper numbered as "chapters," entitled "I Was a Negro in the South for 30 Days." The first column, situated above the fold of the paper, accompanied a large picture of a slouching Sprigle, presumably but not immediately recognizable as a black man, in what looks like a field. The following prefaces his column: *"All of the incidents described are factual, but Mr. Sprigle has in some cases changed the names of persons and places for the protection of the individuals involved."*[3] In each installment, Sprigle detailed his hopefully prize-winning journalistic experiment. The series—expanded into the book-length memoir *In the Land of Jim Crow* in 1949—is comprised primarily of short portraits of southern black life, from sharecropper's cabins and dilapidated elementary schools to churches and juke joints. Written from the perspective of a northern white man's encounter with the "iniquitous Jim Crow system,"[4] Sprigle's experiment indexes postwar anxieties about the place and value of black bodies in a nation still reeling from the horrifying consequences of biological racism in Europe. As the United States sought to solidify itself as an emerging world superpower, there was growing pressure to attend to the hypocrisy of American racism. As Sprigle crosses both the color line and the Mason-Dixon line, he betrays the wishful idea that the U.S. brand of racial terror was a peculiarly southern institution. Ultimately, Sprigle's investigation rests completely on a convenient idea of the South—one defined by Jim Crow segregation and fueled by an inversion of southern nostalgia and the myth of northern innocence. This chapter will establish and define three primary theoretical components of empathetic racial impersonation: "Dixie terror," the failed white ally, and the Myrdalian scaffolding of this genealogy. It will also critique the limits of Sprigle's empathy resulting from his class-constrained, fear-based persona of a "good nigger."

Dixie Terror and the Geographies of Blackness

Martin Raymond Sprigle was born white on August 14, 1886, in Akron, Ohio, to Emmanuel Peter Sprigle and Sarah Ann Hoover. After growing up in northeast Ohio, Sprigle briefly attended Ohio State University before embarking on a career in journalism in 1906. He wrote for a number of southern and midwestern newspapers, and by 1911 he had established a thriving journalistic career in the steel town of Pittsburgh, Pennsylvania, with the *Pittsburgh Post-Gazette*. Sprigle quickly rose through the ranks of the paper to city editor but was fired because of his overt affiliation with the International Workers of the World, a radical labor union. Unemployed, Sprigle enlisted in the army and edited a military newspaper in Virginia during World War I. In 1918, Sprigle returned to the *Post-Gazette* as an investigative crime reporter, and later he was reappointed to city editor. Sprigle made a name for himself primarily through his undercover journalism. Because of his style of mixing facts with unfiltered opinion, Sprigle was described as a "shrewd," "hard-digging, hell-for-leather newsman," and a "muckraker."[5] By the time Sprigle decided to be reborn as black, he had a national reputation as Pittsburgh's most famous reporter and "ranked among the country's elite" journalists.[6]

After receiving permission from the newspaper's co-publisher and editor, William Block and Andrew Bernhard, respectively, Sprigle began the process of becoming his black alter ego, James Rayel Crawford. The name was easy and familiar; he had used it during previous undercover assignments.[7] However, looking black was far more difficult than he anticipated, and the search for a suitable method of embodiment took nearly six months. Sprigle complains, "This thing of suddenly switching races after more than half a century of life as a white man has its problems and difficulties." He continues, "Remember all those romances you've read in which the hero is going to turn Hindu, or Arab or one of the other darker races. Remember how almost invariably he goes to 'an old woman' . . . and she gives him a lotion that turns him dark for weeks or months. Well, my trouble, I guess, was that I couldn't seem to find one of those old women. And in more than six months of searching I couldn't find any lotion or liquid that would turn a white hide brown or black and still be impervious to perspiration, soap and water and the ravages of ordinary wear and tear."[8] Without a magical old woman, Sprigle consulted chemists at the Mellon Institute of Applied Science. They recommended phenol compounds that would indeed change his skin. However, they warned, the chemicals would kill him in the process. Undiscouraged, Sprigle decided on his own less fatal transformation: he attempted to darken his skin with the juice of walnut hulls, along with "iodine, argyrol, pyrogallic acid, [and] potassium permanganate." Unfortunately, "come a little perspiration and I'd find myself striped like a tiger or spotted like a leopard."[9] Finally, he settled for an easier alternative—a tan. After three weeks sunbathing in Florida, Sprigle became a self-described "reasonable facsimile of a light-skinned Negro from the North."[10]

Although Sprigle worried about his ability to look black enough, he quickly realized that "most of my concern over acquiring a dark skin was so much nonsense. Everywhere I went in the South I encountered scores of Negroes as white as I ever was back home in Pittsburgh."[11] Sprigle concluded that his blackness required not a physical alteration but, more important, a willingness to face the precarious vulnerability of "being" black in the Jim Crow South. He writes, "Southern whites have long taken the position that when a man says he's black, so far as they are concerned he is."[12] Sprigle maintained his sun-made color, a shade he described as "coffee-with-plenty-of-cream," and coupled it with Jim Crow segregation to produce a black identity.[13]

On an evening in May, Sprigle decided he was ready. He left Florida for Washington, D.C., to board a segregated railroad coach that would carry his suntanned body back south to Atlanta. Before boarding the train, Sprigle had to tone down his eccentric sartorial style. When not undercover, Sprigle sported a ten-gallon sombrero, silver-ringed cane, and corncob pipe. However, on that particular night in 1948, he swapped his signature hat for a droopy, checkered one, put on oversized, black-rimmed glasses, and traded his sharp black suit and tie for a drab, but still respectable, brown suit. He traveled light—with just one small brown bag. He had already shaved both his head and mustache. He was sixty-one.

Over the next four weeks, Sprigle was introduced to a different South, subsequently learning how blackness is not always immediately legible on the body, and that racial identity and belonging have as much to do with how one negotiates the legalities and geographies that produce difference and its consequences. He writes, "I quit being white, and free, and an American citizen when I climbed aboard that Jim Crow coach in Washington's Union Station. From then on, until I came up out of the South four weeks later, I was black, and in bondage—not quite slavery but not quite freedom, either."[14] As he navigated the Jim Crow South by strategically relinquishing unfettered access to restrooms, water fountains, waiting rooms, and the more amorphous and intangible realms of convenience and privilege, Sprigle experienced how segregation structures black life, or what he called "'passing,' in reverse."[15]

The name Sprigle gives to his racial experiment is useful. His phrasing, "passing, in reverse," prompts us to consider how the longer history of passing—from black to white—impacts his narrative. Passing is legally defined by Randall Kennedy as "a deception that enables a person to adopt certain roles or identities from which he would be barred by prevailing social standards in the absence of his misleading conduct."[16] Although that "deception" can extend to a number of identity categories, its most common, trenchant, and revelatory manifestation in American history has been race. Colloquially referred to as "crossing the line," racial passing is a contested negotiation of race troubling the categories of identity. Although we reify these categories with the belief in the supposedly clear boundaries of identity, racial passing is a reminder of how fluid and mercurial identity really is. Kennedy continues, "The classic racial passer in the United States has been the 'white Negro': the individual whose physical appearance allows him to present himself as 'white' but whose 'black' lineage (typically only a very partial black lineage) makes him a Negro according to dominant racial rules."[17] Complementing Kennedy's definition, Allyson Hobbs, in *A Chosen Exile: A History of Racial Passing in American Life*, makes the compelling argument that "racial passing is an exile." She writes, "To pass as white was to make an anxious decision to turn one's back on a black racial identity and to claim to belong to a group to which one was not legally assigned."[18] She continues, "A study of passing uncovers a phenomenon that, by definition, was intended to be clandestine and hidden, to leave no trace."[19]

Throughout the African American literary canon, black-to-white passing remains a persistent theme for black writers negotiating blackness,
blood, racism, authenticity, economics, love, law, opportunity, segregation,
and politics to various ends. The most exemplary passing narrative is Nella
Larsen's 1929 novel *Passing*, but racial passing finds expression in the work
of authors as varied as Charles Chesnutt, Ellen and William Craft, Harriet
Jacobs, Paul Lawrence Dunbar, James Weldon Johnson, George Schuyler,
and Langston Hughes.[20] One can conclude that the African American literary canon has a preoccupation with passing, beginning in early novels like
William Wells Brown's 1853 *Clotel: Or, the President's Daughter*, and Frances
Harper's sentimental and dogmatic 1892 novel *Iola Leroy*. Passing in African American literature is a persistent and consistent preoccupation present in even more contemporary memoirs, like those by Bliss Broyard and
Toi Derricotte.[21] Ultimately, passing offers a thematic way to read the en-
tirety of the African American literary canon. Such a reading reveals a consistent negotiation of passing and its dangers, an anxiety about race and
authenticity, and the haunting manifestation of the passer as an archetypal,
tragic figure like Clare Kendry in Larsen's *Passing*, as well as more recent
attempts to disrupt and revise the archetypal tragedy of the racial passer, as
in Danzy Senna's 1998 novel *Caucasia*.

Whereas both Kennedy and Hobbs define crossing the line through histories of black-to-white passing, in *Passing Strange: A Gilded Age Tale of Love
and Deception across the Color Line*, Martha Sandweiss details the strange story
of famed white geologist Clarence King, who for more than a decade passed
for black as a Pullman porter and steelworker in order to common-law
marry his wife, Ada Copeland, a black woman born into slavery. Sandweiss
writes, "King's secrecy speaks to his desire to preserve his reputation. But
it speaks also to the very real constraints of public opinion" in the late
nineteenth century.[22] "The practice of passing," Sandweiss makes clear,
"generally involves adopting a particular identity to move *toward* greater
legal and social privilege."[23] She continues, "Rather than moving *toward* legal
and social privilege, he moved *away* from it. He glimpsed something he
sought in Ada Copeland and her African American world, and he acted to
seize the promise of that rich emotional life."[24] Although white King and
his black persona, James Todd, might seem to be the historic precedent to
Sprigle's racial impersonation, King passed for love. Sprigle did not.

Sprigle is not passing as many black authors represent it, or as Kennedy,
Hobbs, and Sandweiss define it. Although Sprigle's temporary blackness is
informed by, but then deviates from, the theatrical burnt cork of the black-

face minstrel, he does not embody blackness for love, safety, convenience, or as a way to avoid discrimination and segregation. Instead, Sprigle embodies blackness to place himself in the harrowing way of Jim Crow. Since Sprigle aims to reveal something about discrimination and racial terror in the South, he spectacularly advertises the manner and method of his four-week black dalliance. In other words, Sprigle intends to leave the sizable trace Hobbs insists is contrary to the exile necessary for black-to-white passing. Since racial passing is dangerous, secrecy rather than self-promotion is required. Recognizing the precarious threshold a black-to-white passer must meet to pass successfully, Sprigle is not passing. Instead, he temporarily breaches blackness by proudly advertising what he hopes will be a historic boost to his career. Consequently, this project insists that the white impersonators in this genealogy are not passing; instead, they "become black" only to exploit their temporary impersonations.

Sprigle crosses the color line with a suntanned, facsimile blackness, but his resulting narrative places far more emphasis on the hazards of crossing another line: the Mason-Dixon. Accustomed to the industrialized spaces of the Midwest, and far from journalistic impartiality, Sprigle writes: "I deliberately sought out the worst that the South could show me in the way of discrimination and oppression of the Negro. I spent most of my time in Georgia, Mississippi and Alabama. I ignored Virginia and North Carolina, where the greatest progress in development of civilized race relations has been recorded. How can you correct evil until you find it? I deliberately sought the evil and the barbarous aspects of the white South's treatment of the Negro. It is of that only that I write."[25] As Sprigle sought a provocative, Pulitzer-contending story, he did so by writing a story about the South. In so doing, he trafficked in and perpetuated a fantasy about the South that had been evolving long before he crossed the Mason-Dixon.

Beginning shortly after the Civil War, northern white folks created a premodern, pastoral image of the South to assuage anxieties about a modernity that was increasingly, and for them distressingly, urban and industrial. That image was solidified in the national imaginary through popular culture, epitomized by 1939's Academy Award–winning *Gone with the Wind*, the grotesquely romanticized height of this southern fantasy. Such imagery benefited both North *and* South. As the South became a popular vacation destination for winter-weary northerners, many cities and sometimes states, increasingly dependent on the revenue generated by northern tourism, willingly corroborated and perpetuated it. For example, as Karen L. Cox describes, in 1932, the Garden Club of Natchez, Mississippi,[26] created the Natchez Pilgrimage, a "weeklong event," "providing tourists with the chance to see large antebellum homes filled with furniture from bygone days, tours by women in hoopskirts, and 'mammies in bandanas.' Festivities included a Confederate ball, tableaux of historical scenes re-created in the mansions, and local black citizens singing black spirituals . . . it attracted northern and midwestern tourists by the thousands."[27] As local white residents nostalgically re-created a revisionist projection of the best of the Old South, the Natchez Pilgrimage reveals that these vacations were never simply about escaping northern winters for sunnier climates but were also about the sale and consumption of a collaborative white supremacist fantasy. White southerners presented their South as they wished it had stayed, and northerners delighted in the privileges of whiteness via an alibi of rest and relaxation.

At first glance, Sprigle's southern tour seems strikingly different. He left the North purposefully seeking lynchings rather than magnolia blossoms, and racism rather than hospitality. However, his ideas about the South and its racial terror were unsustainable without the well-established fantasies of the South as old-fashioned, quaint, and clearly different from anywhere else in the country—especially when it came to race relations. Sprigle could only become Crawford if the land he traveled was imbued with what Houston Baker and Dana Nelson compellingly theorize as the South's symbolic geography as "national but alien."[28] Despite the fact that Sprigle had previously traveled throughout the South on other undercover assignments as Crawford, he insists, "It was a strange, new—and for me—uncharted world that I entered when, in a Jim Crow railroad coach, we rumbled across the Potomac out of Washington. It was a world of which I had no remote conception. . . . The world I had known in the South was white. Now I was black and the world I was to know was as bewildering as if I had been dropped on the moon."[29] Since it was his first experience on the wrong side of segregation, Sprigle spent considerable time describing this spatial disorientation. His time on that overnight train was the first test of his new blackness, and rather surprisingly, even to himself, Sprigle finds the black coach with its reclining seats both "comfortable" and the segregated car "surprisingly good."[30] He even describes the restroom as "really luxurious," and the passengers as "courteous and quiet . . . even the inevitable drunk."[31] With details like these, the segregated accommodations of 1948 sound better than what readers might imagine or expect. However, Sprigle contrasts his own descriptions of the seemingly seductive comfort of segregation immediately. He writes, "But—even excellent accommodations are not going to reconcile intelligent, cultured Negroes to Jim Crow."[32] His insistence here on Jim Crow's incompatibility with specifically "intelligent, cultured Negroes" is disturbing, a focus on respectability that will become more revealing as his columns continue.

According to Sprigle, even amid decent conditions, it only took hours for him to awkwardly mimic the assumed posture, what he calls "the pattern"[33] of black survivability in the face of Jim Crow. He writes,

> We staggered through the swaying Pullmans past the white folks but careful not to jostle or bump any of them.
>
> Already I was in the pattern. Already I was experiencing the thing that was to grow upon me through the succeeding weeks. These whites already were a people entirely alien to me, a people set far apart from me and my world. The law of this new land I had entered decreed that I had to eat apart from these pale skinned men and women—behind that symbolic curtain. For 300 years these people had told each other, told the world, told me, that I was of an inferior breed, that if I tried to associate with them they would kill me.[34]

No. Neither Sprigle nor his kin had been told he was "inferior." However, his rhetoric is strategic. He borrows the pattern, the affect of blackness, as he maneuvers his body from the dining car back to the colored one without disturbing "the white folks." In so doing, Sprigle describes the effect and affect of moving through awkward and arbitrarily segregated spaces. His description of segregation is poignant and, notably, not necessarily wrong. However, in order to write and right himself into the wrong side of segregation, Sprigle spuriously situates himself in a history and psychology of blackness that rhetorically feels too immediate. He details an easy and quick psychic transformation, an already-ness where the once "white and free" Sprigle seamlessly becomes precarious and vulnerable Crawford. As Sprigle insists, 300 years weigh down on his facsimile black body, and this assumptive assimilation is bound up in and enabled by his characterization of the South and his identity as a *northern* black man.

Sprigle's Jim Crow South, which he often refers to as the "Southland," is displaced as another country, described not only as strategically foreign but also as inaccessible and outside history. He writes, "The towers and turrets of the great cities of the Southland, painted against the falling night, as we rolled along the highways, represented a civilization and an economy completely alien to me and the rest of the black millions in the South."[35] Just as he describes the South as alien in the first chapter of his series, he uses similar language to detail "becoming [part] of an alien people" in the third chapter. Sprigle's disorientation coupled with his lush description of medieval architectural relics erects a gothic castle wall between North and South, delimiting the South solely through its relationship to histories of racial terror. With his startlingly bold habit of consistently referring to himself as black while appropriating the consequences of racial and racist histories, Sprigle insists it was not the Mason-Dixon line but "the Smith and Wesson line to us black folk."[36] The violence implicit in this renaming renders the South simultaneously a spectacle, a bounded repository for the racial sins of the past, and a ready excuse for those of the present and future. Sprigle's language could easily have been used to market this "otherworldly" space as the Natchez Garden Club did, a fantasy playground modernity forgot. However, instead of selling the innocently bucolic, Sprigle rebrands the South a "pastoral in blood."[37]

Sprigle's deliberate search for uniquely southern racism is instructively emblematic of what I call "Dixie terror," an imagined construction of the South shaped by racially motivated violence. Whereas the phrase "racial terror" rightly names the often-fatal consequences of racism both in and beyond the Jim Crow South, "Dixie terror" highlights an obsession with a peculiarly southern type of racism. It insists that while debates remain about how to define the geographical South,[38] "Dixie" cannot be found on a map. "Dixie" is a cultural fantasy, a distortion and projection of the South framed and enabled by nostalgia and bolstered by the myth of northern innocence. That fantasy is evident in the lyrics of the often still whistled 1859 Confederate anthem "I Wish I Was in Dixie's Land."[39] Even as the lyrics pledge whistlers will "live and die in Dixie," the "away down South" of "Dixie land" is geographically unspecific and impossible to locate. As a result, Dixie terror relies on the national penchant for constructing fantasies of the South. Unlike the Natchez Garden Club's attempt to erase histories of racism, Dixie terror highlights that history by insisting that racial violence is a peculiar and uniquely southern tradition—the inverse of mint juleps, stately mansions, happy darkies, and seersucker suits. Dixie terror is embodied by the uncomplicatedly evil and sadistic cruelty of Simon Legree, the static villain of Harriet Beecher Stowe's 1852 novel *Uncle Tom's Cabin*. Like Stowe, authors, including Sprigle, rely on Dixie terror to make racism, black suffering, and black death into an uncomfortable spectacle. Dixie terror then is simultaneously perverse and sought after, horrifying and glorified, all for the sake of a compelling narrative. Although deployed to incite moral outrage and invoke the "right" feeling about the horrors of racial violence, Dixie terror traffics in and ultimately exploits racism for its titillating marketability. It revels in accounts of racism with unflinching details of the most disgusting and grotesque displays of it, coupled with hyperattention to the violence exploiting black bodies and their suffering rather than the individuals brutalizing them or the systems enabling and sheltering such violence.

For example, Sprigle recalls a disturbing secondhand account by a "friend" who witnessed "white men bind a black man to a stake ... [and] when the flames burned through the bonds of the screaming Negro and he rolled out of the fire, white men armed with fence rails thrust him back until he screamed and crawled no more."[40] For Sprigle, spectacles of Dixie terror enable his personal investment in cross-racial empathy since, without Dixie terror, black bodies are not legible. In the logics of Dixie terror, only violence and suffering render black bodies worthy of attention and pity. In order to paint a picture of Dixie terror, Sprigle feels the need to also describe a southern landscape already popular in the northern imaginary. Despite his own conservative Republicanism, Sprigle introduces his intended progressive, white northern readers to rich depictions of southern racism as well as lush descriptions of southern land. He writes, "Under a blazing Georgia sun we begin our journey of 3,400 miles through the black South. Cotton is greening the blood-red soil of the endless fields. It's cotton chopping time, when the cotton plants must be thinned out. Family by family the Negro share-croppers are in the fields, children of seven or eight and grandmothers and grandfathers who totter when they walk but still are able to swing a hoe."[41] Sprigle situates black labor against a southern pastoral, nearly plantation landscape, populating that landscape with stereotypical tropes such as the mammy. For example, on the train from Washington, D.C., he cannot help but write about a black family complete with "a navy petty officer—spick and span" dad, "pretty and fashionably dressed" wife ... "[and] their baby had everything hung on him that the magazines say a well-dressed baby ought to have." This is an innocuous description of a traveling black family until Sprigle continues, "And then there was the baby's grandmother—also right out of the old South. She wore a turban just like the one in the pancake ads. I noticed that her hands were hard and knotted and gnarled. . . . They get that way from long hours on a hoe in the cotton fields."[42] As that well-dressed baby's grandmother is read through the commercially available iconography of the mammy, Sprigle ensures that Dixie terror rests not only on fantasies of violence but also on commodified images and plantation stereotypes of a fantasied Old South.

My theory of Dixie terror builds on Saidiya Hartman's work on humanism and the exploitation of black suffering in nineteenth-century American literature and history, what she calls "scenes of subjection." In *Scenes of Subjection: Terror, Slavery, and Self-Making in Nineteenth Century America*, Hartman indicts our cultural participation and investment in black dehumanization. Opening with the "terrible spectacle"[43] of Aunt Hester's beating in Frederick Douglass's 1845 *Narrative of the Life of Frederick Douglass*, Hartman refuses to "reproduce Douglass's account . . . in order to call attention to the ease with which such scenes are usually reiterated."[44] Hartman instead questions the political utility of exploiting and reexploiting the black body in pain. She writes, "Suppose that the recognition of humanity held out the promise not of liberating the flesh or redeeming one's suffering but rather of intensifying it? . . . I am interested in the ways that the recognition of humanity and individuality acted to tether, bind, and oppress."[45] Hartman's query reveals one of the limits of empathetic racial impersonation. Recognizing the perversity of Dixie terror does not undermine the politically important project of condemning white supremacy in all its forms, but it also helpfully calls out Dixie terror for its perversely delightful penchant for splaying broken, bruised, and bloodied black bodies across the page, whether for sympathy or sales.

Despite Sprigle's characterization of the South, what Sprigle often forgets during his hellish descent into Jim Crow as Crawford is the reality that African Americans often traveled to and throughout the South both by force and by choice. In fact, the South is an unavoidable space of physical, historical, and psychic importance for black life. Trudier Harris acknowledges how "African American writers cannot escape the call of the South upon them. The African American literary tradition is adept at narrating the value of the South to African America. The American South, therefore, becomes a rite of passage for many African American writers."[46] For Harris, black writers "exhibit both an attraction and repulsion to the South,"[47] and it is a duality exemplified by James Baldwin's 1972 text *No Name in the Street*. Baldwin writes, "In the Deep South—Florida, Georgia, Alabama, Mississippi, for example—there is the great, vast, brooding, welcoming and bloodstained land, beautiful enough to astonish and break the heart."[48] The South's astonishing beauty is also captured in Richard Wright's litany of southern memory in his 1945 semiautobiographical bildungsroman *Black Boy*. He writes, "There was the vague sense of the infinite as I looked down upon the yellow, dreaming waters of the Mississippi River from the verdant bluffs of Natchez. There were the echoes of nostalgia I heard in the crying strings of wild geese winging south against a bleak, autumn sky."[49] Much like Wright's beautiful literary descriptions of the South as black homespace, the region also resonates through its soundings—from slamming screen doors, the pop and hiss of a skillet of fried chicken, and the soulful, bass-full chitlin circuit music resonating from Memphis to Atlanta and from Houston to the Mississippi Delta.

As black writers, musicians, and cultural producers nuance the delicate paradox of the American South through a different type of nostalgia, Dixie terror demands a strategic disavowal of southern foodways, music, and literature, and the South's place as home. Seeing only horror, Sprigle's bloody South contrasts sharply with his far more forgiving depictions of the North. To fully understand his investment in Dixie terror, it is crucial to return to the argument Sprigle establishes in his first column:

> In the North the Negro meets with rebuff and insult when he seeks service at hotels and restaurants. But, at least in states like Pennsylvania and others, he can take his case to court and he invariably wins.
>
> But in the South he is barred BY LAW from white hotels and restaurants. He is fined and jailed, and frequently killed, if he seeks to enter a railroad station through an entrance reserved for whites, to ride in the forward end of a street car or bus, or railway coach sacred to the white man. His children are barred from white schools and denied an adequate education in the tumbledown shacks in which little black citizens are forced to seek learning.[50]

Although Sprigle mentions the race riots in Detroit, Chicago, and Springfield, Illinois, as occurring from "time to time," he still insists, "But in the North, both black and white rioters go to prison. In the South only the black ones climb the steps to a gallows or serve time in a cell."[51] Sprigle makes his defense of the North and indictment of the South plain: "Don't anybody try to tell me that the North discriminates against the Negro, too, and seek to use that as a defense against the savage oppression and the brutal intolerance the black man encounters in the South."[52] Sprigle refuses to construct the North as equally complicit in the history of racism he insists is far worse in the South: "Discrimination against the Negro in the North is an annoyance and an injustice. In the South it is a bloodstained tragedy." Sprigle concludes, "In short, discrimination against the Negro in the North is usually in defiance of the law. In the South it is enforced and maintained by the law."[53] Characterized only by the "annoying" consequences of U.S. racism, including lynchings and riots, Sprigle's "innocent" North appears like a bastion of racial compassion and empathy in comparison to the much more sickening spectacles of racism in the South. Sprigle renders inconsequential the violent rash of race riots during the red summer of 1919 in cities such as Chicago and Omaha, the 1930 lynchings of Thomas Shipp and Abram Smith in Marion, Indiana,[54] and the 1943 race riot in Detroit. He does so while seedily anticipating similar spectacles of what he deems exclusively southern terror. For Baker and Nelson, "To have a nation of 'good,' liberal, and innocent white Americans, there must be an outland where 'we' know they live: all the guilty, white yahoos who just don't like people of color. . . . 'The South' comes to the rescue of U.S. wholeness."[55] Sprigle's rhetorical strategy structures and contours the South, first as a geography of Dixie terror rescuing U.S. wholeness in the Baker and Nelson sense and consequently as a geography of potential intervention and empathy. In Sprigle's columns, the South is constructed as the any and only place where real and consequential Dixie terror happens. Thus, the South is the geography where white reporters and investigators, and not just liberal ones, can most readily intervene. In an article contextualizing the *Post-Gazette's* fiftieth-anniversary reprint of all of Sprigle's columns, called "Sprigle's Secret Journey," Bill Steigerwald writes, "Though he was a lifelong friend of the underdog, Sprigle was no softhearted liberal. He was no moralist, no precocious civil rights crusader, no longtime champion of the cause of the Negro, North or South. He was a staunch conservative Republican who hated FDR and the New Deal. All he wanted his southern investigation to do, [Sprigle] said later, was to see 'that justice was done to a group that is grossly oppressed.' "[56] However, this lifelong friend of the underdog, "hell-bent" on uncovering the Deep South's Dixie terror at the excuse of northern culpability, did so not only by writing a story of the South but also by carefully crafting the persona of James Rayel Crawford. This persona proved to be a stunning tutorial in an undercover journalism marred by fear.

How to Be a Good Nigger

Before Sprigle boarded that Jim Crow train as Crawford in May 1948, he knew it would be foolish to travel alone. He writes, "Of course I realize that if I tried to make my way through the black South on my own, alone, I would have met with suspicion and rebuff on every hand from black and white alike. Fortunately, though, I didn't have to go alone into the black world of the South. Walter White, executive director of the National Association for the Advancement of Colored People, took care of that."[57] Sprigle later elaborates in *In the Land of Jim Crow*: "Scores of times Walter White has traversed the South from end to end, posing as a white man, risking his life every mile and every minute of his journeyings. And here was a white newspaperman from Pittsburgh who wanted to reverse the process and turn Negro. The idea caught his fancy."[58] While not "unmistakably a Negro," Walter White was a good choice.[59] For ten years, born black White used his light skin and blue eyes to investigate lynchings and race riots on behalf of the NAACP and northern newspapers. While passing for white, White collected pertinent data on forty-one lynchings and eight race riots, including the infamous 1921 riot and black massacre in Tulsa, Oklahoma. White traveled through rural communities seeking and gathering information both during and in the aftermath of racial terror and black death. Although White's undercover exposés required feigning sympathy with extralegal mobs and self-described vigilantes and, in the case of Tulsa, volunteering as a city deputy, he still faced threats of violence when his curiosity or identity seemed suspicious. Ultimately, White's investigative work demonstrated the political utility of racial passing as well as the NAACP's willingness to employ it as a civil rights strategy. By endorsing Sprigle's project, White revealed not only the potential value in exposing communally sanctioned racial violence but also the need for white sponsorship of, and audiences and allies for, testimonies to that violence. Although the black press, cultural producers, and educators had long narrated both the banal and extraordinary circumstances of black life in the United States, White anticipated that Sprigle, armed with the methods of undercover journalism and empathetic objectivity, could reach a larger audience.

However, by the time Sprigle sought his guidance, White had already ended his undercover career with a 1929 piece in *American Mercury* outing himself as a lynching investigator.[60] So, he introduced Sprigle to John Wesley Dobbs, or, as Sprigle writes, "Out of his vast store of friendships of Negroes, North and South, [White] chose a man to lead me through the warrens of the black South."[61] Although Sprigle kept Dobbs anonymous to protect him from reprisal and reactionary violence, it is clear that Dobbs was not just any southern black man. By 1948, Dobbs was already a civic and political leader, and his success and commitment are now well memorialized throughout his hometown of Atlanta, Georgia. The street boasting his childhood home has been renamed for him; his six Spelman College–educated daughters, including Mattiwilda, a notable opera singer, are still celebrated among the college's alumnae; and his grandson, Maynard Jackson, was elected the city's first African American mayor in 1973. With a man like Dobbs at his side, Sprigle assumed he was guaranteed to experience black southern life. He writes, "And if there is any commendation due anyone for these chronicles, surely the lion's share must go to that companion of mine. I doubt if there is a man living who knows the South, black and white, as he does. . . . If I learned anything about the life of the Negro, it is because he took me to the places, the men and women from whom I might learn."[62]

In unequivocal terms, Sprigle lauds his traveling companion. He recalls how Dobbs impressed him as they traveled together through those endless southern nights. Sprigle continues:

> We'd roll along through the night, our destination the Negro section of a town perhaps 200 miles away and for hours I'd listen while he recited long passages from *Macbeth* and *Hamlet*, [Robert] Ingersoll's essay on Napoleon—page after page from the best in English literature. All his life he has fought against the oppression, the injustice and the discrimination weighing on his people. But there is no bitterness, no hatred in the man. To him his "Southland" . . . is the fairest country in the land. He loves his Georgia above all other states—he would live nowhere else in America.[63]

Here, Sprigle seems immediately impressed by Dobbs's ability to cite liberally from the canon of "great books." However, his unequivocal love for Georgia is difficult for Sprigle to understand. Since Sprigle crossed the Mason-Dixon to document the South's most horrifying examples of racism, a prestigious black man unabashedly proclaiming his love for Georgia contradicts Sprigle's investment in Dixie terror.

In 1948, Dobbs's prominence and influence spread beyond the metropolitan spaces of Atlanta to the rest of the South. Consequently, the "Dobbs" name opened doors for Sprigle wherever the two traveled, even as Dobbs's love for Georgia challenged Sprigle's persistent judgment of the South as the home of Dixie terror. Sprigle reconciles this paradoxical contradiction with Dobbs's prominence, education, prestige, and stature. For Sprigle, the South can be seen as a palatable and laudatory homespace only through the dynamics of black respectability and exceptionality. Rather than a lesson in the visuality of blackness in the Jim Crow South, with Dobbs's tutoring, Sprigle underwent a course in survivable southern blackness in general and black masculinity more specifically. Dobbs ensured that Sprigle encountered a very particular snapshot of black life, enabled by the instructive tutorial of Dobbs and his circle. Sprigle writes, "Here are the things they [Dobbs and his circle of friends] stressed in their instructions to me—repeated over and over again. 'Don't ever fail to say 'sir' when you speak to a white man. . . . Don't ever strike back if a white man hits you—whether he's drunk or sober. . . . Don't ever speak disrespectfully or familiarly to a white woman. . . . Don't ever argue with a white train or bus or streetcar conductor, or with any white man. Do as he tells you and keep quiet.' "[64] As Jonathan Scott Holloway writes, "The companion [Dobbs] was the director for Sprigle's staged performance. He taught Sprigle how to act (right) and how to hit his marks."[65] In *In the Land of Jim Crow*, Sprigle elaborates on this training in a chapter aptly entitled "Fear Walks with Me." In this longer account, Sprigle details these countless protective "don'ts" received from men who successfully navigated the peculiarities and pitfalls of the segregated South, concluding: "The black man in the South lives in fear."[66] He continues, "There were towns in the Delta where my companion wouldn't even take me. Don't think I gave him any argument on it, either. These black friends of mine back in Jackson, Mississippi, had talked too much about what had happened and what could happen to a black man in Mississippi."[67] In the fourteenth chapter, Sprigle elaborates: "Back in Jackson, the night before we started our expedition into the Delta, half a dozen Negro leaders briefed us on tactics, strategy and general behavior for our Delta tour as if we had been going into an occupied country to join the Underground. 'Don't talk to share-croppers either at work or along the roads.' 'Don't argue if a 'rider' stops you and asks questions.' ('Riders,' by the way, are the mounted patrols that plantation owners maintain as field foremen and general overseers. Mounted field foremen frequently are trusted Negroes. Overseers are white.)"[68] Since Sprigle already braced for Dixie terror, fear structured Sprigle's travel throughout the Southland, and his rhetorical use of *plantation* riders reinforced the idea that the South was still bound and defined by an archaic past. It was this socialized anxiety about the wages of blackness and black masculinity coupled with Dobbs's shepherding guidance that would ultimately buttress Sprigle from the firsthand experiences with racism he supposedly wished to encounter.

Sprigle's fear and anxiety were real. He rigorously held to Dobbs's daunting list of "don'ts" except once, when he, as Crawford, accidentally subverted the entrenched mores of Jim Crow segregation. After alighting from that comfortable Jim Crow train and already improbably conditioned by 300 years of history and black servility, Sprigle went ahead of Dobbs to hail a cab. As he boldly walked through the front of the Atlanta train station, Sprigle heard a cautionary voice: " 'Wait a minute,' I heard my friend call.

'This way.' I back-tracked and he led me through a door branded 'For Colored,' to a small littered waiting room. . . . Here was no wide portico, no line of cabs. In fact, no cab."[69] Sprigle's mistake, the crime of walking obliviously through a white entrance while black, gave Dobbs an idea: "[Dobbs] led me around to the front of the station and we defiled the white folk's entrance by going through it. Nothing happened. So we tried again. Still nothing happened. . . . 'Seriously though,' [Dobbs] told me while we waited for our Jim Crow cab, 'ordinarily we'd have been stopped and told to go to the colored entrance. . . . If you have any idea you can walk through the white folks' entrance by going through it. . . . And I'll stand back and watch— and bail you out.'"[70] Clearly, Sprigle's defiance was met with disappointment, blamed on Atlanta's seemingly lax Jim Crow protocol, and what Sprigle deemed "police inefficiency": "My friend was all set for minor adventure and then the Atlanta police force let him down."[71] Here, Dobbs hoped for a moment when Sprigle could move from observer and witness to participant and maybe ally. Dobbs imagined a moment when Sprigle as Crawford might experience the real legal consequences of segregation, a moment that never occurred. "Politely I declined [Dobbs's] challenge," Sprigle writes. He then confirms, "That was the first, last and only time I disobeyed the white folks' law during all my stay in the South."[72]

As Sprigle and Dobbs crisscrossed the South together, Sprigle indulged in platters of his favorite fried chicken while listening to stories of black suffering—tales giving fleshly description to his columns. To that end, Sprigle's columns often ended in overly sarcastic or provocative one-liners and questions that rhetorically hung in the air for his presumptive white, northern readers. For example, Sprigle uncomfortably details the unjustified and retaliatory lynching of forty-two-year-old Henry Gilbert through the traumatic memories of his grief-stricken widow, Carolyn. As "sobs shake her,"[73] Sprigle steps outside his Crawford persona to conclude: "Me, a white man— even though she thinks I'm black—pray for Carolyn Gilbert! Who would listen?"[74] Sprigle often implores his readers through this type of address.

As a whole, the columns comprising "I Was a Negro for 30 Days" often challenge and/or undermine either the hope or futility of the previous one. It is what Pittsburgh's ace reporter does well, mixing the supposed objective witness of undercover work with a bitter and controversial tone. This is the rhetorical hallmark of Sprigle's writing, for which he became nationally renowned. However, his biting prose cannot fill the gaps of experience. So, while Sprigle insists he "ate, slept, traveled, [and] lived"[75] black behind the curtain of segregation, he also admits: "In all my sojourn in the

South, in 4,000 miles of travel by Jim Crow train and bus and street car and by motor, I encountered not one unpleasant incident. Nobody called me 'nigger.' Nobody insulted me. Nobody pushed me off the sidewalk."[76] While those made most vulnerable by Jim Crow might consider this negotiation of the South a "success," Sprigle laments, "This would be a far better story if I could show some scars left by the blackjack of some Negro-hating, small-town deputy whom I'd failed to 'sir.' Or a few bullet holes, mementos of an argument with some trigger-happy Atlanta motorman. I could have gathered them, all right. Just by getting 'fresh' at the right time and place. But for me, no role as hero. I took my tales of brutality and oppression and murder at second hand."[77] He later continues, "I saw to it that I never got in the way of one of the master race. I almost wore out my cap, dragging it off my shaven poll whenever I addressed a white man. I 'sirred' everybody, right and left, black, white and in between. I took no chances. I was more than careful to be a 'good nigger.'"[78] Although he traveled across the South to experience its "evil and barbarous aspects," Sprigle never learned what it meant to be a black man.[79] Instead, he learned how to be a "good nigger."

The offensively horrific, but supposedly comic, one-liner "the only good nigger is a dead nigger" does not apply here. Being a "good nigger" keeps Sprigle not just alive but out of harm's way—too far out of harm's way. Sprigle writes, "Came morning—and Atlanta. Now I had been briefed for days on my manners and behavior as a Negro."[80] Here, Sprigle succeeds in a performance of shuffling subservience and unquestioned deference to white authority and supremacy. A "good nigger" might go by other names, like "Uncle Tom," "house nigger," or the more contemporary epithet "oreo."[81] Sprigle's good niggerhood did not go unnoticed by his own contemporary critics. In a review of *In the Land of Jim Crow* for the *Atlanta Daily World*, Stetson Kennedy writes, "The idea of sending a white reporter into the South as a Negro was such a good one, I almost fell for Ray Sprigle's series. . . . But when the publisher sent me a complete set of advance proofs on all 21 articles, I decided they should be titled, 'I Was an Uncle Tom.'"[82] As Sprigle clutched his checkered hat in his dutiful hand and constantly bowed his newly shaven head, he revealed the tension in his project. Sprigle's Crawford yessir'd and shucked his way across the South, thereby avoiding the Dixie terror he purportedly came to uncover, experience, and document.

Although the respectability politics of "good niggerhood" can never completely protect a black person against Dixie terror, Sprigle's investment in it deeply influences his interactions in both white and black southern communities. He admits that, except for the word "sir," "I'd scarcely spoken to a white man."[83] Meanwhile, and importantly, his performance of obedient black masculinity impacted his interactions with southern black folks. Couched among the warnings about the dangers of sassing white men and women, Sprigle was also instructed not to "stop to talk to field hands."[84] However, because of his sustained interest in sharecropping over a number of columns, Sprigle does talk to field hands. In so doing, he reveals, almost accidentally, both structural racism and class determinism. Despite his commitment to "good niggerhood," Sprigle cannot help but uncover how race conspires with class in the Jim Crow South.

Accidental moments like these balance the failures of Sprigle's empathetic racial impersonation. For example, Sprigle reports the story of Henry Williams, a sharecropper for twenty-nine years, in the seventh chapter. With a narrative picture of Henry's relationship to southern home and land, Sprigle writes, "You begin to get a better idea of what it means to be a black share-cropper in the South as you sit on a home-made stool in the two-room shack of Henry Williams in Sumter county on the road to Americus in the Georgia cotton country. No northern farmer would keep his cattle in a shanty like this. And this place of Henry's is far and away better than hundreds of others we have passed on our travels. It at least has one window in one room. . . . Henry, however, has no fault to find with his mansion."[85] Since Sprigle admits to disagreeing with Henry about the number of rooms in the Williams home—Sprigle's two against Henry's four—the description of Henry's home as first a "shanty" and then cheekily a "mansion" rhetorically exposes the economic realities of sharecropping against the more recognizable idealization of a mythic American dream. Sprigle goes on to detail how Henry is caught in an economically oppressive cycle dominated by the whims of "the Man" and his fuzzy, racist math. Recognizing the impossibility Henry faces when trying to get a fair wage for the labors of his production as a sharecropper, Sprigle writes, "In all his share-cropping, Henry has never seen any kind of an account of his operations. 'The Man' never gives him a statement—no figures—just hands him a check or a bundle of cash."[86] He continues, "Here is the pattern through the South. Every Negro knows it and accepts it. It's a custom, a tradition, just as basic as Jim Crow. No Negro dares buck the system. Everywhere I went, and I talked with at least a score of sharecroppers, I heard the same expression: 'If you go to figure behind The Man you're gonna git trouble.'"[87] Although he learns all too well that trouble is the quickest detriment to black survivability in the South, Sprigle forcefully and damningly concludes: "This share-cropping in the South is grand larceny on a grand scale. And the Negro is the victim."[88] Even though Sprigle tries to be a "good nigger," he still stumbles on the ramifications of institutional racism. As a racial impersonator, Sprigle pivots between the aspirational dreams of the black men he meets, the constricting guidelines of his impersonation, and his signature journalistic style. For example, Sprigle challenges the despondent conclusion of this column with the hopefulness of his next one.

After indicting the sharecropping system's treatment of Henry, Sprigle opens the next column with a heads-up to his readership: "This is a 'tough' town in a 'tough' county."[89] Tough as it is, Sprigle hopefully narrates the life of a typical landowner, Jared Buford, lauding him as atypical and exceptional. Sprigle describes how "Jared rents himself a hundred good acres from a white planter and pays cash rent for it,"[90] making money on his land while also running a "picturesque juke joint" for black folk on the profits from his rented acres.[91] Sprigle is clearly smitten with Jared's ability to successfully navigate the arbitrary pitfalls of Jim Crow. He writes: "It takes an exceptional Negro to succeed in the desperate struggle from sharecropper to tenant farmer."[92] However, Jared attained "exceptional Negro" status by strategically avoiding white people. In a subsection entitled "Jared's Philosophy," Sprigle quotes him: "Ain't no Negro in this country going to be hurt or killed as long as he keeps his place. . . . White folks here ain't going to make trouble for the sake of trouble like they do some places. I never had any trouble and I ain't going to have no trouble. I got my place here and on the farm, and the white folks got their place."[93] Consequently, Sprigle concludes: "Here is a man, it seems to me, who has just cut himself off from white civilization. And is doing all right at it, too."[94] Read sequentially, Jared's quasi-triumphant story undermines the previous one about Henry. Sprigle narrates Jared's tale as a triumphant example of the American dream even under the economic and social regimes of segregation and the debt peonage of sharecropping.

For Sprigle, Jared modeled a "good niggerhood" strategically self-segregated from white authority. Sprigle then reinforces the possibility of exceptionality in spite of the sharecropping system only columns later with the story of Dave Jackson, a man Sprigle describes as a "one in ten million" Negro.[95] Despite that Dave began as a "penniless" sharecropper, Sprigle applauds him for his struggle to own 1,000 acres of the most fertile land in Adel, Georgia, a small part of Cook County. Along with those acres, Dave "owns two blocks of business property in Adel, and a score of houses. He's a stockholder in the newly formed bank. He lives in a 10-room modern home."[96] Sprigle's accolades continue for paragraphs in Sprigle's eleventh column. Like Jared, Dave is exceptional. However, Sprigle recognizes, "Let nobody get the idea that there's anything typical about the career of Dave Jackson or any other successful Negro farmer in the deep South. There are only a handful like him. . . . To produce a Dave Jackson in the South you've first got to have a white community tolerant enough to sit back and let a Negro succeed. Then of course you've got to have an exceptional Negro."[97] He prefaces Dave's story: "Given the right kind of white neighbors, the right kind of a community, the right kind of land and a terrific capacity for hard work, once in a while a Negro can do pretty well for himself in the deep South."[98] Here, Sprigle clearly recognizes the implausible rarity of this "perfect" southern environment, yet, in his insistence on fully portraying exceptional southern black life, "good niggers" are instructive.

Knowing the unlikely conditions enabling Jared's strategic segregation, Dave's precariously awkward and measured respect by the white law in Adel, and the carefully contoured, respectably classed parameters structuring Sprigle's interactions with black southerners, it becomes even more difficult to accept Sprigle's righteous insistence that he authoritatively experienced the variegated contours of black southern life and labor. Despite his lament, he "encountered not one unpleasant incident." There remains a persistent emphasis throughout his writings—he has seen it all: "Don't anybody try to tell me anything about the lot of the Negro in the South," he defensively challenges, "That much at least I know. And nobody told me. I saw it for myself."[99] Without experience, Sprigle relies on testimony. However, most often what he heard, rather than saw, was grief.

Since Sprigle's narrative of black life needed Dixie terror, he supplemented it with secondhand tales of brutality. Instructively, we return to his fifth column, about Georgian farmers Henry and Carolyn Gilbert. He opens with a description of Carolyn, describing her body and grief well before he gives readers her name, first referring to her only as "she." He writes,

> She is worn and aged and bent beyond her time. Nearly a quarter of a century behind a plow and a mule under blazing Georgia suns have done that to her.
> In a haze of dull despair, this broken, hopeless Negro farm woman sits in this little parlor in Black Atlanta and tells her tale of murder.
> "When the white folks gave him back to me he was in his coffin. I held his head in my hands when I kissed him. And I felt the broken pieces of bone under the skin. It was just like a sackful [sic] of little pieces of bone.

I put my arms around him for one last time as he lay there. All down one side of him there were no ribs—just pieces that moved when I held him."

That was her husband she was talking about—Henry Gilbert, 42 years old, Negro farmer, murdered by the white folks of Harris and Troup counties, Georgia, May 29, 1947.

Henry Gilbert was victim of the mores of the white Southerner. When a Negro kills a white man and escapes, somebody has to pay. Henry Gilbert just happened to be the Negro picked for slaughter.[100]

Sprigle later writes, "Here is what the undertaker found when he fixed Henry Gilbert's body up for burial: His skull was crushed to a pulp both in front and the rear. One leg and one arm were broken. All the ribs on one side were smashed into splinters. He was riddled by five bullets fired at close range. That is what Georgia justice officially describes as 'justifiable homicide in self-defense.'"[101] Sprigle condemns the horrifying murder of Henry Gilbert by Troup county policeman Willie H. Buchanan, highlighting this egregious miscarriage of justice in the wake of Buchanan's court-earned "innocence." However, in order to do so, Sprigle overwhelms his readers with the excruciating details of Henry's broken body. Ultimately, readers know little more about Henry Gilbert than his identity as a corpse, and Carolyn is only legible through grief. Notably, Sprigle elaborates the picture of Carolyn's sorrow in his book-length adaptation: "She is worn and aged and bent beyond her time. Her hands are warped and gnarled as she wrings them helplessly. . . . Terror and tragedy seemingly have wrung her dry of emotion."[102] Carolyn's gnarled hands are like those of so many daughters, sisters, wives, and friends wringing in the wake of white supremacist violence. Carolyn's hands are reminiscent of the "knotted and gnarled" ones Sprigle noticed on that "mammy" from the Old South in that Jim Crow car. He writes, "I was to see many hands like that on little old colored women in the weeks to come."[103] Rather than see the hands of those black women as capable of nurture or resistance, Sprigle can only see them clasped in sorrow, just as he sees Henry's black male body as a mourned-for sack full of bones.

The Epistemology of a New Black Man

Although Sprigle's black southern grooming ensured he would never experience authentic Dixie terror so he must relate hearsay tales of it, Sprigle still positions himself as an authority on the southern black experience. Although inundated with a number of only secondhand tales of Dixie terror, Sprigle defiantly opens *In the Land of Jim Crow* with a definitive, epistemological conclusion: "Now I, a 'white' man, know, as well as any white man may, what it means to be a black man below the Mason and Dixon line."[104] This "knowing" goes beyond the perspective of the witness. It is hubris thwarting the intentionality of the ally. This hubris is the corrosive and seductive deception of empathetic racial impersonation. Sprigle's secondhand experience of a stymied, bourgeois blackness stands in place of the full spectrum of black, southern life. Even in the face of the commercial failure of *In the Land of Jim Crow*, Sprigle maintains he fully understands what it means to be a black man in postwar America. Here, he confuses black epistemology, experience, and narrative authority with making a few new black friends.

What Sprigle fails to understand is what James Baldwin makes plain in his essay "Stranger in the Village." He writes, "It is one of the ironies of black-white relations that, by means of what the white man imagines the black man to be, the black man is enabled to know who the white man is."[105] Baldwin reminds us how power is always at work in the American racial imaginary. Sprigle's racial imagination is limited not only by his "good nigger" search for Dixie terror but also by the privileged notion that the "other" is fully and thoroughly knowable, even when knowing is reduced to four weeks of tempered interactions. As Toni Morrison illuminates, "Black slavery enriched the country's creative possibilities. For in that construction of blackness *and* enslavement could be found not only the not-free but also, with the dramatic polarity created by skin color, the projection of the not-me. The result was a playground for the imagination."[106] She furthers Baldwin's incisive critique by unpacking the "Africanist presence"[107] haunting the canon of American literature: "What rose up out of collective needs to allay internal fears and to rationalize external exploitation was an African-Americanism—a fabricated brew of darkness, otherness, alarm, and desire that is uniquely American."[108] As Sprigle plays in the playground of the "not me," he does so using a dialectical desire of "love and theft," as Eric Lott so aptly describes blackface minstrelsy in *Love and Theft: Blackface Minstrelsy and the American Working Class*. Sprigle "knows" blackness in the South without knowing or finding interest in the panoply of black experience or cultural production, qualifying the besieged nature of black life in spite of Jim Crow while disregarding the cacophonous and expansive conditions of black humanity.

To be fair, Sprigle's conclusive knowing in the opening lines of *In the Land of Jim Crow* could be dismissed as just a provocative teaser for his narrative, an introductory conclusion the rest of his reporting would presumably challenge or undermine. However, Sprigle's racial knowing—as a qualified "white" man—expands beyond both his columns and his memoir. On November 8, 1948, Sprigle was featured on a public radio show also newly broadcast on television, *America's Town Meeting of the Air*. As a show about national issues, that particular episode focused on a then controversial question, "What should we do about race segregation?"[109] a question Barbara Dianne Savage rightly describes as "politically untouchable."[110] Along with Sprigle, the panel featured Walter White and southern journalists Harry Ashmore and Hodding Carter. Savage writes, "The first speaker to try to answer [moderator George] Denny's question was Ray Sprigle. . . . Sprigle spoke as if still in his assumed identity, taking liberty of talking 'from the standpoint of the Southern Negro.' He described segregation as part of 'the whole vicious and evil fabric of discrimination, oppression, cruelty, exploitation and the right to an education.'"[111] Emboldened by his brief blackness, Sprigle offers a clear and decisive invective against the horrors of Jim Crow for this national audience. Ultimately, that *Town Meeting* audience met Sprigle's persona, James Rayel Crawford, instead of the renowned Pittsburgh reporter. Sprigle's Crawford persona proved a lucrative one. As an expert on the black experience, his *Town Meeting* appearance garnered Sprigle his requested $400 honorarium, a sum far exceeding the $100 Walter White earned for the same appearance.[112]

That Sprigle went temporarily black in a bid for a second Pulitzer and then went on to make money by parroting his version of southern black masculinity is uncomfortable. Coupling that with his insistence, both on and off the page, that he knows the intricacies, vulnerabilities, and precarious paradoxes of southern blackness makes Sprigle's time as Crawford even more unpalatable—so much so that Sprigle could be easily dismissed. However, although his Crawford blackness is rendered uncomfortable at best and offensive at worst, his frankness about how this empathetic racial impersonation changed his perspective on whiteness and white supremacy is still instructive. Unlike his previous undercover assignments as a mentally ill patient in Pittsburgh's troubled psychiatric hospitals or his time spent as a black market butcher, "being" Crawford wrought a psychological change in the reporter. With provocatively qualifying quotation marks around his formerly easy and unrepentant racial positionality ("I, a 'white' man, know"), Sprigle's four weeks as Crawford forced him to question his whiteness. In his third column, right after that eye-opening overnight train ride from D.C. to Atlanta, Sprigle writes, "Already I had begun to dislike them. It did no good to tell myself that I was white—or that I would be white again four weeks hence. I was beginning to think like a black man."[113] Sprigle's shifting perspective continued under the subtitle "A Psychological Change": "In weeks to come I was to become seriously concerned about the psychological change that was taking place in my thinking. There were to be nights when I had sat for hours listening to grim tales of injustice, and cruelty and the wanton shedding of innocent blood, that I began to be worried over the problem of turning my mind white again. To tell the truth, I doubt if I ever regain the satisfied, superior white psychology that I took South with me."[114]

Importantly, Sprigle's questioning of whiteness prompted the then First Lady of the United States, Eleanor Roosevelt, to mention Sprigle's black sojourn in her own reflective daily column. On August 12, 1948, Roosevelt wrote, "[Sprigle's] articles ought to add to the understanding and enlightenment of our white people. . . . The subtle way in which this reporter's feelings changed and he began to dislike his own kind, as he identified himself more and more with the colored people, is very enlightening. That is a subtle way of telling us how every colored person feels who has had to endure segregation and discrimination."[115] Of course, Roosevelt finds resonance in Sprigle's impersonation since she had also publicly imagined herself black five years earlier. On October 1, 1943, as part of a series of very popular columns in *Negro Digest* entitled "If I Were a Negro," Roosevelt speculated: "If I were a Negro today, I think I would have moments of great bitterness. It would be hard for me to sustain my faith in democracy and to build up a sense of goodwill toward men of other races." However, as Sprigle would demonstrate later, the First Lady undermines this seemingly progressive racial imagination with a number of qualifying statements. "I think, however," she admits, "I would realize that if my ancestors had never left Africa, we would be worse off as 'natives' today under the rule of any other country than I am in this country where my people were brought as slaves." She, rather predictably, advocates for full military service, hard work, and the overall patience of her fantasied racial community. She ends her article by putting the burdensome consequences of racism back on the black community. She imagines, "I would try to remember that unfair and unkind treatment will not harm me if I do not let it touch my spirit."[116] Eleanor Roosevelt's column in the "If I Were a Negro" series "became the best-selling issue in the [*Negro*] *Digest*'s short history."[117] As Holloway writes in

Jim Crow Wisdom: Memory and Identity in Black America since 1940, "The popularity of Roosevelt's contribution, specifically, and 'If I Were a Negro,' more generally, speaks to the high level of fascination that each race held for each other."[118] Along with Roosevelt, Sprigle also holds and exploits that fascination. Sprigle's anxiety about recovering his white psychology marks him as a failed ally. He longs again for his whiteness and, subconsciously, the power behind it. Although his early columns rhetorically reveal an all too easily absconded whiteness, it was not Sprigle's physical change but his psychological change that lingered. To borrow the titular language of cultural critic Mark Anthony Neal's *New Black Man*,[119] Sprigle's Crawford is not about *if* he was Negro but how he embodied a temporary, new black man who still craved a return to his prior, old white manhood.

Sprigle as Crawford as Eliza

Over the course of his four weeks, the violent, racist misadventures Sprigle anticipates never materialize. Although Sprigle's failed heroic opportunity might have been the consequence of the protection of White and Dobbs and the "good nigger" performance encouraged by middle-class aspirations, Sprigle still craved southern-style racial violence—the Dixie terror necessary to guarantee the salaciousness of his columns and subsequent narrative. Perhaps if Sprigle had traveled alone, been courageous enough to confront terror firsthand, or been exposed to a different class of less accommodating and probably less successful black men, his articles and subsequent book would have been more marketable. This is not to suggest Dobbs and company incorrectly schooled Sprigle on the precarious consequences of southern black masculinity but recognizes how Sprigle was right to insist on some authentic Dixie terror. Sales of the book-length *In the Land of Jim Crow* were disappointing, and his series in the *Post-Gazette* failed to garner the second Pulitzer Prize nomination his newspaper's staff so heavily campaigned for on his behalf. However, this "failure" is not only a matter of book sales. Sprigle is often overshadowed in the annals of empathetic racial impersonation by the much more popular John Howard Griffin, who "became" a black man in the South a decade later.

Backed into a rhetorical corner where he lacks the experience of Dixie terror while still holding onto it as a concept, Sprigle turns to sentimental literature as his remedy. In the last chapter Sprigle writes, "All my life I've regarded Eliza's stunt of crossing the Ohio on floating ice floes, with bloodhounds baying at her heels, as a pretty heroic adventure. Not any more.

The night I came up out of the deep South in a Jim Crow bus, I'd have been glad to take a chance crossing on the ice if anything had happened to stall our jolting chariot on the Kentucky shore. And there'd have been no need of any bloodhounds to put me into high gear."[120] Sprigle replaces his lack of experience with the citation of Eliza's escape from slavery, an iconic literary scene standing in for Stowe's novel *Uncle Tom's Cabin* and its discursive legacies. Here, Sprigle anticipates a readership familiar with Eliza as a character, so much so that Sprigle does not see the need to contextualize Eliza's story. Eliza is the beautiful, white-looking, fugitive slave mother, heroically evading slave catchers by desperately crossing the icy Ohio River with both agility and grace. In "Poor Eliza," Lauren Berlant helpfully investigates the value of sentimentality in the dramatic adaptation of Eliza's harrowing ice walk in the 1956 cinematic depiction of the Broadway musical *The King and I.* She writes, "Almost every adaptation of the novel involves an elaborate dramatic staging of the scene where [Eliza] crosses the Ohio River riding rafts of ice. This event takes less than two pages in the text. Yet it is a powerful scene, electrified by the awesome power of the mother to harness her own sublimity to the sublimity of nature, thus transforming herself into a species of superperson."[121] Since Sprigle never mentions Stowe or the novel's title, Eliza's place in his series trades on what Berlant calls the "supertext" of nineteenth-century American sentimental fiction. Berlant's naming of *Uncle Tom's Cabin* as a "supertext" ultimately reveals how the novel dominates the cultural and historical imagination. Subsequently, Sprigle's unattributed citation of both Eliza and Stowe solidifies *Uncle Tom's Cabin* as a cultural and literary touchstone that supposedly illuminates the consequences of race and racism, although the novel is infamous for its fraught and racist representations of blackness.

Sprigle restages the scene of Eliza's crossing for presumably familiar audiences. However, as a southern Ohio spring replaces the frosty winds of a February night, and suspended bridges rather than ice floes carry him to "freedom," Sprigle disrupts the iconicity of the scene by replacing Eliza's tender and agile feet with a Jim Crow bus, and her black woman's body with his white male one. By placing himself at the center of this scene, Sprigle does not identify with either Eliza or the danger she confronts. Instead, too-good-a-nigger-to-be-a-hero Sprigle usurps Eliza's place, attempting to gain purchase from her superheroism. Since Eliza's escape highlights the transregional vulnerabilities at the heart of the 1850 Fugitive Slave Act, Sprigle's substitution anachronistically collapses the fictional rendering of nineteenth-century fugitive slave life onto the 1948 realities of Jim Crow segregation.

Importantly, Sprigle appropriates not just any representation of black womanhood but one mired in the complexities of white-authored narratives of black experience and empathy. The fictional Eliza was an exceptional slave, "a petted and indulged favorite," characterized by Stowe's fetishized "refinement . . . [and] softness of voice and manner . . . [of] the quadroon and mulatto women. These natural graces in the quadroon are often united with beauty of the most dazzling kind."[122] Thus, it is telling that Sprigle does not appropriate the bodies or legacy of historical figures such as Harriet Tubman or Sojourner Truth. Rather than ground his own racial impersonation in the experiences of real and heroic black women, he locates his empathetic experiment in Stowe's problematic ideal of black womanhood. As Baldwin wrote of Eliza and her husband, George, a century after the novel's publication, "We only have the author's word that they are Negro and they are, in all other respects, as white as [Stowe] can make them."[123] By choosing Eliza, Sprigle restages his "good nigger" masculinity as a palatable black femininity.

Sprigle strategically positions *Uncle Tom's Cabin* as his literary predecessor by explicitly situating his narrative as one of *Uncle Tom's Cabin*'s "hard-boiled descendants."[124] In so doing, Sprigle revels in what Baldwin, in his 1949 essay "Everybody's Protest Novel," vehemently denounces as sentimental literature's "fantasies, connecting nowhere to reality," the fantasies Stowe specializes in and nearly trademarks. In a trenchant critique, Baldwin writes, "Sentimentality, the ostentatious parading of excessive and spurious emotion, is the mark of dishonesty, the inability to feel; the wet eyes of the sentimentalist betray his aversion to experience, his fear of life, his arid heart; and it is always, therefore, the signal of secret and violent inhumanity, the mask of cruelty."[125] Sprigle's complicated desire for, but ultimate fear of, the consequences of black life in the wake of Dixie terror explicit in his "good nigger" posturing is clearly an "aversion to experience." Since Baldwin's concern is with what he calls "the protest novel," a category encompassing authors from Stowe to Richard Wright, he argues that the protest novel relies on a formula to answer its generic demand: "the necessity to find a lie more palatable than the truth."[126] Baldwin critiques how the protest novel "exemplif[ies] this terror of the human being, the determination to cut him down to size,"[127] coupled with a nearly gleeful, persistent, and grossly entertaining catalogue of black disenfranchisement, trauma, and death. It is a formula framing the ideologies of the protest novel as well as Sprigle's postwar narrative of cross-racial empathy.

Although Baldwin rightly calls this "unflinching" documentation of violence "senseless" and "unmotivated,"[128] Sprigle's work reveals how the protest novel and its descendants always traffic in the logics of Dixie terror. Thus, they are inseparable from and shaped by the work of sentimentality. To borrow language from Baldwin, Sprigle offers a "catalogue of violence . . . explained by . . . [a] laudable determination to flinch from nothing in presenting the complete picture; an explanation which falters only if we pause to ask whether or not [this] picture is indeed complete."[129] As he did with Henry Gilbert, Sprigle offers up the dead black male body, that "Negro picked for slaughter," to incite readers' pity. Consequently, Sprigle brings sentimentality's most perverse renderings of race and racism to the political consequences of postwar empathy. Berlant continues, "When sentimentality meets politics, it uses personal stories to tell of structural effects."[130] In other words, sentimentality primes us for that heaping, bitter dose of liberalism's "good" medicine. Berlant emphasizes sentimentality's ability to use the personal to spuriously reveal the structural aspect of racism, but empathetic racial impersonation often purposefully obscures its institutional aspect. She continues, "The original impulse behind sentimental politics . . . is to see the individual effects of mass social violence as *different from* the causes, which are impersonal and depersonalizing."[131] In Sprigle's invocation of Stowe's sentimentality, he obscures causes by capitalizing on sentimentality's potential to facilitate a project of racial empathy. Sentimentality guarantees liberalism's success by placing a seductive affect around the sociopolitical ideologies of postwar American liberalism. Through coerced feeling, sentimentality establishes the necessary emotional conditioning for the suturing of a palatably raced subject to the postwar American nation.

Sprigle's hubristic substitution of his body for Eliza's can be read through the postwar logics of empathy. Gunnar Myrdal's *An American Dilemma* (1944), his supposedly comprehensive study on "the Negro problem," determined that solving the woeful gap between America's democratic ideals or "creed" and its demonstrable racism rested "in the heart of the [white] American."[132] This moral conclusion insists that "problematic" black bodies are wholly separate from the national conversation about who can claim, constitute, and embody ideal American citizenship. According to Nikhil Singh, Myrdal assumes that "White Americans were capable of more mature and capacious judgment. Even as he elevated racial matters into a position of unprecedented centrality ... Myrdal interpreted [that] active, broad-minded, self-reflective ... white Americ[a] ... held the capacity for reform *within itself.*"[133] It is well documented that Myrdal relied on, and egregiously erased, the vastly important research contributions of numerous black intellectuals and academics, such as Ralph Bunche, W. E. B. Du Bois, and E. Franklin Frazier.[134] Similar to his erasure of the black academic labor enabling his spurious single authorship, Myrdal strategically ignores the capacity of African Americans for narrating, critiquing, understanding, and negotiating their own histories of oppression and survival. By denying black agency, Myrdal's conclusion renders the problem of black bodies as a white burden.

Such is the burden Sprigle adamantly, and enthusiastically, undertakes. He considers Myrdal's implicit query—who is the Negro?—by answering Myrdal's Dixie terror–enabled, implicit question, how does the Negro, specifically the Southern Negro, suffer? In the foreword to *In the Land of Jim Crow*, novelist Margaret Halsey offers a way to situate and understand Sprigle's postwar empathetic efforts. She writes, "Mr. Sprigle has not turned up any new material. All his facts have been reported before in such research volumes as Gunnar Myrdal's *An American Dilemma*, and others. But in the scholarly disquisitions, the facts are necessarily arranged in graphs and statistics and cautious footnotes. In Mr. Sprigle's book they are personal and vivid—the spontaneous, unstudied reactions of a self respecting white American trying to live from one dawn to the next under the disabilities imposed on colored Americans."[135] Sprigle literalizes the empathy Myrdal demands by turning internalized, "heartfelt morality" outward—into a superficial politics of the skin. For Sprigle, then, temporarily walking in black skin enables authority and understanding. If I know *some* black people, the thinking goes, then I know black people.

Importantly, these narratives of cross-racial empathy are done in good faith; they are not racist but instead "social experiments." It is a defense Baldwin anticipates in his critique of the protest novel: "The avowed aim of the American protest novel is to bring greater freedom to the oppressed. They are forgiven on the strength of these good intentions, whatever violence they do to language, whatever excessive demands they make of credibility. It is, indeed, considered the sign of frivolity so intense as to approach decadence to suggest that these books are both badly written and wildly improbable. One is told to put first things first, the good of society coming before niceties of style or characterization."[136] Bringing Baldwin's language to this descendant of the protest novel, Sprigle reveals that although paradoxically well intentioned, maddening, misguided, exploitative, but somehow sincerely pursued, these experiments expose both the potential and failures of sentimentality and empathetic racial impersonation. Sprigle's ideological kinship with Myrdal allows us to reconsider *An American Dilemma* with attention to the work of sentimentality. As an oft-disparaged literary mode characterized by grotesque excess, sentimentality seems disciplinarily far from Myrdal's celebrated study. Although Myrdal's presumed objectivity, coupled with the disciplinary demands of the social sciences, renders the genre strangely inappropriate among obsessively documented facts and figures, sentimentality structures the data and analysis while priming *Dilemma*'s readers for its conclusion.

Myrdal's research is a text full of the charts, graphs, and appendices that render social scientific evidence legible to those who are not social scientists. With social science, it attempts to invoke the "right" feeling to provoke reflection and possible action. To that end, Myrdal concludes his analysis with a laudatory nod to his formal discipline. He writes, "We have today in social science a greater trust in the improvability of man and society than we have ever had since the Enlightenment."[137] This glowing disciplinary allegiance is disrupted only pages before as he articulates America's potential for exceptionality:

> Mankind is sick of fear and disbelief, of pessimism and cynicism. It needs the youthful moralistic optimism of America. But empty declarations only deepen cynicism. Deeds are called for. If America in actual practice could show the world a progressive trend by which the Negro became finally integrated into modern democracy, all mankind would be given faith again—it would have reason to believe that peace, progress and order are feasible. And America would have a spiritual power many times stronger than all her financial and military resources—the power of the trust and support of all good people on earth. *America is free to choose whether the Negro shall remain her liability or become her opportunity.*[138]

That a famed economist makes a sentimental appeal to white America through faith and the "spirituality" of American power is incredibly important. *An American Dilemma* hails falsely universal categories of "mankind" and "American," hallmark characteristics of the sentimental literary genre, to make American exceptionality possible amid the real and imagined threats to its status as an emerging superpower. For Myrdal, America has the potential to inspire a redeemable global citizenry of "good" citizens who refuse to let the Negro remain its only barrier to global dominance. Ultimately, reconciling the "Negro problem" becomes a moral, domestic imperative through the embrace of black bodies into an explicitly American, liberal project, ironically dedicated to power and empire building.

Although Sprigle's original motivation was his career, he does his part to fulfill Myrdal's dogma. Sprigle stretches the affective boundaries of sentimentality, pushing beyond simple imagination to actually become the "other" Myrdal prompts white folks to merely pity. It is a strategy refusing real political change: "Because the ideology of true feeling cannot admit the nonuniversality of pain, its cases become all jumbled together and the ethical imperative toward social transformation is replaced by a civic-minded but passive ideal of empathy."[139] In sum, being empathetic is often a singular goal since we can pat ourselves on the back for simply acknowledging the reality of the "other." Sprigle's brand of empathy not only refuses to challenge the reality of black second-class citizenship, it actually *requires* it.

As a case in point, Sprigle attempts to intervene after hearing a testimony of racial discrimination that shakes him to his very core. He writes of a "little, straggling Negro cemetery . . . on the edge of this Mississippi Delta town of Clarksdale" and finds a "magnificent sarcophagus of white Alabama marble."[140] In his fifteenth column, Sprigle describes how "this beautiful tomb out here on the edge of the cotton fields is a monument to the cold-blooded cruelty of the white man; to the brutal mandate of a white world that black men and women must die rather than be permitted to defile a cot or an operating table in a white hospital with their black skins."[141] He then documents the story of Marjorie Hill, the pregnant wife of wealthy dentist Dr. P. W. Hill. Although Marjorie planned to birth a healthy baby at home, something went wrong during labor to force a life-saving Caesarean section. Sprigle writes, "Clarksdale boasts of a small but adequate hospital. But it is sacred to white patients. Dr. Hill didn't even seek admission for his wife and unborn baby. Just before midnight he put them into an ambulance and started a mad drive north to Memphis and its Negro hospital, 78 miles away, in a desperate race with death. Death won."[142] After hearing the tale, Sprigle challenged Dr. Hill's commitment to his wife and the veracity of fatally segregated hospitals. " 'But, Doctor,' I insisted, 'you didn't even try. You didn't even ask Clarksdale Hospital authorities to admit your wife.' " Both Dr. Hill and Dobbs interrupt Sprigle's query: " 'In the South,' they told me, 'when you're black you don't try to fight the pattern. Hospitals are for white people. White people do not admit black folk to their hospitals. Black folk do not even ask for admission. They just die.'"[143] Even in the face of Hill and Dobbs's frank attempts to get Sprigle to understand the perilous reality sick and dying southern black residents face, in a striking moment of defensiveness, Sprigle writes, "But I wasn't satisfied." For the reporter, black testimony was not enough. He continues, "Back home, and a white man myself again, I decided that here was one barbarity charged to my race that I'd disprove."[144] After sending wires and registered letters to the director of the hospital, Louise Francis, to confirm the horrible practice of Clarksdale Hospital's refusal to receive black patients under any circumstances, Sprigle received nothing but silence. Even after hearing similar stories about critically injured black patients turned away from other segregated hospitals in both Tennessee and Georgia, Sprigle still tried to contact hospital personnel to find out if the stories he heard were true. Again, however, he never received an answer to his queries. Ultimately, Sprigle failed. Although seemingly laudable, Sprigle's dogged pursuit of "truth" is not evidence of his journalistic diligence. Neither is it evidence of his desire to change the system. It *is* evidence of his admitted desire to challenge the "barbarity charged to my race." His intervention, a hollow empathetic gesture, is therefore nothing more than a defensive disbelief of black testimony.

As the series winds down, there is one other thing Sprigle vehemently disbelieves. In the newspaper's penultimate chapter, Sprigle writes, "Strangely enough, the Negro in the South doesn't hate the white man."[145] He continues, "But what he does hate with all his heart is the discrimination and the oppression that dog his footsteps from the cradle to the grave. He hates most of all the fact that he is but half a citizen."[146] After brutal tales of Dixie terror featuring the splaying of broken and bloodied black bodies across the series, Sprigle admits: "Give me another couple of months, Jim Crowing it through the South—forever alert never to bump or jostle a white man—careful always to 'sir' even the most bedraggled specimen of the Master race—scared to death I might encounter a pistol-totin' trigger-happy drunken deputy sheriff or a hysterical white woman—and I'm pretty sure I'd be hating the whole damned white race."[147] Sprigle then distinguishes Crawford's imagined hatred from the feelings of black folks who know there are "decent, humane, tolerant white men and women in the Southland."[148] Those Negroes are reassuring, establishing the accommodating rhetoric of his final column.

Perversely, the conclusion of "I Was a Negro in the South for 30 Days" puts potentially anxious postwar readers at ease with pacifying recommendations about race and racism. Sprigle concludes:

And finally, too, one last word to the white man in the South from a Negro, even though a temporary one.

Don't be concerned that the Negro seeks to rise to the stature of manhood and American citizenship.

Don't worry about him defiling either your hotels or restaurants or, above all, your race. Not one Negro did I meet who wanted to associate with white folks. True, all of them condemned segregation bitterly. But as they talked on, it developed that it was discrimination rather than mere segregation that they hated. Every man and woman I talked to, field hand or educator, betrayed the fact that he wanted as little contact with the white world as possible.

But here are a few things with which, it seems to me, no decent southerner could quarrel.

Quit killing us wantonly just to try out a new gun, or to teach us that it's not good for us to try to vote, or just because you "don't like a damn nigger no how."

Next, let us exercise the franchise guaranteed us by the Constitution and the Supreme Court. You'll never see a Negro party in the South. You'll find that the Negro vote, when there is one, is going to split along the same lines as the white vote.

Give our children a decent chance at a decent education—the same kind of an education that you want for your children. And give our young men and women a chance for a university education—in law, medicine, and engineering. We might even be of service to you.

Surely none of that is going to destroy the way of life of the white South. It probably won't even appreciably dent white supremacy.[149]

This quotation is stunning. It is brazen in its use of "us" and "we," a grammar of inclusion and belonging that Sprigle uses to position himself as a spokesperson for southern black communities, the very position he would again take months later for the *Town Meeting* audience. He imagines not only a black South but also black descendants—generations of black children he will never father or shepherd through the precariousness of southern black life. Here, his rhetorical persona of Good Nigger Crawford knows few bounds. While Sprigle acknowledges, "I don't know if anybody in the South will read these articles," he exclusively addresses an imagined white southern reader. Sprigle's list of demands is disturbing and tepid, again excusing the North as innocent. Pittsburgh's most dogged reporter, known for his aggressive mix of journalistic reporting and opinion, offers a flaccid acquiescence to white supremacy, denying the basic humanity of the very community he speaks for by clearly stating that "the Negro" doesn't want "manhood," "citizenship," or true integration. In so many words, Sprigle argues that the dangerous and dehumanizing logics of separate but equal would be enough. Sprigle's conclusion feels similar to Booker T. Washington's 1895 address at the Atlanta Cotton States and International Exhibition, a speech famous for his imploring demand to white southerners to "cast down your buckets where you are" into the readily available sea of black labor. Even in the late nineteenth century, Washington's plea to southern whites was incredibly controversial. For some he articulated an unfortunate but necessary compromise, whereas others viewed his speech as an egregious, personally beneficial "selling out" of the black community. Sprigle's similar insistence that "we might even be useful to you" feels dated, even for 1948, and it fails to strike even a strategic compromise. Instead, he unabashedly heralds the uninterrupted continuation of Jim Crow. Twenty-one columns and a book later, Sprigle ensures the safety of white privilege. To that end, a reviewer for the black periodical *Atlanta Daily World* forcefully critiques Sprigle in a column entitled "No Help to Our Cause":

> It would be fair to say that [Sprigle's] series not only [does] not present any new angle or thought on the race problem in the South, but will give flesh and substance to the cause of Dixiecrats, who are seeking by every means, both honorable and discredited, to set back the cause of mutual advancement between the races.
>
> Moreover, we believe Mr. Sprigle is guilty of the common blunder of a great number of other northern whites. A white man who is sincerely interested in promoting the advancement of the Negro in the South need not make any apology for being white. There are hundreds upon hundreds of southern white liberals who make no pretense of being friendly to the cause of the Negro. . . . And never once have we heard of them changing their racial identity in order to accomplish their desired ends. They work in season and out of season to achieve harmony, and not just 30 days under disguise.[150]

This reviewer rightly articulates the political consequences of Sprigle's empathetic racial impersonation, and they are not the conclusions progressive or liberal readers might hope racial impersonators espouse or intend. This *Atlanta Daily World* critique recognizes the southern whites Sprigle describes as "decent, humane, [and] tolerant." However, Sprigle then knocks those same southern whites "[as] lack[ing] courage." He continues, "and it would take courage of a high order—to take a definite stand against the more vicious forms of discrimination. [The Negro] knows that they lack the courage to spearhead a movement to jail, indict, try and hang the trigger-happy 'nigger-killers' who are the men who actually set the pattern for race relations in the South."[151] Sprigle's erasure of the antiracist southern white liberals the review mentions forces uneasy questions about Sprigle's decision to become Crawford in the first place. Imagine if Sprigle traveled south to learn how to become a northern ally to southern black and liberal white communities seeking substantive and systemic change instead of how to be a "good nigger." Admittedly, this imaginative revision of Sprigle's thirty days can be dismissed as a useless exercise in the hypothetical. However, this imaginative restaging might offer the possibility to learn, and ultimately know, a more complicated southern experience—one without racial appropriation, an investment in Dixie terror, or the desire to speak as an authoritative mouthpiece for southern black communities while troublingly also advocating a questionable agenda for black folks both in print and onstage. This imaginative restaging might also avoid the lauded invocations of a spurious northern innocence that came to frame both Sprigle's impersonation and his portrait of the South.

Since we know Sprigle did embody "Good Nigger Crawford" during those thirty days, what remains strikingly clear is how badly Sprigle wanted to return north and how disorienting crossing back over that symbolic line of segregation felt. Shedding his persona of Crawford was not a smooth Superman to Clark Kent transition. About that return Jim Crow ride, Sprigle writes:

> We rolled out of Kentucky across that old Ohio River bridge into Cincinnati—into safety and freedom and peace. Again I was free with all the rights of an American citizen. Again I was no, not white. Not yet. It wasn't that easy. Down South my friends had done too good of a job making me into a Negro.
>
> For many days I'd been looking forward to an elaborate meal in a luxurious restaurant with fancy food and prices and service and attention. I found one. And then—take it or leave it—I didn't go in. I found a little lunch counter and ate there.[152]

Describing the affect of crossing back into whiteness, Sprigle continues: "I took a cab to the Hotel Stinton—my first cab in four weeks that didn't have 'For Colored' on the door. And, safely delivered at the hotel, I hesitated again. So I went down a block, found a telephone, called the hotel, made a great point of the fact that I was a *Post-Gazette* man from Pittsburgh, asked for a room and got it."[153] He later writes, "I'll bet I know one thing that no other white man in America knows. That's how a white skinned southern Negro must feel when he quits his race, 'crosses over' and turns white."[154] Although Sprigle might rightly describe the awkwardness of becoming white, he certainly is not accurately describing how "a white-skinned Southern Negro must feel when he quits his race." What Sprigle feels, this anxious hesitation and self-doubt, is because Sprigle is becoming white *again*, the return to his normal life and the power and meaning invested in his waiting whiteness and privilege. His experience is not exemplary of how "white-skinned" black folks crossing the color line for myriad reasons *feel*. The color line for the "white-skinned" Negro is a dangerous, tenuous, vulnerable, precarious, and sometimes fatal one—and was so even in 1948. For black folks, physically usurping the legislation of segregation by crossing the line does not establish unquestionable whiteness. Although Sprigle recognizes how the psychic and spatial realities of the Jim Crow South orient him toward blackness, it surely is not so easy for the "white-skinned black" in the North or South. At the end of his temporary blackness, Sprigle is able to slowly shed his "disguise" in Ohio. Despite his narrative discomfort at the thought of eating at "luxurious restaurants" or once again sleeping safely ensconced in the comfort of a reputable hotel, Sprigle still immediately accesses the power arbitrarily assigned to his "authentic" identity as a northern white man. Even as he hungrily eats at that chosen lunch counter, Sprigle is no longer black. He eats heartily, once again as a white man.

Perhaps tangential to Sprigle's lunch counter meal, but arguably not tangential at all, Sprigle echoes bell hooks's definition of empathy as "eating the other." For hooks, "eating the other" always fails. Sprigle's black Crawford persona, coupled with his longed for, eagerly anticipated shedding of his too vulnerable thirty-day blackness, "reinscribes and maintains the *status quo*."[155] In other words, Sprigle readily consumes the idea and ideal of an award-winning, facsimile black masculinity only to regurgitate his new black man self after he gratefully crosses the proper racial ordering of the Mason-Dixon line. Once again on the right side of the Mason-Dixon, white Sprigle is righted by the power of his journalistic reputation, the comfort of a supposedly innocent North, and his waiting white privilege.

Warning: whiteness is hard to shake.

CHAPTER TWO

The Missing Day

John Howard Griffin and the Specter of Joseph Franklin

In the Preface to his 1961 book *Black Like Me*, John Howard Griffin offers this assurance to his readers: "This began as a scientific research study of the Negro in the South, with careful compilation of data for analysis. But I filed the data, and here publish the journal of my own experience living as a Negro. I offer it in all its crudity and rawness."[1] Although *Black Like Me* portends to be the unfettered daily account of Griffin's famously iconic empathetic racial impersonation, the text is missing a revealing and deeply personal day, Saturday, October 31, 1959—the day after *Sepia* magazine's editorial director, Adelle Jackson, and its owner, George Levitan, green-lit Griffin's temporary racial experiment as a black man in the South. Now, with the security of *Sepia*'s financial support and in the privacy of his journal, Griffin admits, "The intellectual, scientific fascination remains unabated, but the emotional dread increases to a point of sickness now."[2] He continues, "In truth, if you look at it objectively, I will be the same person, only dipped in a vat and changed in appearance; and yet, I will no longer be John Howard Griffin—no. I feel I will in reality be Joseph Franklin; that my interior as well as my exterior will change."[3] None of what Griffin anxiously wrote late that Halloween night was ever published in the *Sepia* series, its book-length follow-up, *Black Like Me*, or his later memoirs. Fueled by insomnia and alone in his Mansfield, Texas, writing studio, Griffin confesses to some deeply uncomfortable assumptions about the blackness he would soon embody and perform. Only in the pages of his typed journals would Griffin ever mention the fantasy persona of Joseph Franklin, and, in many ways, "Joseph" stands in for a template of assumptive black masculine becoming. This chapter details how the haunting absence of this missing day structures each generic iteration of Griffin's empathetic racial impersonation—from his unpublished journals and articles for *Sepia* to both the literary and film versions of *Black Like Me*. By tracing this strategic avoidance, and sometimes heavily revised references to October 31, 1959, Griffin's archive uncovers the imagined specter of black masculinity shaping the most iconic example of empathetic racial impersonation.

John Howard Griffin on the April 1960 cover of *Sepia* for the first installment of "Journey into Shame."

White Like That

Before he imagined himself as Joseph Franklin, John Howard Griffin was born white on June 16, 1920, in Dallas, Texas. Throughout his long career as a writer and lecturer, Griffin represented his upbringing in rigidly segregated North Texas as that of a "genteel Southerner."[4] The second son of four children born to John (Jack) Griffin and Lena Mae Young, Griffin describes his childhood as follows: "I had the black mammy, the summers in the country. . . . We were taught to be good and kind."[5] Robert Bonazzi, Griffin's longtime biographer, corroborates the goodness of the Griffins by concluding that they "were not overtly bigoted."[6] Although John's mammy remains forever anonymous, a black woman lost to history, Griffin explicitly recounts the first moment he became conscious of race and racism in the Preface to his 1977 memoir, *A Time to Be Human*, his last book published before his death. Within its first few paragraphs, Griffin makes it clear that *A Time to Be Human* "[does] not represent myself as a spokesman for black people or for anyone else."[7] Instead, it is a self-described "personal book," beginning with a raw recollection of his early childhood in the segregated South. Griffin writes, "My first vivid memory in life begins with the word 'nigger.' As a very small child I used that word in speaking to a black man in my grandfather's grocery store in south Dallas. I had scarcely spoken when I was jolted by a hard slap across my face and by the anger in my grandfather's voice as he snapped, 'They're people—don't you ever let me hear you call them niggers again.'"[8] Griffin never acknowledges where he might have first heard the word "nigger" or how he knew, as such a small child, when to deploy it. What we do know is that this is Griffin's racially empathetic origin story—the corrective undoing of the milk-taught racism of a kid growing up on the white side of Jim Crow. At first read, Griffin's anecdote satisfactorily establishes the roots of his dogged commitment to uncovering the truth about southern racism. Although this moment seems uniquely prescient, it is not.

In *Separate Pasts: Growing up White in the Segregated South*, Melton A. McLaurin unravels the instructive heroism of Griffin's anecdotal slap. McLaurin writes,

> I knew, for I had been told since birth, that whites were superior to blacks.... On the other hand, I had also been taught that one should never mistreat a black, insult a black, or purposely be rude to a black. One was never to behave badly toward blacks, partially because of moral imperatives....
>
> Such moral considerations, however, rarely influenced the behavior of upper class whites toward blacks. The more compelling reason why one was expected never to abuse blacks ... had little to do with the admission that blacks were fellow humans. Rather, it was because superior people never treated their inferiors in an unseemly manner. For example, one didn't say "nigger," not because the use of that word caused blacks pain but because to do so indicated "poor breeding." "We don't use that word in our family"—this was the standard response.[9]

Both Griffin and Bonazzi cloak the Griffin family in a better class of southern whiteness, defiantly rejecting racial terror; however, as McLaurin describes, the refusal to deploy the word "nigger" is not at all about black humanity. Instead, it is a rhetorical distinction supposedly proper southern gentility makes between themselves and distasteful and disgraceful white trash. Through the helpful lens of McLaurin, Griffin's anecdote about a formative racial awakening is not about the devaluing, sometimes fatal, consequences of Jim Crow suffered by black communities in the South; rather, this southernness is staged solely along the *intra*racial boundaries of class. Griffin himself corroborates McLaurin: "Many of us in the South had a formation that built racial prejudice in us and at the same time persuaded us that we were not prejudiced. Often we were taught to look down on the viciously prejudiced, to view them as 'white trash.'"[10] In the logics of kind white supremacy, only "white trash" torment black folks for fun and without provocation; and only "white trash" lynch black men for looking too long at a white woman or disrespecting a white man. Supposedly, then, only "white trash" protest moments of unwanted or "go slow" integration with mouths wet with spit and venom. "White trash" is the specious alibi available for a certain class of southern white folks on whom the most egregious aspects of racial terror can be blamed. Then, supposedly genteel southern hands can zealously attempt to cleanse themselves of their own trash, as if those hands were ever, or would ever become, clean.

As much as Griffin presents a typical moderate white southern upbringing, his mid-twentieth-century childhood is far from typical. A dissatisfied teenager bemoaning the lack of language and science education in North Texas, Griffin left home at fifteen to attend Lycée Descartes in Tours, France, on scholarship. Graduating fluent in French, Greek, and Latin after only two and a half years, Griffin enrolled in medical school at the University of Poitiers, specializing in psychiatry. His time in Europe was spent learning both psychiatry and musicology, during which he worked as an assistant in the city's psychiatric hospital. When World War II broke out in Europe, Griffin defiantly stayed in France to help Jewish children escape the Nazis by disguising them as mentally ill patients. He was later forced from France, but his time there undoubtedly expanded and shaped his worldview on the consequences of difference. Still, Griffin stubbornly "refused to see the same social mechanisms at work in the suppression of American blacks"[11] back home. He returned home to Texas learned and restless. Eager to serve his country and see the world again, Griffin enlisted in the Army Air Force in 1941. While Griffin was an Air Force sergeant stationed on special assignment in the South Pacific, a shrieking shell exploded near him during an air raid, rendering him unconscious for days. Griffin awakened to find he had lost most of his eyesight. After returning to France to pursue musicology and classical composition while he still retained limited sight, he finally returned home to Texas in 1945. He was completely blind.

Since disability contoured his life for more than a decade, Griffin's empathetic origin story would not be complete without contextualizing his blindness. Far beyond the physical changes and accommodations he was forced to make, blindness became one of the most salient ways Griffin came to understand difference. According to Bonazzi, "during his sightless years . . . 'racism became a preoccupation'[12] . . . without eyesight, [Griffin] was forced to perceive human beings simply as human beings. 'For the blind man, the whole issue of racism on the basis of inferiority according to color or race is solved axiomatically,' wrote Griffin in his *Journal*. 'He can only see the heart and intelligence of a man, and nothing in these things indicates in the slightest whether a man is white or black, but only whether he is good or bad, wise or foolish.' "[13] Idealistically, Griffin found, through disability, a humankind where race has no markers but color. It is curiously naive but still instructive. Bonazzi cites Griffin: "Past experiences, my religious encounter and academic studies came together with the personal experience of blindness, and the evil of racial discrimination was revealed by all of that in such a way that struck me a tremendous blow."[14] Griffin's most extensive writing about his blindness, the posthumously published *Scattered Shadows: A Memoir of Blindness and Vision*, details the incredible moment when he regained his sight on January 9, 1957. Since blindness had been such an important part of his understanding of humanity, a supposed unlearning of the arbitrary scopic logics of racialization, Griffin does not immediately revel in his newly recovered sight. In a chapter entitled "What It Means to See," Griffin writes, "Many people wondered what it might be like to see again after a decade of blindness. Sight does not return full-blown suddenly. You have to learn to see again, like a newborn infant. You have to learn to use muscles, to focus. The adjustment back to sight was as complex as the adjustment to blindness had been. The simple mechanics of living had to be learned over again. How to eat, how to walk, how to look at people. I kept forgetting that I could see, and that in seeing I could do many things that I had put out of my life."[15] This is a vulnerable articulation of the transition to sightedness, one Griffin interestingly equates with the tabula rasa of infancy. Race was one of those things Griffin allegedly put out of his life, but in his country home in Mansfield, Texas, his relearning undoubtedly included the visuality of race.

Griffin's blindness, years spent navigating the world without racialized sight, bolstered the myth about his own racial objectivity. He furthers this mythmaking by recounting how *Black Like Me* came to be. Griffin writes about his time working as a research assistant for a sociologist from the University of Texas in 1959. He was tasked with gathering surveys about the supposed rise in "suicide-tendency rates" among black southerners. Griffin clarifies, "This did not mean that black people were committing suicide directly. Rather it concerned a rise in violent incidents that were not connected, incidents in which blacks would appear to go berserk and lash out against whites, often strangers, for no apparent cause. The blacks would then make no attempt to escape and when caught would say something to the effect that they did not care if they lived or died."[16] To investigate what is clearly described here as racial stress, Griffin attempted to collect responses from a survey sent to an interracial sample of "educators, business and professional people and community leaders."[17] About the replies from white respondents, Griffin writes, "Almost everyone remarked that my study was 'ridiculous,' since it was racially characteristic of blacks that they never committed suicide. 'They are just naturally a happy-go-lucky people,' one said. Another wrote, 'When something troubles a Negro, he goes out and finds himself a shady spot under a tree and sleeps it off.' "[18] Embarrassedly, Griffin admits harboring some of the same racist stereotypes revealed by these responses while also recognizing the "sincerity of these people" since "we have been brought up believing this myth about blacks."[19] Griffin was not surprised by the "inevitab[ility]"[20] of these white responses.

However, Griffin says, "When the questionnaires came back from black people, I was astonished to note that not one contained any answers to my questions. The few that were returned were blank. . . . For the first time one of them used a term I had never heard before, but I found it accurate and illuminating. He said, 'You probably can't help it, but you think *white*. . . . We don't believe it's possible for a white man, even one trained in the sciences, to interpret his findings without thinking white and falsifying the truth."[21] Although Griffin could identify with the expected paternalistic racism behind the white responses to the questionnaire, he is slapped again, but this time not by his grandfather. Griffin's astonishment was less about what he calls the "justified"[22] nonresponse of the black subjects he polled but more important the galling assumption that he, after being slapped and blind, was still thought of as white . . . like that; or, in other words, white *like a racist*. Importantly, before "becoming" black, Griffin thought both his thinking and southern hands had been cleansed of the ideological stains of white supremacy. "We are, after all, 'Southerners,' " he writes, but then distances himself from racist whites by describing himself and his family as "'fringe southerners' living in a land where our whole lives, our pasts have been surrounded by the tainted atmosphere of white superiority; with ingrained reactions to the Negro. . . . Intellectually we have liberated ourselves from this concept—intellectually we KNOW better and are on the side of perfect justice."[23] He continues in his journal, "I who thought I had not an ounce of prejudice, find myself falling into deep gloom—I think this experiment will reveal many terrible things about us and our convictions."[24] Although these are Griffin's private thoughts, they are revealingly naive. Although both Griffin and McLaurin write about being indoctrinated into the classist lies of Jim Crow, a gentility somehow excusing them from past and present legacies of racial terror, Griffin perpetuates the myth that white southerners can be wholly removed from the psychic and emotional holds of white supremacy just as he thought he was. However, in these private moments, he deeply fears what his experiment might reveal about his own unexamined racism.

Importantly, those black questionnaires were not all defiantly blank. Griffin writes, "Across two or three of those blank questionnaires, black people had written that the only way I could ever hope to understand anything about the plight of black people would be to wake up some morning in a black man's skin."[25] Throughout his career, Griffin wrote multiple, shifting accounts about why he initially wanted to "become" black, but none was more thoroughly staged than this last account in 1977. For his original *Sepia* readers, Griffin introduced his motivation as a nagging desire for cross-racial knowing: "For some years an idea has haunted me. I have wondered what it is really like to be a Negro in the South."[26] In the opening lines of *Black Like Me*, Griffin repeats the claim of a haunting blackness, but this time, in the first entry on October 28, 1959, he confesses to being haunted "more insistently than ever."[27] According to Mark Pittenger, in neither version did Griffin acknowledge that his blackness had "been suggested—even authorized—by thoughtful African Americans who distrusted the standard procedures of social science."[28] In 1977, Pittenger continues, Griffin "cast himself as a white man who listened to black voices and heeded their advice, learning from them that a scientific method embedded in racist assumptions, whatever its pretensions to universalistic objectivity, would not produce truth."[29] Allegedly, this is when Griffin's idea for empathetic racial impersonation was born—only after these helpful anonymous black responses. *This* Griffin knew the late 1970s would be less tolerant of the idea of a white man hauntingly pursued by the idea of temporary blackness. His ability to stage and restage the motivations behind his blackness, a self-revisionist lore based on the changing sociopolitical needs of each moment and audience, reveals one of the main reasons Griffin remains the most iconic figure in this genealogy.

WHITE MAN EXPERIENCES LIFE AS A NEGRO IN THE DEEP SOUTH

JOURNEY INTO SHAME

© Copyright John Howard Griffin, 1960

By John Howard Griffin

PART VI

SYNOPSIS: In five preceding chapters, John Howard Griffin, a white author from Mansfield, Texas, told of his masquerade as a Negro on tour of the southern states. All his life, Griffin had heard stories and reports of the extreme racial prejudice and mistreatment afforded the Negro in the south.

As a white man, he had seen, and yet, not seen, the conditions of second class citizenship under which the Negro lives in the South. Griffin realized that in order to fully understand the situation, he would have to see it as a Negro sees it. He would have to turn his skin dark and find out for himself how the whites would treat him.

He took internal medication and ultra-violet ray treatments. It didn't take Griffin long to realize that he had made more than a mere change in the color of his skin. He had made a transition into an entirely different world.

His first stop was in New Orleans where he worked as a shoeshine "boy" for an old man. From there he went on into Mississippi. He got his first taste of discrimination on public carriers in the South, when a bus driver refused to let him get off at Hattiesburg to use the restroom.

In Poplarville, where a demented white mob lynched Mack Charles Parker, he found the Negro section of town in a grip of complete terror. He was hustled into a quarter room over a cafe by what he termed an "underground" system. A strange Negro in town is always subjected to close scrutiny by the police and the system served to keep the Negroes from being arrested without due cause.

He visited a friend of his in another Mississippi town. The friend, a white newspaper editor, is fighting a losing battle against white prejudices. After a lengthy discussion they came to the conclusion that the only solution is in an appeal to the religious nature of the whites.

Being the object of the "hate stare" was by now a daily occurrence for Griffin, and he found that one cannot

"get used" to it. There is no spoken word, just a stare of pure hatred. He found that even the most devout churchgoers use the stare as a silent means of "keeping the Negro in his place."

Once a white man gave him a ride in a pickup truck, and immediately began a one-sided conversation about his sexual relations with Negro women. The man made no bones about the fact that segregation ends at the women's bedroom doors. He stated frankly that he had had relations with several Negro women, in fact he made it a prerequisite to employment at a plant that he owned. Griffin bore the man's boasting during the ride in almost complete silence.

He realized that the man was showing a side of his nature that other white men never saw. The man told him that he was a grandfather, and Griffin tried to picture him at home with his grandchildren. By his outward appearance it wasn't too hard to do. He had a kind face, patient blue eyes and it was easy to see that he smiled a lot.

But now the man's words belied the fact that he had a shred of human decency. A man that, once the lust for blood had arisen, would never show an ounce of mercy to a Negro he thought "should be taught a lesson."

Griffin told how lonely a Negro becomes in a white man's world where he is forced to set himself apart from the rest of the populace. How he passed a restaurant, looked at the menu in the window, and driveled, but he didn't dare try to enter.

There were a lot of things he didn't dare try as a Negro, such as tarrying too long to look at the pictures of the white women in front of movies. He didn't look at them at all. He felt that sooner or later some white person would walk by and say, "What are you lookin' at, nigger?"

He learned that simple things such as food and water are a major problem for the Negro. He couldn't stop just

---

ABOUT THE AUTHOR

John Howard Griffin's first two novels, THE DEVIL RIDES OUTSIDE and NUNI have earned him international reputation. "For sheer talent, power and virtuosity of craft, Griffin ranks very high among the new writers, but he has deeper powers than these," comments literary historian Maxwell Geismar in his AMERICAN MODERNS.

Griffin was born in Dallas, Texas in 1920. He attended grade school in Texas, high school and university in France. Studying medicine in preparation for psychiatry, he became interested in musicology while experimenting with sound in the treatment of the insane. This led to studies with Nadia Boulanger and to historical research with the Benedictines of Solesmes. He is a recognized authority on Gregorian Chant.

In 1947, with a total loss of vision, he returned to America to attend schools for the blind. He then moved to a farm at Mansfield, Texas and divided his time between raising pure-bred livestock and writing books. He continued studies of philosophy and theology under the direction of the Discalced Carmelite Monks and the Basilian Fathers of Canada.

The first page from John Howard Griffin's final chronicle of "Journey into Shame" in *Sepia*.

The Missing Day

Despite the revisionist framings in the *Sepia* articles, *Black Like Me*, and *A Time to Be Human*, Griffin cannot escape the frank truths exposed by his own private journals. Griffin kept meticulous, largely unpublished journals, numbering a couple of thousand pages, even throughout his decade of blindness. Two years after regaining his sight, Griffin's plan to "become" a black man and document his experiences with racism throughout the South was fully backed by *Sepia*'s Jackson and Levitan. Griffin had been writing for *Sepia* since 1957, although he presents his idea in *Black Like Me* as a simple pitch to a friend in the publishing business and never acknowledges his already established relationship with the magazine as both an editor and part-time writer. *Sepia* was only one of the titles published by The Good Publishing Company, headquartered in Fort Worth, Texas, an "international black-magazine empire."[30] George Levitan, a plumbing supplier originally from Michigan, bought the then six-year-old publishing company in 1950. Shortly thereafter, Levitan built a large pressroom, keeping everything from the editing and writing to the publishing in-house. Consequently, it was "the only self-contained, black-magazine publishing facility in the nation."[31] The Good Publishing Company put out a number of titles, including *Bronze Thrills*, a tawdry, confessional-style periodical with headlines like "Make-Believe Bride" and "I'll Take Anybody's Man." The rest of the magazines, *Jive*, *Soul Teen*, and *Soul Confessions*, were similar pulpy confessionals about teenage tramps, dope fiend lovers, and ladies who "lived on lust." *Hep* was Good Publishing's often fictionalized account of celebrity romances. With a readership based largely in the South and on overseas military bases, the flagship magazine, renamed from *Negro Achievements* to *Sepia*, was modeled after the photojournalism of *Look* and attempted to compete with *Ebony*, despite its modest circulation of a little more than 61,000 subscriptions. First published in 1947, *Sepia* featured stories on politics and race relations along with celebrity profiles and reporting on the civil rights movement. Although it was the flagship magazine, writers often resorted to cheap journalistic tricks to create content. For example, according to sportswriter Mike Shropshire, "When [he] would interview a black athlete after a football game—Jim Brown, for example—he would take the liberty of writing a *Sepia* story on the player with fabricated quotations about the athlete's feelings on life. . . . 'We did it knowing full well that Jim Brown was never going to see *Sepia* magazine.'"[32] Ultimately, the magazines' often pulpy and smutty content could not compete with either the black respectability of *Ebony* or its subscription numbers.

Now, with both funding and publishing commitments, Griffin returned to his home office to contemplate the weightiness of his decision to embark on this black experiment. Late on that 1959 Halloween night, Griffin wrote a deeply uncomfortable account of his anxieties about the experiment as well as his own personal motivation for "becoming" black. Mostly, he meanderingly riffed on the imagined consequences of his new blackness:

> I skirt all around the reasons, but I must face them. Our intimate reactions—what this will do to my family—my parents and my wife and children; not only in the unpleasantness that we anticipate; but in some deeper realm ... but can one ever root out the deeper reactions of the gut. Am I not myself, all in having studied the situation of racism, loathing injustice, etc., still filled with the clichés that form our concept of the southern Negro. Yes, and do I not loathe even more deeply the prospect of becoming a Negro; and I must be clear here—not because of the reprisals, not because of the subterfuge, which I shall minimize, but because there is the deeper taint within me, as though becoming a Negro will do some profound damage to my humanity; and still more terrible, will perhaps forever alter my intimate relationships with my family—my wife, especially (who is thoroughly behind me in this) and God forbid, later my children. The truth is that we have come to the terrible, unspoken conclusion that I will not be a disguised Negro, but that I will be, in effect, a Negro; and God knows how this ramifies in the deepest recesses of our beings; and we cannot foretell how it will be afterwards.
>
> I am still not saying it.
>
> Today, when I talked of this with my mother; I saw the look of terrible dread on her face—not again because of what I was to do, but because of some deeper intuition that I will never again escape the marks, the "Negroness." ...
>
> Why am I so nervous, why do I find the project so profoundly offensive now that I must face the reality of it. Perhaps because I fear that the physical change will drag along with it a total transformation of identity, even interior identity.[33]

It is not a coincidence that Griffin is experiencing his identity crisis on Halloween, a day of masquerade, costume, childish revelry, spooky scares, and the ability to either hide or expose true selves. However, unlike the temporary costuming of the holiday, Griffin fears his blackness will be permanent, as if this experiment will indelibly stain him and his family, penetrating his bones and psyche—not just his skin. This missing day, the one he refused to reproduce in either *Sepia* or *Black Like Me*, challenges Griffin's insistence during his blind years that race is somehow immaterial, and it reveals his deep anxiety about what color really means. He knows he will be *seen*, both in his own mirror and by others, as a black man. His fantasied persona, Joseph Franklin, is like his October 31 thoughts he never makes public. In sum, becoming Franklin is part of his most closely held fears about empathetic racial impersonation. While Griffin "decided not to change my name or identity [and] would merely change my pigmentation and allow people to draw their own conclusions," the consequences of becoming Joseph Franklin haunt him and his new black psyche.[34] Here, Griffin echoes the rhetorical strains of his unacknowledged precedent, Ray Sprigle: "I began to be worried over the problem of turning my mind white again," Sprigle writes.[35] More than embodying blackness, Griffin, like Sprigle, fears somehow staying black and the complete loss of his white self. Unlike Sprigle, though, Griffin fears how his empathetic racial impersonation will also impact his family.

In the pages of that missing day, Griffin writes about never being able to return home white again. He recalls a conversation with his wife, Elizabeth, earlier that night:

> "I promise I won't come back while I'm a Negro; but if I did—if some emergency made it necessary—and we went to bed together—would you be able to overcome what you saw, conceive of me as the husband you've always known; or would you have the impression you were committing adultery with a Negro man?"
>
> She couldn't answer. "You'd feel like you were committing adultery with a stranger, wouldn't you?"
>
> "Yes . . ." she said softly, regretfully.
>
> "Isn't it insane—I'd feel the same way," I said.
>
> I did not pursue this with her, did not ask her if the idea excited her equally, in this weird situation where intercourse would be legal, morally okay, but give the illusion of being a profoundly *forbidden* and even monstrous act. . . . I did not want to oblige her to admit anything further along this line. . . .
>
> "Let's say that next Sunday I'll be gone, I'll be a bald-headed Negro somewhere in a rooming house or hotel room. . . . When you think of me next Sunday, how will you see me—as the man you've

known or as some bald-headed Negro in that room?" "As the Negro," she said. "I can't help it, I know that's how it'll be."

That was the death sentence to me—and how can I explain it? I told her: "God damn, if you don't visualize me, see me and remember me as the white John Howard Griffin; then what happens to that man? That's what scares me. Does he just cease to exist; disappear in the air?" . . .

I feared she would always see herself lying not with a Negro, but with a part-nigger.[36]

As Griffin feared Joseph would overwhelm his four decades as John, more worrisome was that, somehow, black Joseph Franklin would fuck his white wife. Like white supremacy in general, this is completely illogical. Sure, maybe the persona of Joseph Franklin might spice up the bedroom with some taboo, interracial sex play, but calling sex with his own wife "adultery" is his own racial fantasy, one coloring all of his interactions during his impersonation. It is a fantasy he tries to expose in other white men while downplaying it in himself. For example, when asked in *Sepia* if his experiment "encourag[es] race-mixing?" Griffin righteously responds, "The Negro does not want to mix races any more than the white man."[37] Joseph Franklin's "excitement" challenges Griffin's claims. Ultimately, Joseph Franklin makes Griffin a liar, which is why it is left to the privacy of his largely unpublished journal. Franklin represents the alienation Griffin anticipates as a black man, and his anxieties are especially curious when placed alongside the fact that while he was blind he married his wife and had children. While blind, Griffin never uses the language of separation and alienation about his relationship with his family he would later use to describe his temporary blackness.

In order to become the private Joseph and the public racial ally John, Griffin sought the medical supervision of a white New Orleans dermatologist. Although Griffin refused to detail "the method of darkening my skin . . . since it is dangerous to the health"[38] in the first installment of his *Sepia* articles, during his treatment, Griffin took an accelerated and potentially dangerous regimen of the vitiligo corrective medication Oxsoralen. Still, Griffin lamented how "the treatment did not work as rapidly as I had hoped, but after a few days I began to have a dark undercoating of flesh tone."[39] Unhappy with a singular prescription for his blackness, Griffin supplemented his treatments with topical stains and tanning lamps to even out the parts of his body; for example, around his mouth, the Oxsoralen refused to darken. Under his doctor's advice, Griffin shaved his head since he "had no curl at all. As I left his office for the last time, the doctor shook my hand and said gravely, 'Now, you go into oblivion.'"[40] In *Black Like Me*, Griffin more fully details his descent into the oblivion of blackness. He reveals that the friend hosting him in New Orleans was not aware of the full contours of his experiment. "What are you going to do—be a Puerto Rican or something?" he asked. "Something like that," I said. "There may be ramifications. I'd rather you didn't know anything about it. I don't want you involved."[41] Griffin does not record his friend's response.

After telephoning home without receiving an answer, Griffin "simmered with dread. Finally I began to cut my hair and shave my head. It took hours and many razor blades before my pate felt smooth to my hand. . . . I applied coat after coat of stain, wiping each coat off. Then I showered to wash off the excess. I did not look into the mirror until I finished dressing and had packed my duffel bags."[42] Rather than debuting Joseph, Griffin insisted nothing but his skin would change. He wondered, "Would they treat me as John Howard Griffin, regardless of my color, or would they treat me as some nameless Negro, even though I was still John Howard Griffin."[43]

Before Griffin first "walk[ed] out into the New Orleans night as a Negro,"[44] and although he would never publicly admit it, Griffin met his new self, Joseph Franklin, in a mirror rather than in public. He writes:

I went to look at myself in the mirror. A fierce looking, bald Negro glared at me from the glass. He in no way resembled me. The transformation was total and shocking. I had expected to see myself disguised, but this was someone else. I was imprisoned in the flesh of an utter stranger. All traces of the John Griffin I had been were wiped from existence. Even the senses underwent a change so profound it filled me with distress. I looked into the mirror and saw reflected nothing of the white John Griffin's past. . . . I knew then that I was not a disguised white man but a newly created Negro who must go out and live in a world unfamiliar to him.[45]

With Franklin in his psychic closet but glaringly in his every reflection, Griffin embarked on a "Journey into Shame," a six-part series that ran from April to September 1960 in *Sepia*. The October issue that followed was dedicated to the aftermath of the articles. The first installment of the series dominated *Sepia*'s April front cover. "Searching for the Truth—He Found It," the cover's title proclaimed: "White Man Experiences Life as a Negro in the Deep South." Wearing a nearly monochromatic brown suit and holding a burning cigarette in his right hand, Griffin sits casually facing the camera with arms crossed. His gaze is paradoxically serious but pleasant. This Griffin, parenthetically described as "(white)," is featured at the forefront of the cover in full color. Aside from *Sepia*'s bold red, white, and grey logo, and its feature title, white Griffin is the only colored image on the cover. Behind him are black and white photographs from Griffin's time as black. To the left of white Griffin's dominant image, a smaller headshot features parenthetically "(Negro)" Griffin with a shaved head, darkened skin, and shaded glasses. Also framing him are smaller images of Negro Griffin shining shoes, standing in front of a segregated colored entrance, window shopping in front of a bookshop, and patiently waiting for service at what looks like a lunch counter. In a small section called "Our Cover," on the contents page, Griffin is described as "truly a bold and fearless man behind his modest exterior. This montage of photos on our cover this month portrays Griffin in the various phases during his 'new life.' Griffin toured the southland to search for the truth concerning the conditions of the Negro. Many people will remember Griffin unbelieving as they recall the tall, husky 'Negro' with glasses and shaven head. They will recognize themselves in Griffin's by-line story that begins in this issue of *Sepia*."[46] Twelve pages into the magazine and alongside advertisements for small radios, bop style glasses, and a hair crimper, Part One of Griffin's series is listed in the contents under "Adventure," along with a number of "Feature" articles such as the "Slow Death of a Famous Street," about Central Avenue in Los Angeles, Detroit's "Motor City Shutterbugs," and an article entitled "The Day I Ran as a Negro," by history-making Olympian Jesse Owens. Griffin is listed as an editorial consultant on the issue.

Griffin's seven-page spread features as many images as pages, the photographs having been taken by established (also white) photojournalist Don Rutledge and staged after Griffin turned white again. Griffin details the awkwardness of once again donning temporary blackness. On November 9, he writes, "In New Orleans I resumed my Negro identity and we went to all my former haunts to photograph them. Getting photographs proved a problem. A Negro being photographed by a white arouses suspicions.... We had to arrange to be at the same spot at the same time, but pretended to have no relationship."[47] On December 14, Griffin writes in *Black Like Me*, "Finally the photos were taken, the project concluded.... I felt strangely sad to leave the world of the Negro after having shared it so long."[48] Although for *Black Like Me* readers Griffin is sad to leave the black community, for the *Sepia* readership, Griffin strategically acknowledges that he does not presume immediate black kinship: "Few issues have been more clouded by propaganda than the race problem. We have heard that the southern Negro is content with his lot, that he does not want 'The Southern Way of Life' changed any more than does his white neighbor."[49] The "we" deployed in "Journey into Shame" is a pronoun of both cross-racial distance and interest, complicating the rhetoric in the title of the *Sepia* articles. Griffin writes, "I had no precise idea what I would find. I promised myself only one thing—that I would note the truth, as exactly as I could, let the chips fall where they might."[50] Whereas Griffin supposedly offers objectivity, he found and marketed shame. Since shame is not objective but here a deeply internalized feeling of guilt, it works rhetorically for *Sepia*'s black readers while still coloring Griffin's understanding of cross-racial empathy. Paradoxically, while Griffin transformed "we" from a distanced, objective whiteness to a pronoun of assumptive kinship in *Black Like Me*, he felt the duplicity of his impersonation during an excursion with the famed white liberal P. D. East. Although on November 14 Griffin had only been briefly black, he rode uncomfortably in the front seat with East because it was "breaking the 'Southern rule' somehow."[51] "What did we fear? I could not say exactly," Griffin writes, "We merely fell into the fear that hangs over the state, a nameless and awful thing. It reminded me of the nagging, focusless terror we felt in Europe when Hitler began his marches . . . our deep shame of it. For the Negro, at least, this fear is ever-present in the South, and the same is doubtlessly true of many decent whites who watch and wait, and feel the deep shame of it."[52] Fear is the assumptive feeling Griffin projected on all black southerners, and shame was the assumedly proper response of "decent" white folks. Ultimately, his use of "we" attempts to represent communal blackness even during these revealing moments of racial bifurcation.

For *Sepia*, Griffin describes the "abject fear [that] has a taste like salt in the mouth"[53] he experienced as a new black man, and according to the letters to the magazine's editor, those readers overwhelmingly supported Griffin's articles. For example, a reader from Niagara Falls, identified only as "E. V. G.," writes, "I would like to take this opportunity to say 'Bravo.' [Griffin] should be congratulated by every anti-racial discrimination person in America. To Mr. John Howard Griffin, thank you for a job well done. If others considered the importance of equality, brotherly love and fair play our American flag would mean what it stands for."[54] Another reader, Gilbert Smith, calls Griffin's writing "majestic,"[55] and William Trapp offers his appreciation for "making public the persecutions the American Negro is suffering from the South."[56] Griffin then turned those lauded articles into

The October 1960 cover of *Sepia* highlighting the fallout of John Howard Griffin's "Journey into Shame."

Black Like Me. That memoir has remained consistently in print as a paper-back since 1962, "selling over a million copies in fourteen languages."[57] The success of *Black Like Me* was as much about the sociopolitical moment as it was about the memoir itself. For decades, Griffin's memoir has been on middle school, high school, and college reading lists as an exemplar of cross-racial empathy and heroic whiteness. In the memoir, Griffin skillfully situates himself among the most recognizable white liberals confronting race, like Lillian Smith and East. Also, because of his devout Catholicism, having converted from his largely agnostic Baptist upbringing, Griffin established himself as an important public ally to the faith-based community during the civil rights movement. Although that movement, a network of grassroots organizing, nonviolent action, and armed resistance, is often strategically reduced to the singular face of the charismatic, religious black leadership exemplified by Martin Luther King Jr., in 1961 it still needed white allies to voice and/or amplify its concerns. Griffin's Catholicism is the final piece in the story of his empathetic mythmaking. Along with his grand-father, blindness, and objective social science, Catholicism framed Griffin's cross-racial empathy. His empathetic racial impersonation, his ultimate moral sacrifice, makes him seem both humble and heroic because he consistently points to the Catholic Church as the remedy to racism. For example, Griffin's most explicit consideration of race, racism, and the Catholic Church is his 1969 *The Church and the Black Man*, a thin, oversized, coffee table–style book filled with full page photographs, some of which Griffin took himself. It begins with an anecdote about how he and activist and comedian Dick Gregory "walked with the campus minister toward the chapel of the University of the Pacific in Stockton, California. . . . Gregory glanced up at the sunlit façade of the chapel. 'God, I hate to go in these pa-gan temples of hypocrisy,' he said quietly."[58] He continues, "We listened that Sunday to a liturgy that struck us as starkly personal. *'O God, sustain my cause, give me redress against a race that knows no piety, save me from a treacherous and cruel foe . . . '* The glances we exchanged expressed clearly what we did not need to say; the 'cruel and treacherous foe' for us was racism, quite particu-larly racism that hid behind the guise of religion. That cruel and treacher-ous foe had killed too many men and women whose lives had been connected with our lives."[59] On that "Passion Sunday" in 1968, Griffin "wondered if others heard the words of the liturgy with the same personal recognition we did. Had any of them known the intimate grief of seeing friends and colleagues calumnied, shot or beaten by racists who called themselves Christians?"[60] Throughout *The Church and the Black Man*, Griffin exposes the hypocrisy Gregory laments by citing "random statements from black priests in different parts of the country."[61] He quotes an anonymous priest identified only as black and southern: "If the Church in the South could be really 'Catholic' we could really change in ten years. It is a hell of a job."[62] Here, Griffin wants to suture the future of racial equality to the promises of "real" Catholicism.

Despite Griffin's religious overtures in 1969, the last installment of the *Sepia* series and the conclusion of *Black Like Me* could not be more differ-ent. Undoubtedly catering to the mostly white readers of *Black Like Me*, Griffin lambasts the growing militancy of black folks. He writes:

The Negro does not understand the white any more than the white understands the Negro. . . . The most distressing repercussion of this lack of communication has been the rise in racism among Negroes, justified to some extent, but a grave symptom nevertheless. It only widens the gap that men of good will are trying desperately to bridge with understanding and compassion. It only strengthens the white racist's cause. The Negro who turns now, in the moment of near-realization of his liberties and bares his fangs at a man's whiteness, makes the same tragic error the white racist has made.

And it is happening on a wider scale. Too many of the more militant leaders are preaching Negro superiority. I pray that the Negro will not miss his chance to rise to greatness, to build from the strength gained through his past suffering and, above all, to rise beyond vengeance.

If some spark does set the keg afire, it will be a senseless tragedy of ignorant against ignorant, injustice against injustice—a holocaust that will drag down the innocent and right-thinking masses of human beings.

Then we will all pay for not having cried for justice long ago.[63]

This condemnation of burgeoning black militancy, particularly by black youth, is a racial blame game spuriously equating black protest and activism with the institutions of white supremacy. Here, Griffin shows his hand as a failed white ally by writing to his audience from fear rather than compassion. He writes what could happen if cross-racial empathy does not happen in the South but unfortunately does so by pretending reverse racism is actually real. While black supremacy cannot exist in the ways he describes, Griffin dogwhistles to white readers of *Black Like Me*, as rhetorically part of a black "we," that black resistance, under the guise of black supremacy, is a credible threat.

The disturbingly racist conclusion of *Black Like Me* is a far cry from how Griffin ends the *Sepia* series. Rather than warning white folks of a burgeoning black retribution, Griffin humbly writes, after recalling the many questions he answered in response to his experiment, that "Journey into Shame" was written to console black readers that white people could understand them, and a white person with a pen could authoritatively author their stories. And when asked, after all the questions and retribution Griffin suffered, he told those southern black folks, "Yes, I would do it again."[64] While Griffin only once again embodied the persona of a black man, to have photographs taken of the embodied psychic specter of Joseph Franklin for *Sepia*, his experiment and persona came to the big screen.

Black Like Me on the Silver Screen

While the title of the memoir *Black Like Me* was being splashed on movie theater marquees in 1964, John Howard Griffin's name was not—not even

James Whitmore as John Finley Horton in the 1964 film *Black Like Me*. Directed by Carl Lerner.

on the theatrical movie posters. Because of the book's success, audiences for the film presumably knew that the harrowing experience of "John Finley Horton" represented the film adaptation of Griffin's racial exploits. Their hunch was confirmed shortly after the theater lights dimmed and the opening credits began scrolling; this is "an actual event," the film prefaces. "John Howard Griffin, a white Southerner, changed the color of his skin, cut and dyed his hair—nothing more—and lived as a Negro, accepted without question by black and white. The characters and names are fictional, the incidents are based on John Howard Griffin's diary, letters and book. One man's strange journey—He happened to be a white man. But it could be *any* man's journey—If his skin were black . . ."[65] Even before the film begins, the silver screen's *Black Like Me* reveals one of the most troubling tensions at the heart of every empathetic racial impersonation—a white impersonator gets a name and individuality up until the moment he "becomes" just *any* black man.

Directed by Carl Lerner and co-written by him and his wife, Gerda, *Black Like Me* was a film with a shoestring budget of $273,000.[66] When James Whitmore agreed to star as Horton, he was already a long-established Tony- and Emmy-winning actor, most famous for his role as Abraham Lincoln Jones in the forty-two-episode television series *The Law and Mr. Jones* (1960–1962). Whitmore would later tell a *Fort Worth Star-Telegram* reporter during a telephone interview: "Oh boy, was the budget ever small. We did it for nothing."[67] What they did for nothing was a story Hollywood studios had long wanted to depict. In a 1964 film review, William Peper wrote, "Griffin said there was interest in the book from movie companies when it first came out. 'But, they suggested things like hiring Lena Horne for a romantic interest.'" Refusing routine Hollywood revisionism, Griffin signed on with a smaller, independent production company based in New York, Continental, a division of Walter-Reade Sterling Inc., concluding: "Now [the film's] been made straight."[68]

Despite Griffin's conclusion, there was little "straight" about either the filming or the content of Continental's *Black Like Me*. Fearing retribution from racists while on location in the South, everyone involved with the film decided to lie. Vernon Scott, journalist for the *Dallas Times Herald*, described the making of the film: "Hollywood will take an unfair rap for slithering into the southern states under false pretenses to film a controversial movie that is sure to cause more strife in that area."[69] He continues, "According to Whitmore, instead of announcing its intentions openly the New York film company invaded the south secretly. While asking various communities and individuals for the use of street scenes and interiors, the filmmakers lied about their movie. Police departments and individuals who assisted the company were doubly duped. First about the picture, secondly that it was being made by a Hollywood company."[70] First, Whitmore defends the production on the basis of fear: "'We made the picture on the Q.T. to avoid publicity,' he said 'We thought we might have encountered trouble if it was known what we were shooting. We might have been troubled by organized picketing and bully boys at worst. Or maybe just annoyed by drunks?'" He then adds, "The picture will be inflammatory to southerners."[71] Betraying the cast and crew's imagined and anticipated southern racism, the assumptive Dixie terror did not sit well with Scott. He defensively pushed back, "Did they give the South a chance to prove otherwise?" he asked. To which Whitmore simply replied, "No." When Scott presses further about "all the double-crossing" and asks why the New York firm said they were from Hollywood, Whitmore tries to downplay the fear of Dixie terror by suggesting the South was "bamboozled" (Scott's description) to hide Whitmore's own fame: "'People recognize me from that television show, *The Law and Mr. Jones*. And we thought it would make people less suspicious,' he said. 'When people asked me why my skin was dark I told them I was playing an FBI man in disguise.'"[72] The reporter again pushes back, asking if Whitmore is "bothered by his own lack of candor in dealing with southerners who graciously made him feel at home? 'What are you, some kind of an honest nut?' [sic] Whitmore flared angrily. 'We might not have had police protection down there. The false pretenses annoyed me a little. But getting the picture made was more important.' Whitmore, who admits he does not believe in the ends justifying the means, said, 'It's different in this case.' But his face was red."[73]

Maybe, as Whitmore concluded, the film would offend southerners. Even before the film's release, its falsified production certainly offended Scott. However, Whitmore's candor here is instructive. Rather than actively search for the worst of southern racism and racial terror as Sprigle and Griffin did in their real-life empathetic racial impersonations, the film sought to avoid that same Dixie terror while simultaneously wanting to restage it. Despite Scott's moral objections, *Black Like Me* was originally released on a double bill with the 1960 horror film *The Hands of Orlac*, about a "concert pianist who receives a hand transplant from a convicted killer and descends into homicidal madness," as Kevin Heffernan describes it in *Ghouls, Gimmicks, and Gold: Horror Films and the American Movie Business, 1953–1968*.[74]

Although Scott saw Whitmore's angrily defensive red face, that same face on the big screen is often shoeshine black. However, before audiences see that black face, we see a road—specifically a shot of a fast-moving dividing line. It is a shot used repeatedly throughout the film as a transitional trope as well as a reminder of the Jim Crow line Horton willingly and heroically crosses. The road is a thematic declaration that this cinematic adaptation is a travel narrative depicting a journey into both blackness and the precariously racist South. Throughout the film, Horton is constantly on the move, echoing Griffin in *Black Like Me*: safety meant "walk[ing] constantly until you could catch a bus, but keep[ing] on the move unless you have business somewhere."[75] Horton is always moving—on foot, as a passenger on segregated buses, and as a hitchhiker in strangers' cars. In the logics of the film, Horton still is not safe. After the road, audiences see Horton on a rambling, segregated bus, awkwardly seated next to a standing white woman. We see her face and those of the other passengers before Horton finally looks up at the woman and gentlemanly offers her his seat. It is his first racial faux pas, a violation of Jim Crow mores to which the woman takes great vocal offense. However, his faux pas is not this scene's most interesting moment.

As Horton lifts his head, his temporarily blackened face fills the camera's frame, and in that moment, the audience should be grateful that *Black Like Me* was shot in black and white. Seeing Whitmore as Horton is a visually jarring moment. Dressed in a suit, one he wears in nearly every scene,

Horton's black skin looks incongruent with his piercingly unchanged, light eyes. His head remains unshaven, unlike Griffin's strategic baldness. *New York Times* film critic Bosley Crowther rightly describes Whitmore as "blackened to look like an end man in a minstrel show—a make-up that would seem a quick betrayal of the pretense he is trying to put across."[76] Horton's cosmetic blackness can only be described as greasy, unevenly applied, and often looking like it just might melt. Too many times we see Whitmore's camouflaged white skin, especially in the creases along his neck and across his wrinkled brow. Such bad makeup is unimaginable in full Technicolor, and its badness is most egregious when Horton shares the screen with real—matte—black bodies. Only in the film's fictional landscape would Whitmore's sweaty blackness be taken seriously. Ultimately, *Black Like Me* on the big screen reinscribes the visual logics of blackface minstrelsy also on the April 1960 cover of *Sepia* featuring Griffin. Much like early advertisements of blackface minstrels, the photographs replicate the iconography of blackface with the dual images of white and Negro Griffin.

The distracting and sometimes laughable failure of Whitmore's unconvincing blackness is excused by the revelatory truth of Horton's experiences while black, or as the tagline of the theatrical trailer demands: "See *Black Like Me*—it's true." As Crowther claims, the film "does not succeed in putting the viewer inside a Negro's skin. Neither does it convince one that its hero is truly passing for black. It simply succeeds in demonstrating some ugly and painful incidents of racial prejudice as witnessed by one man, but it does that very well."[77] Although "very well" is a strong conclusion, *Black Like Me* delivers a wealth of "painful incidents." For example, after being chastised by the rude white woman on the bus, Horton is denied the same bathroom break afforded to the white passengers at a rest stop. Although the other black riders experience this same routine moment of Jim Crow degradation, only Horton challenges it. He angrily disembarks and resigns to walk. For readers familiar with Griffin's account, this moment marks a decisive shift between the textual blackness of Griffin and the visuality of Horton. When Griffin was not let off a New Orleans bus after sounding the buzzer multiple times, he was demure: "'May I get off now?' I asked quietly when the others had stepped down. 'Yeah, go ahead,' [the driver] said finally."[78] On that day, November 14, Griffin had been impersonating blackness for exactly a week, already knowing how to keep his head down. However, Horton did not. Griffin himself commented on Horton's portrayal of his blackness: "He plays it angry all the way through. . . . I couldn't behave that way when I was doing it in real life. I'd have been killed."[79] Griffin rightly acknowledges that while Whitmore describes his fear of racial retribution during the making of the film, he, as an actor, probably would not have been killed, despite his overwrought and overplayed anger.

Horton's painfully racist incidents continue. Although Horton happens on a friendly black man, Bill Mason, who offers this meandering stranger lodging and food, hooligans inexplicably try to run them off the road. Out of breath, they finally make their way safely to the house of Doc Collins, a black man who graciously agrees to host Horton as his family's guest. As Collins complains about the routine racial torment both men just experienced, Horton admits, "I guess I'm not used to this kind of thing." With freshly applied blackness, Horton is obviously unaccustomed to the illogical racism enabled by Jim Crow, even though he did not register the same fear of it on that segregated bus. Alone, Horton is heroic, but, in the company of actual black men, Horton quickly admits his inexperience with the consequences of blackness under Jim Crow. Rather unevenly, the film attempts to dramatize, often overly so, the Dixie terror Horton bravely encounters individually alongside the racism contouring the lives of *any* (read every) black man.

During *Black Like Me*'s 105 minutes, being denied permission to pee and nearly being run off the road represent only two of Horton's experiences across the Jim Crow line. Horton also suffers the humiliation of a random white man telling him to "find yourself another place to set"[80] while eating lunch on a bench next to a white woman and her baby; white managers denying him a job even as wanted signs hang in the windows to lure the unemployed; and white teenagers chasing him into an alley while calling him a "nigger," and ridiculously, since he never changed his hair, a "burrhead."[81] These incidents are most often endured while Horton, alone, is attempting to find stillness while being black—trying to sit and eat, seeking the stability of a job, and attempting to make it back safely to the solace of his rented room. All but one of his most egregious encounters with racism regularly occur in the cars and trucks of the white men providing him rides when he was hitchhiking. Like the shots of a moving road, scenes of Horton as an uncomfortable passenger are a repetitive trope in the film. For example, after Horton is ousted from his lunch bench, he flags down a white driver, who picks him up. In the supposed interracial, homosocial privacy of the truck, the two first make casual small talk about the bird the driver has caged in the back of the cab, a surprise gift for his wife. The casual banter quickly, weirdly, turns from birds to sex. When the driver asks Horton if he is from "around these parts," he answers, "No, Texas." "Then you ought know enough to say 'sir?'" the driver chastises. "Yes, sir," Horton acquiesces. Their conversation continues when the driver asks if Horton's wife is pretty, before crudely querying "She ever had it from a white man?" Even though Horton is upset by the line of questioning, the driver confesses: "Nigger women know they can't get jobs unless they put out to their bosses. I've hired lots of them. . . . I guarantee I've had every one of them before they ever got their pay." Although Horton suggests he "must have lots of colored children" and then angrily asks if he ever "consider[s] th[ose black] women," the driver laughingly dismisses those concerns. He then, braggingly, goes on to insist his serial raping of black women was a boon to the black community and an unremarkable consequence of Jim Crow: "We all do it around here," the driver insists, "we figure we're doing your race a favor, put[ting] a little white blood in it." When Horton refuses to confirm the driver's rapaciousness and/or sexual curiosity, the driver suspects he is in the company of a "troublemaker": "You know what we do to troublemakers here? . . . Kill a nigger and toss [it] in one of these swamps. Nobody ever know anything about it." As he slows the truck, the driver insists: "This is where you get off. I'll tell you how it is down here. We do business with you and your women. Other than that, as far as we're concerned, you're completely off the record." Horton bolts out of the truck. He is repeatedly called "boy" and a "black bastard"[82] before finally throwing a retaliatory rock at the back of the again moving truck. Interactions like these are another way the film, despite Griffin's trusting conclusion about it, is not entirely "straight." If Horton had indulged the driver's racist sexual proclivities, he might have made it safely to his destination.

Instead, Horton walks a dark road lined with live oaks dangling with Spanish moss until a blurred image of his very white wife fills the screen with the now absurd refrain of the racist driver: "She ever had it from a white man?" The faces of the other rapacious and curious drivers besiege him, splitting the screen with the pleasant images of his wife, Lucy. After an emotionally exhausted Horton collapses under the weight of this psychological torment, the film flashbacks to him and his wife together in bed, postcoital, and both white:

HORTON: If I was to come home suddenly, how would you feel?
LUCY: Delighted to see you.
HORTON: No. No. No. I mean, while I'm changed.
LUCY: You always did look good with a tan.
HORTON: I'd be a Negro.

LUCY: I don't understand.

HORTON: If I were to stay with you would it be like sleeping with a Negro?

LUCY [startled]: John!

HORTON: It excites the hell out of me.[83]

While this dialogue is on one hand a tender conversation between lovers, it reveals the sexual anxieties and racial fetishes Griffin detailed in the missing day. With access to Griffin's journal, the Lerners staged a sanitized version of that day as an important moment in the arc of the film. In this romantic moment, Horton admits to being turned on by the thought of making love to his white wife as a black man. It is a scene mired in fantasies around the taboos of interracial sex much like the kinds of uncomfortable sexual queries and confessions black Horton raged against as a passenger in the cars of the white men supposedly not like him. Unlike Griffin's carefully curated memoir, the film version of *Black Like Me* allows the fictional Horton to expose a small bit of Griffin's secret sexual proclivities—that he is white *like that*.

Ultimately, then, *Black Like Me* on the big screen is not only a travel narrative. It is a story of sexual fantasies and anxieties at the color line. It heavy-handedly images the homosocial, cross-racial encounters between black Horton and white men; the brief flirtation between Horton and a black woman on a blind date; and the psychological barrier Horton experiences as a temporary black man with his permanently white wife back at home. Only a few years before *Loving v. Virginia*, the 1967 Supreme Court decision that struck down the remaining bans on interracial marriage, bootblack Horton is unable to communicate with Lucy as he earlier promised. In a melodramatic scene, Horton tries and fails to write his white "Darling." Hounded by the looming consequences of Jim Crow, Horton cannot help but recall the instructions he received early in his impersonation from Bill Mason to not even look at a picture of a white woman while in the South. Alone in his room, a longing and frustrated Horton ignores Mason and stares at a picture of his white wife and child. The film then jumpcuts to a flashback of Horton being chased, again inexplicably and without provocation, by two white boys yelling racial epithets. After ducking into an alley with balled fists, Horton angrily threatens the youths to "come on" and meet him in the alley while also whispering a frightened prayer of protection to Saint Jude. When the youths back off, Horton slowly emerges from the alley and runs, full-speed, back to his room. He then shatters the mirror in his room that mocks the black skin responsible for this racial terror. While doing so, he accidentally spills either ink, or possibly the greasepaint used to touch up his black face, on the photograph of his family. Rather than crying or attempting to clean the photograph, Horton maniacally laughs. Here, Horton's fear finally comes true; his blackness spills beyond himself, contaminating and ultimately destroying the last anchor to his preblack self and the only tangible link to his white family. It is Horton's racial breaking point. In " 'Black Like Who?' Cross-Testing the 'Real' Lines of John Howard Griffin's *Black Like Me*," Kate Baldwin writes about Griffin's memoir, "Despite his intentions to break the color barrier, [he] finds himself—a white Southerner—policing the very line he presumably set out to sever."[84] Baldwin's words are also applicable to the film. Whereas white Horton could admit to the exciting possibilities of interracial sex in ways creepily similar to the white drivers he finds racist and repulsive, and much like Griffin on Halloween, bootblack Horton is imprisoned by the mores of Jim Crow compelling him to uphold the sanctity of allegedly pristine southern white womanhood.

Finally, the not "straightness" of *Black Like Me* is confirmed by one of Horton's last encounters with a white man—this time a northerner. Horton meets Charles Maynard, a graduate student researching southern race relations for his dissertation, at a small, black-owned diner. Maynard is immediately fascinated by Horton's intelligence and nags him enough that Horton reluctantly agrees to accompany Maynard back to his room for a nightcap. It only takes one or two drinks for Maynard to expose his racist hand. Wrapped in the alibi of research, Maynard spouts his assumptions about black folks: they are inherently more sexually free, lack inhibitions, have unstable family structures, and "large number[s] of illegitimate births." Horton angrily insists that the moralities of black and white communities are not different, and that Maynard's facts are the result of environment rather than racial determinacy. Maynard's scientific interest insistently turns to the now familiar harassing curiosities about sex and black masculinity. Maynard wants to know how large Horton's johnson might be, going as far as to suggest they compare the sizes of their penises since they are roughly the same age. Full of rage, Horton leaps on Maynard and begins choking him, only letting him go after Maynard implores him to stop. "I'm no queer," Maynard insists. Surprisingly dazed by his own capacity for violence, Horton leaves the room and heads for the nearest Catholic Church.

In the film's logics, this scene is palpable evidence of how Jim Crow corrupts men who happen to have black skin. Here, blackness was not about kinship, history, or belonging but instead about what happens when racist whites see blackness, a conclusion bolstered by the decision to change nothing about Whitmore but his skin. This decision corroborates once-blind Griffin's own conclusions about race. The film instructs its viewers that a good white man who only wants to understand racism from deeply held moral convictions can descend into violent madness just because of how his skin is seen. Rather than the shame Griffin describes in *Sepia*, Horton's rage is the inevitable consequence of being viewed as a black man in the South. After casually confessing to a priest that he just tried to kill someone, Horton reveals himself as a white man impersonating blackness for "three months now"—much longer than Griffin's actual racial experiment. "It horrifies me," Horton tells the priest, "It's as though I was no longer myself. I look like a stranger. I live like a stranger. Now, I'm beginning to feel like a stranger. 'Tis though I lost my immortal soul." The priest reassures Horton he could never lose his soul, and the only thing lost while black was "pride of self."[85] The priest sympathizes as a similarly not too prejudiced white man in the South and promises to pray for him, a nod to the redemptive power of Griffin's real-life Catholicism. "Being" black for months had not only separated Horton from his family but also separated him from himself. "I find myself acting like an inferior colored man filled with anger and hatred," Horton insists. This stranger, perhaps a hate-filled Franklin, was far from the kind of black man, Burt Wilson, the shoeshine man Horton entrusted with his racial experiment early in the film, instructs Horton to be. Wilson taught Horton "how to act right" by first modifying Horton's physical appearance by suggesting he remove his coat and tie and roll up his sleeves. After this, Wilson critiques: "You got to learn how to act. . . . You talk too educated one way and in another way you got to get smarter. Ugh, you're gonna be a problem. You think it's easy being colored?" At first, as a self-described "not drinking man," Horton chuckles at the question. However, as the film nears its end, Horton is far from laughing. He all too quickly becomes a defensive, liquor thirsty attempted murderer.[86]

After even more encounters with racism on a beach and in yet another bus terminal, now repentant Horton finds one last gracious black family to shelter him—the house of Pops and his politically involved son, Tom. Whereas Pops immediately ingratiated himself to his temporary guest, Tom was skeptical. After finding out that Horton wrote about southern race relations, Tom asks if Horton made a lot of money on his stories, not so subtly implying that Horton's stories were merely tabloid fodder for northern black folks who refuse to support southern black protests but still

In the 1964 film *Black Like Me*, John Finley Horton defends his empathetic racial impersonation to Tom and Pops. Directed by Carl Lerner.

delight in reading gory accounts of segregation. Horton counters, "What I write, I write for the South," defending himself with a replica of the magazine. The titular banner of the issue remains outside the camera's frame, but audiences see a brief but clear close-up of the rest of the cover: "Travel for the Truth: White Man Lives Life As a Negro in the South U.S.A." With its unnecessary addition of "the South U.S.A.," the cover implies the magazine had a sizable international readership that exceeded *Sepia*'s real southern readership. Otherwise, the magazine stayed true to *Sepia*'s original layout. Horton is featured prominently as a white man on the right side, and "Negro" him, imaged only in profile, flanks his other side.

As Horton presents the magazine exposing him as white, Tom is simultaneously skeptical and incredulous: "Well, how do you like that," Tom retorts. "I knew there was something phony about you. You got a lot of nerve coming into people's homes pretending you're 'folks' . . . sneaking in here all painted up." "Will you let me explain?" Horton implores. Tom, the idealistic civil rights protester, begins to angrily recount the demonstrations he participated in: "You know what it woulda meant for one white man to support us at that time? And I don't mean just talk." A less angry but still insistent Horton responds, "I do now. Why don't you read what I've written before you twist it all around?" "Because it won't make any difference," Tom counters, "That's just words." Their interaction continues to escalate:

TOM: One single white man in each county willing to give up his life for justice. You know what a difference that would make?

HORTON: [The] white southerner has to know what it's like to be a Negro. Really know.

TOM: And you know what it's like, huh? After ten weeks or three months or whatever it is, you know?!

HORTON: No, I don't know. And I can never know any more than you can know what it's like to be inside my skin. . . . We got to keep trying.

POPS [interrupting]: So, that blackness on your face, it'll come off won't it? You wipe that blackness off, they'll treat you like a man. We black—in a white man's country. Ain't nothing we can do about it. If you don't understand that, you don't understand nothin'. I know how Tom feels. I know how come he talk that villainous. Tom know though that that ain't no way to talk. He been taught different. [Turning to his son] Tom, the man tryin' to help.

TOM [with a raised voice]: We don't need his help! What we want we'll get by our own strength.

HORTON [also with a raised voice:] I'm doing this for myself! I want the South to be a fit place for my children to live. Can't you understand that?!

This conflict between the three men reflects both generational and interracial differences as well as the momentous sociopolitical changes during the timeline of the publication of the *Sepia* articles in 1960, the memoir in 1961, and the film's release in 1964. Months before the Civil Rights Act of 1964 passed, and years before May 20, the day of the film's domestic release, four college students defiantly sat down at a segregated lunch counter in Greensboro, North Carolina; the Student Non-Violent Coordinating Committee was founded; Freedom Riders crisscrossed the South to protest segregated transportation; Medgar Evers was assassinated; the Mississippi Freedom Summer for voter education and registration saw the lynchings of three young people; Martin Luther King Jr. delivered one of the most important speeches of the twentieth century; and the country was still reeling from the assassination of John F. Kennedy. To find its audience, *Black Like Me* had to account for the national interest in the civil rights movement and this changing sociopolitical and racial landscape. In short, the articles and memoir had to be updated to include its own critique. Tom, played by Al Freeman Jr., the same actor who would play black botanist Howard in the 1968 film version of *Finian's Rainbow*, was that critique.

Much like the missing day, this scene is absent from Griffin's memoir. However, unlike the missing day, this absence does not result from Griffin's careful curating of his text. Tom, or any character like him, is not buried in Griffin's journal. Rather, he is a character made necessary by the timing of the film. Ultimately, the inclusion of Tom remains the most forceful internal critique of the logics of *Black Like Me*, and Horton's selfish motivations for empathetic racial impersonation. Tom reveals how Horton is a failed white ally who only experiments with blackness to further his personal investment in his own white family. By extension, Horton, as a Griffin cipher, uncovers how *Black Like Me*, as both memoir and film, also reveals that this empathetic racial impersonation was about white folks rather than the betterment of black folks. It finally reveals that Horton writes for the white South to help usher in a fit and/or safe South for his white family and not a better South for any black communities. However, even with the inclusion of Tom, the film stays true to the spirit of Griffin's racial sacrifice. After a few more tense minutes between Horton, Pops, and Tom, Horton finally admits that although he does not know everything about being black, he promises to tell the "folks back home" what he has found. Horton believes the authority of his whiteness coupled with his revelatory white words trump Tom's critique and his permanent blackness. Although Tom faced the punitive consequences of protesting Jim Crow, all Horton wants him to do is sit down and read his articles to understand the righteousness of his temporary blackness. Like a self-appointed missionary, Horton defiantly concludes the conversation with his commitment to spread his not so good news to a rather ambiguous audience: "All I know is, I'll tell them." The "them" is unclear; however, we can assume "they" are the not yet as empathetic white southerners Horton imagines can only be reached and changed by his racial travails—the whites *like that*. The film's final shot captures Horton crossing that ubiquitous dividing line on the road, this time representing his crossing back into whiteness. Since audiences never see his transition back to whiteness, viewers are left to only imagine Horton's racial homecoming, and Pops's reassurance that Horton would once again be treated like a man, not only by racists but, more important, by his own wife.

Taken together, Griffin's *Sepia* articles, unpublished journal, bestselling memoir, and the fictionalized feature film offer a compelling archive. Assuredly, some of his popularity results from the nearly perfect sociopolitical timing of the publication of the memoir. However, that cannot singly account for the decades-long persistence of Griffin's impact. For example, I happened on the DVD of *Black Like Me* prominently displayed among other more contemporary films in a Tallahassee Target store. I was shocked. My shock quickly turned to questions like "why?" and "who, other than me, would want to buy this DVD in 2012?" After a longer, admittedly more thoughtful pause, I asked myself: "What can Griffin still teach us about empathy?" I bought the DVD.

A decade before Griffin, Sprigle understood his blackness through the logics of "good niggerhood," a shuffling, servile performance of black masculinity learned from the successful southern black men who instructed him.[87] However, Sprigle's inability to earn another Pulitzer Prize with his columns "I Was a Negro in the South for 30 Days" for the *Pittsburgh Post-Gazette* and the lack of commercial success for his memoir *In the Land of Jim Crow* largely resulted from the fact that although he articulated the link between racial impersonation and masculinity, he was more cowardly than heroic.

In contrast, Griffin's blackness reveals the vulnerable anxieties and instabilities of heteronormative masculinity, particularly in spaces of homosocial, interracial contact.[88] As demonstrably portrayed in the film and also described in his memoir, while hitchhiking from Biloxi, Mississippi, to Mobile, Alabama, Griffin experienced assumedly unexpected curiosity as well as unwanted sexual advances from the white men willing to give him a ride. In *Black Like Me*, Griffin writes, "It quickly became obvious why they picked me up. All but two picked me up the way they would pick up a pornographic photograph or book. . . . All showed morbid curiosity about the sexual life of the Negro, and all had, at base, the same stereotyped image of the Negro as an inexhaustible sex-machine with oversized genitals and a vast store of experiences, immensely varied. They appeared to think that the Negro has done all of those 'special' things they themselves have never dared to do. They carried the conversation into the depths of depravity."[89] Here, Griffin details how homoerotic, white supremacist stereotypes of virulent, hypersexual black masculinity dictated these interracial interactions between men.[90] No longer able to rely on the respectability and power conferred on white heterosexual masculinity, Griffin, quite to his surprise, is queered by blackness. Again, no iteration of *Black Like Me* was ever "straight." Unlike Sprigle, Griffin put himself in harm's way, relating the numerous consequences of his new black masculinity under the regimes of Jim Crow, including being hanged in effigy in his hometown of Mansfield, Texas, after he returned to whiteness.

Arguably, Griffin could be, and often was, taught as a real-life version of Atticus Finch, at least before 2015, when Harper Lee's controversial sequel to *To Kill a Mockingbird*, *Go Set a Watchman*, unraveled the fictional sanctity of American literature's most cherished protagonist of white ally-ship in ways similar to how the missing day complicates Griffin's legacy. However, even James Whitmore put Griffin on a sanctified pedestal of cross-racial empathy well after he portrayed Horton. "John was as close to a saint as any man I knew," Whitmore lauds, "What he did was just extraor-dinary. We didn't do him justice . . . John was way ahead of his time."[91] In the hopeful future of imagined racial harmony, Griffin performs, for many readers, a representative tutorial on how to make that future possible. How-ever flawed, selfish, improbable, and even unknowingly racist he may be, Griffin remains instructive. Ultimately, what we learn about empathy from Griffin is much like what in the film Horton tells Tom in defense of his impersonation: "We got to try." Griffin's empathetic racial impersonation represents a desire for models of trying, even when they fail, like Finch ul-timately does. Even as Griffin stands as the most exemplary mid-twentieth-century mouthpiece for cross-racial understanding, his biographer Robert Bonazzi still describes him as a "reluctant activist."[92]

Warning: blackness might make you famous.

CHAPTER THREE

A Secondhand Kind of Terror

Grace Halsell and the Ironies of Empathy

> As Lorraine Hansberry had observed, it's a special time to be
> young, gifted, and black.
>
> —GRACE HALSELL, September 16, 1969

When Grace Halsell cited Lorraine Hansberry's affirmation of a talented generation of black youth, she had only recently become a white woman again. On July 9, 1968, armed with the curiosity and mobility of a freelance journalist, the economic security of a former staff writer for Lyndon B. Johnson, the mentorship of John Howard Griffin, and the reckless courage of the daughter of an infamous cowboy and westward expansionist, Halsell abandoned the presumed comforts of southern white womanhood by beginning a course of medication to darken her skin and become a black woman. Halsell was not motivated by a desire to challenge the structural racial inequalities exposed by the era's growing tumult; she had no grand aims of easing the escalating racial tension of the late 1960s. Instead, she chose blackness "to open my mind, my eyes, my pores, to the dilemma of race in America, and to share my experiences,"[1] selfishly suggesting, "I need this experience."[2]

Although a self-described "descendent of slave-holders and Civil War veterans,"[3] Grace Eleanor Halsell was no belle. Born white on May 7, 1923, in Lubbock, Texas, to a sixty-three-year-old father and thirty-year-old mother, Ruth Shanks, Halsell was encouraged to "exert free will"[4] by her father, whose 1957 *New York Times* obituary was headlined, "Harry H. Halsell, 96, Indian Fighter, Texas Rancher Who Once Outfoxed Geronimo Dies." Despite growing up near native communities, Halsell retroactively insisted that "color was not a conscious fact in my early years."[5] She did not become "personally interested"[6] in either the ethical or legislative gains made by the civil rights and black power movements, or even the lives of any people of color, until a book recommendation at a State Department reception in January 1968 made race personal.[7] Although she had never heard of *Black Like Me* or its author, John Howard Griffin, Halsell writes: "I bought *Black Like Me* and plunged into it, discovering that Griffin talked to me like an inner voice, calm, suggestive." Deeply moved, she concludes, "I could do that . . . I could be black."[8] And Halsell did, committing to impersonating a black woman living in both Harlem and Mississippi for six months.

More than a year later, reflecting in her private diary on Hansberry's motto "to be young, gifted and black"—the title of both a posthumously produced play and a literary mosaic of unfinished works, interviews, and journals—Halsell did so by appropriating the powerful rhetoric of a burgeoning black power movement. Halsell's six black months allowed her to imagine herself among the intended audience of Hansberry's loving and urgent charge to a new generation of black writers. Hansberry affirmed, "Though it be a thrilling and marvelous thing to be merely young and gifted in such times, it is doubly so, doubly dynamic—to be young, gifted *and black*." She beseeched her audience, "Write about *our people*: tell their story. You have something glorious to draw on begging for attention. . . . This nation needs your gifts."[9] With her once temporarily black body coupled with the hubris of privilege, Halsell positioned herself as uniquely available to tell her story in her 1969 book *Soul Sister*, the formal conclusion of her experiment. That memoir boasts over a million copies sold, five translations, and a paperback reprint celebrating its thirtieth anniversary.

Halsell's timing was terribly ironic. Paradoxically decontextualizing Hansberry's charge, Halsell gave birth to her "special" and "gifted" blackness just as black separatists began to question and reject the place of white liberals in the civil rights movement, especially as that movement started to address issues beyond southern segregation, including white supremacy, capitalism, and the U.S. imperialism of the Vietnam War. While many white liberals hailed the end of de jure segregation as the solution to racial inequality in the United States, it became clear in the wake of the passing of the 1964 Civil Rights Act that, however historic the legislation, the institutionalized oppression facing African Americans reached beyond Jim Crow to include the persistent issues of economic security, housing, and employment. Subsequently, the radicalized youth comprising the Left, including the white-led and -dominated New Left, represented by Students for a Democratic Society (SDS) and the highly visible activists in the burgeoning Black Power movement, grew more skeptical of those same white liberals who fought for integration but balked at more militant pronouncements of racial sovereignty and class reform. Dissatisfaction with what many saw as the failed promises of American liberalism erupted in a 1968 that saw 125 urban riots protesting the status quo as well as the assassinations of Martin Luther King Jr. and Bobby Kennedy. Invoking Gunnar Myrdal's 1944 description of America's "Negro problem" as the country's "dilemma," Halsell's sojourn into black womanhood coincided with this decisive sociopolitical shift from the integrationist tactics structuring civil rights strategies to the more radicalized demands of black power. As Carol A. Horton writes, "The old Myrdalian paradigm, it seemed, had been pushed to the breaking point. Either the American dilemma—now reformulated to demand not simply the end of formal discrimination, but the eradication of entrenched socioeconomic inequality—had to be resolved, or its contradictions would destroy the democratic spirit of the nation."[10] In this historical context, Halsell's six-month experiment as a temporarily black woman can be understood.

Halsell's temporary blackness gave her a disorienting perspective on twentieth-century U.S. race relations, providing not only a warped interpretation of what black womanhood meant at the end of the 1960s but also a perverse opportunity to unmoor herself from the pedestal of southern white womanhood. As an independent, mobile, employed divorcee, Halsell already teetered on the edge of that pedestal, and her "need" to experience blackness represents a desire to shed what those southern ideals represented. So, when Halsell's former boss, President Johnson, wrote a blurb for *Soul Sister* proclaiming it a text to be "read by all Americans," his seemingly straightforward endorsement betrayed the central, intriguing, and uncomfortable irony to which this chapter attends. Johnson insisted that the text was for "all Americans" at a moment when the concept of who was allowed to constitute an "American" was becoming more fractured, and blackness was becoming more diversely understood. Engendered by the once oxymoronic claim that "black is beautiful," Halsell's ill-timed eagerness to "open" herself and "share" her new blackness is premised on a convenient and disavowing erasure of narratives by black women, revealing the imbalanced power dynamics in the empathetic gesture. By detailing Halsell's racial experiment and self-miscegenation as well as the relationship between Halsell and her masquerade mentor, John Howard Griffin, this chapter reveals the pervasively perverse assumptions about the meanings of black identity and the utility of cross-racial empathy. It contends that these meanings are rendered most explicitly at the crossroads between the anxieties of white liberalism and the urgent necessity for a redefinition of blackness. Ultimately, this chapter insists that such fetishized assumptions of blackness and womanhood are matters of life and death.

A Kind of Lady *Black Like Me*

Published in 1961 by another Texas native, *Black Like Me* chronicled Griffin's iconic sojourn into what he calls "oblivion," his trek through the Jim Crow South as a black man. Halsell found in the pages of *Black Like Me* the cure for acute racial myopia: empathetic racial impersonation. Inspired by Griffin, Halsell began an intimate correspondence with him in March 1968 that would last until Griffin's death in 1980. "I want to know you," she writes in a telegraph.[11] "How nice of you to write me," Griffin writes on March 22, 1968: "I know who you are and would be pleased to meet you."[12] Halsell received her chance to meet Griffin on April 3 since he was delivering a lecture at the University of Baltimore that day. "Thank you so much for your kind letter," Halsell responded on official White House letterhead, "Could I pick you up after your lecture on the third? And perhaps drive you to the airport on the fourth?"[13] Although Griffin acknowledges many readers of *Black Like Me* sought his encouragement and advice for their own racial experiments, it was this initial meeting and ensuing friendship that convinced Griffin that Halsell could and should attempt blackness. Notably, in a May 23 letter to Robert Gutwillig, editor of the New American Library, a division of Penguin Books, Griffin introduced Halsell, hoping his recommendation would proffer publishing support for her proposed memoir: "Let me just say that many people have approached me about such a [racial impersonation] project and I have consistently discouraged it, because it is dangerous and it takes very special gifts of perception.... When Grace Halsell suggested this to me, I jumped at the idea enthusiastically, because she combines the experience and the perception and the 'feeling' more than any person I know:—I urged her to do what I have always discouraged everyone else from doing."[14] With the support and mentorship of the man she would eventually call "Soul Brother Number One Howard,"[15] Halsell prepared herself for her experiment, an updated version of *Black Like Me*, initially conceived as a year-long project.

Even before physically transforming herself black, Halsell began learning how to perform blackness by enrolling in what could be described as John Howard Griffin's correspondence course, "Empathetic Racial Impersonation 101." Responding to her queries on how to affect the "identity . . . in mind,"[16] Griffin offered this advice: "I think the best thing is to keep the story as near the truth as possible . . . (We must avoid giving the racists the material to discredit you later—they will love to put on that you went there [Mississippi] under false pretenses.) Certainly with Negroes, I would tell the exact truth, that you are doing a kind of 'lady' *Black Like Me*; you are from Fort Worth. Once you are in the Negro community it is just assumed that you are Negro, so you will not need to make any explanations because none will be asked.... If Negroes ask questions you can give honest answers; if whites (especially strangers) ask questions, just assume that cold-staring 'sullen' attitude and mumble the minimum replies ... this is what most Negroes do now, when the questions are unwarranted."[17] Here, Griffin instructs Halsell in a performance of blackness, one he caricatured as a "sullen" and "mumbl[ing]" suspicion. Griffin's tutorial is assuredly excavated from the stereotypes of the white male imaginary and then filtered through his former experience as a temporary black man. Griffin's advice to Halsell is haunted by the racial experiences and conclusions recounted in his narrative—from being trapped on a segregated bus unable to disembark at his requested destination and hearing testimony of the harrowing tales of Mississippi brand Dixie terror to the "hate stare" visually trapping him within the dangerous and confining racial stereotypes structuring his new blackness.

Although Griffin made his own connections with members of the black community both before and during his black weeks and encourages Halsell to speak honestly with members of her new racial community, he does so by positioning himself as her race mentor. With assumptive authority, Griffin never advises Halsell to seek out any black women before she becomes one. Black women's bodies, interests, and collaboration are not only conveniently absent but also rendered unnecessary. Instead, Griffin schools Halsell in a set of racial templates standing in for a "real truth" about the performance, consequence, and performativity of race and racial difference.[18] He then explicates the presumed schism between the public and interior lives of African Americans, suggesting blackness must be staged for the appeasing benefit of white audiences. In *Real Black: Adventures in Racial Sincerity*, John Jackson writes, "Classifications by race, class, gender, sexuality, ethnicity and nationality are all such shortcuts, templates we use in lieu of absolute interpersonal transparency. We employ them to get at the truth of the world, to get at *the real world*."[19] While the structural regimes maintaining difference demand that the assumptions, stereotypes, and ideologies collectively creating these templates be naturalized to the point of invisibility, empathetic racial impersonation exposes these templates as already memorized scripts, guiding and interpreting cross-racial, interpersonal relationships in lieu of a more complete understanding of how difference is structurally maintained. Consequently, Griffin's and Halsell's impersonations reveal assumptions of what it means to not only *act* black but also *be* black under the spuriously faulty visual logics of race. Following Griffin's instruction, being "taken for" and "assumed to be" black will give Halsell experiential and moral authority. Appropriating a mixture of methodologies borrowed from the presumed intimacy of anthropological fieldwork, the exoticizing conceits of the travel narrative, and the supposed objectivity of investigative journalism, Griffin claims, as participant observer, exclusive insight on the black experience, or what Gayle Wald calls the "fieldwork of passing."[20] However, without acknowledging the performance and performativity of racial difference and its structural and institutionalized mandates, Griffin obscures *intra*racial anxieties about black authenticity and belonging often played out at the precarious intersections of gender, class, and sexuality. Before Halsell's intervention, empathetic racial impersonation was an enterprise of white men, specifically Ray Sprigle and Griffin. Wald writes, "The gendering of white passing [is] an enterprise of 'heroic' masculinity."[21] Although rife with the baggage of white masculine privilege, Griffin's encounters with queered sexual vulnerability, like his disturbing experiences with curious white men during his own experiment,[22] along with his other encounters with racism, structure his anxious mentorship of Halsell.

While readying Halsell for her curtain call on the stage of black life, both she and Griffin were motivated by the gendered insight Halsell could bring to a white readership's understanding of black America. "After all," Halsell writes, "*Black Like Me* was written by a man. . . . I wondered if it were possible for a white woman to expose herself to that mind-deadening malady of second-class citizenship and report its effects," a dystopian and telling assumption about blackness.[23] In the same letter to Gutwillig, Griffin heavily markets Halsell's womanly perspective. He writes, "I have also felt that this [impersonation] should be done by a woman, and felt my own work deficient because I believe there are insights that only a woman can get."[24] Selling Halsell to this potential publisher with gynocentric ideals of female intuition, Griffin recognizes his blindness regarding the experiences of black women in his own exposé.[25] However, he paradoxically still positions himself as the guiding authority on how to perform black womanhood. While supposedly speaking to the differences between his experiences as a briefly black man and what he anticipates Halsell will encounter as a briefly black woman, Griffin cautions Halsell on the threat of sexual violence. It is a caution that recalls his own experience of sexual vulnerability. "Always act suspicious," Griffin warns, "especially of men asking questions, and especially of the police, suspicious, uneasy and ready-to-run; because certainly the fear of rape is widespread."[26] Griffin is ambiguous here. Who is Halsell to fear exactly? And why? Perhaps it is the memory of his own sexual vulnerability that prompts this cautionary advice. Perhaps, as "Soul Brother," Griffin specifically worried about his little "Soul Sister's" safety. Or, perhaps this is Griffin's socially conditioned, white masculine instinct to protect southern white womanhood in general from the lecherous virility of black masculinity. The latter hypothesis seems much more likely since in his own memoir black Griffin was psychologically unable to write a letter to his *very own* white wife. Griffin resigns, "My conditioning as a Negro, and the immense sexual implications with which the racists in our culture bombard us, cut me off, even in my most intimate self, from any connection with my wife."[27] However, and through either scenario, Griffin insists that an understanding of the widespread threat of sexual violence is an essential part of constructing a recognizable and legitimate performance of black womanhood.

Consequently, throughout *Soul Sister*, Halsell interprets Griffin's warnings through her long-conditioned fear of black male sexuality. "Yes," she admits, "I've packed all of my old fears, right in with the nylons and hairbrush. I'm not *supposed* to go [to Harlem]."[28] Halsell continues, "No telling what's going to happen to a good white woman like me."[29] Whereas white men accost Griffin in the pseudo-private, transitory space of the automobile with vulgar and untoward curiosities about the virility of the black male body, Halsell anticipates rape by black men. She writes, "The white man says the black man is a beast and marauder, he will rape you, rob you, he is mean as the devil (you know the devil has got to be black)."[30] Here, Halsell simultaneously animates the myth of the black male rapist while attempting to rhetorically distance herself from complicity with sexual racial terror by invoking "the white man." This is a discursive move Halsell employs throughout *Soul Sister*—a reading of white supremacist stereotypes, conveniently excusing herself specifically and "good" white womanhood in general from the consequences of race. Halsell summons this readily available, hyperbolic template of the black male rapist as a white male fantasy, one recognized as a particularly, but not exclusively, southern fiction. As Riché Richardson reminds in *Black Masculinity and the U.S. South: From Uncle Tom to Gangsta*:

The myth of the black rapist that emerged in the South in the wake of Emancipation functioned in some ways as the obverse of the Uncle

Tom and was rooted in even more explicitly perverse scripts of the black masculine body and sexuality. It was a myth that cast black men as sexually pathological, hyperbolized their phallic power, and construed them as inherently lustful and primitive. It was rooted in the growing panic about racial intermixture in the South that emerged after slavery ended, reflected the region's obsession with protecting white womanhood to ensure the purity of the race, and served as a primary rationale for lynching in the region.[31]

Richardson later concludes that the myth of "the black rapist is one of the most virulently racist stereotypes of black masculinity in this nation's history."[32] Subsequently, Halsell's southern white womanhood is predicated on the paranoid expectation of a pathologically rapacious black masculinity. While supposedly ensuring that whiteness is protected from miscegenation, this racial anxiety produces a vulnerable white womanhood. It is as if the rapaciousness of black sexuality would undoubtedly hunt down and uncover the "truth" of her whiteness. In other words, she may "become" a black woman but would always be a white rape victim.

On July 9, 1968, after completing Griffin's cautionary and epistolary empathetic impersonation workshop, Halsell began her transformation into a black woman. It was a medical blackness developed and maintained by a team of renowned dermatologists: Robert Stolar of Doctors Hospital in D.C., John A. Kenney of the Howard University School of Medicine, and Aaron B. Lerner of the Yale University School of Medicine. Under their guidance, Halsell began a regimen of Tsiroralen and the topical ointment Zetar. These medications condition the skin to receive sunlight by enlarging the secretory cells responsible for injecting pigment into the skin. The medications are most often prescribed as a corrective remedy for vitiligo, a dermatological disease that results in an uneven loss of pigmentation characterized by random blotches on the skin.[33] Along with these medical and topical interventions to her skin, long-held racial mythologies still impact how Halsell chooses to embody her synthetic blackness. Or, as Halsell exclaims in a September 2, 1968, letter to Stolar, "I'm beginning to see several benefits in being a man! I could wear long-sleeved shirts and trousers and just have a dark face and dark hands."[34] Halsell fantasizes herself both black and in drag, longing for the masculine privileges of Griffin's seemingly easier black embodiment. Griffin never anticipated the need to display his entire body to the gaze of anyone aside from his own reflection, and prepared his blackened body to pass only in public—much like how blackface minstrel performers used burnt cork just on their face and hands. In contrast to the theatrical blackness confined to Griffin's face, torso, and hands, Halsell supplements her medication with a week basking in the tropical suns of Puerto Rico during a month of bikini sunbathing and almost overdosing on vitiligo corrective medication in the desperate attempt to get an even coloring on her entire body. Her attempt at physical blackness reveals her conclusion that to successfully perform black womanhood, her *entire* body must be able to withstand the scrutinizing gaze of racial surveillance. Once Halsell's body reached a "beautiful color (good enough to eat I suppose—*if* you like caramel),"[35] as she described herself to Lerner, she added a few more physical changes to her bodily landscape, including hair dye and black contacts. By readying her whole body for the private sphere, Halsell gestures toward the vulnerability of black women, eerily foreshadowing, as we will see, the uncomfortably ironic end of her memoir. Finally caramel from the Puerto Rican sun, but also still worried about her physical transformation, Halsell saw Dr. Kenney one last time before moving to Harlem to begin her (mis)adventures in blackness. "*To reassure myself,*" she writes about her physicality, "*I put my arm against his. He is Negro, but I am still darker.*"[36] It is a move white girls still do against the arm of a black friend to ensure their vacation tans are satisfactory.

Abandon All Hope Ye Who Enter Harlem

Satisfactorily dark, Halsell completes her look before getting on a bus headed to Harlem from the nation's capital. She writes, "I put on a simple cotton dress and flat shoes, insert the black 'eyes,' and tie a kerchief over my hair."[37] Halsell continues, "And I pack—the same bag I've always handled with insouciance I now pack with portentous dread. Harlem, only four nonstop bus hours away, seems distant and awesome, a land of menace and fear. . . . Soon be there! In that ghetto that everyone wants to 'study,' and no one wants to understand, that largest black metropolis in the world. I have never seen it except in a cluttered, symbol-ridden mind's eye."[38] On entering blackness, she also writes, "I have been on the outside looking in. I have smelled the colored people's collard greens and their living-up-close-together smells. I am now going to knock on their doors and say, black people let me in there with you!"[39] Imagining the wafting and iconic black neighborhoods of Harlem as a restricted "black enclave," Halsell refuses the slumming fantasy of the culturally rich, endlessly accessible Harlem that drove the curious white middle class uptown for exotic nights of jazz and

gin during its Renaissance. Instead, she constructs Harlem as an urban wasteland marred by the blight of overindustrialization and the accumulating
detritus of modernity.[40] "So the bus moves towards Dante's inferno," she
writes. "No, not Dante's but Claude Brown's, James Baldwin's, Billie Holiday's. And through my roiling mind: *Abandon All Hope Ye Who Enter Here*."[41]
Unlike how she distances herself from the black male rape fantasies of white
men, Halsell constructs her move to Harlem by imagining herself within
the alien and alienating space of a decidedly urban black landscape, one
"peopled by Dickensian elements, drunks, pushers, thieves, murderers, dope
addicts, the deprived, the predator."[42] The sonic markers of aesthetic
poverty reinforce this hellishness. She describes her first night: "At first I
listen to the noises. . . . The sirens that wail endlessly. Another overdose?
Another stabbing? A .38 in the chest? A murder? A fire? All night the sirens
tell the story of Harlem—a cacophony of heartache, tragedy, trouble."[43]
Harlem's cacophonous soundings resurrect nightmarish fantasies of urban
blackness, complete with the stereotyped images of black rage, criminality,
and violence already haunting the white imaginary of the late 1960s, most
specifically the mournful and rage-filled riots protesting the death of Martin
Luther King Jr. on April 4, 1968—a moment briefly acknowledged by Halsell as the day after she first met with Griffin. Still, black humanity is absent from Halsell's Harlem, another world of the dying and marauding
undead, and a "pantheon of villains."[44] It is this exotically dangerous and
terrifying image of a seedy black metropolis that structures Halsell's urban
blackness.

Clutching her travel bag on that bus, Halsell moves to Harlem full of the
psychological ghosts of racism and white supremacy. Anticipating a geographical, physical, and psychic shift of being and perspective once she
alights, Halsell writes: "In Harlem I will no longer carry my identity card
that has always provided me with special status: white American, member
of *the* club. I will be going to a black country, where in all directions, uptown, downtown, and crosstown, there will be nothing but black faces. I
will no longer be the person I have always been, and to enter into this new
world I will have to ask to be accepted. I will be knocking on the ghetto
door, beseeching: let me come in, accept me as one of you, a black among
blacks."[45] Halsell is first dropped off in Midtown Manhattan, overwhelmed
by how everyone seems to know where to go. Vaguely knowing that Harlem is uptown, she braves the subway, finding herself on Harlem's iconic
125th Street. Her first impressions of the neighborhood are telling: "I get
off at 125th Street and climb toward the light. Here before me is the ugly,

awful, open wound that is Harlem. Early afternoon. I see the nodding, bobbing addicts, the drunks swinging empty bottles around their heads like lassos, crap shooters, pushers, and strewn through the streets like mines on a battlefield, the broken, jagged liquor bottles."[46] I "can hardly believe what I see," she writes.[47] Overwhelmed by too many "sights, sounds, [and] smells,"[48] Halsell walks the streets for four hours, "feel[ing] a special gray death . . . hanging over my spirits."[49] Halsell attempts to find a reputable place to stay the night. She calls friends and asks strangers. However, to her, "Every person here appears *condemned*."[50] Exhausted, she finally finds a hospitable $5 room in the Douglas Hotel at St. Nicholas and 151st street. After flinging her tired body on the bed, the noises of strange men moving through the halls intimidate her to the point of emotional and psychic suffocation: "I can't breathe," she writes.[51] With Griffin's warnings about rapacious black men ringing in her ears, she takes her chances back on Harlem's streets. However, after fleeing the phantom threat of heavily footed men at the hotel, she still seeks the help of a black man.

During her first Harlem dinner of pork chops and collard greens, Halsell repeatedly calls Jim Hamilton, a contact she made in Puerto Rico during her aspirationally black sun worship. After many missed calls, they finally arrange to meet around 10.30 P.M. Since this nightcap is indicative of the tensions between white liberals and a burgeoning black radicalism, their interaction is quoted here at length. About a supposedly casual drink between acquaintances, Halsell writes:

> Jim . . . a proud Afro . . . undoubtedly foresaw only a pleasant, uncomplicated interlude, with beer in hand, and a superficial conversation. . . . What he got was my frustration and fear and thwarted plans and painfully innocent notions spilled all over his nice manner and his composure. I told him everything, adding, "I need your help."
>
> Just as frankly he replied that I would not get it. He let me know that he and others like him were sick and tired of white liberals coming to "study" and help the Negroes. "You help as long as *your needs* hold out, and then when you've eased a guilty conscience your help is finished."
>
> He said that not for one second would he condone such romantic notions as a desire to go poking my nose into his friends' lives "to discover more of your untruths." And he added, "No, no indeed, I won't open up any of my friends' closets—for your inspection!"

"Jim . . . I want a closet of my own." I was being womanly—logical in the way that so infuriates a man. But I recognized in Jim Hamilton the indignant black man who is sick of the white liberal who seeks self-identity through little pitying acts of condescension, running up to Harlem to make himself more compatible with his conscience.

He'd been perfectly willing to drink a quiet beer with me as someone who was only female. Now he saw me as the activist and he hated me, hated me for all that whiteness represented, a sluggish callousness, yet with ego bent on action and the "right" to lead the struggle, to guide the Negro, and with the additional right to be cheered, recognized, for having always done "so many good things" for the colored folk. He hated me because he now saw me as part of the System that has permitted America to concern itself with poverty, discrimination, and deprivation around the world without applying its vast resources to sickness at home.

Well, stay out! Jim was saying to me.

"Jim," I told him, "if I had only come to drink a beer with you, that would have been all right. Or, if rather than seeing me on the day I arrived in Puerto Rico, *white*, you had seen me later, with dark skin and black lenses, then you would have accepted me. But you have raised the huge Off Limits sign only because I was frank with you, only because I have told you I want to educate myself, and *to write* about it."

He was off on another tirade. "No, no! Your timing is just *too right*. Just at the time Harlem closes itself to the white press, you come up, to make your 'study,' no doubt to report on 'Negro violence,' while the violence against black people is taken for granted, like the weather!

Why don't you write about the System and the Establishment? Why don't you reveal who controls all the importation of narcotics in this country? Why don't you write how the mass media perpetuate the evils of slavery?

You can't understand me, you can't understand the man or the woman of Harlem because *you* can't have known the special burden of being black in this country. You can't have known the person you're trying to write about when he was a child of five, a child of ten—and all of the years, or all of the evils of the society that can oppress a man, make him so ashamed that he is among the oppressed, rather than the oppressors!"

Jim's rage struck me in the face and heart. Feebly I tried to defend my position: "I'm not trying to understand or write about *your* life, but only to live awhile in Harlem and relate *my* experiences."

He again repeated that no "truths" could come from that.[52]

This is a painfully poignant interaction, detailing the widening gap of distrust between activists on either side of the black/white binary. In this scene, Halsell is defensive, coy, and flirtatious. While definitely not an activist, Halsell wants to be seen as doing something different from those white liberals Jim critiques, repeatedly citing her need for a personally transformative experience through black womanhood. However, Jim recognizes the spuriousness of Halsell's claim, confronting her assumption that a "truthful" cross-racial epistemology can come from her temporary impersonation. As Jim reminds her, Halsell does not have the context of growing up undeniably and permanently black in the United States, and he challenges Halsell's assumption of blackness as a readily available catalyst for change.

"Jim's rage" stems from deep-seated frustrations about being part of a community continually devalued as merely the subject of white curiosity and scholarship marred by the stereotypes of black pathology. Consequently, his anger can be contextualized as both an indictment of Halsell and a useful response to Daniel Patrick Moynihan's liberal call for national action to remedy the supposedly pathological instability of the predominately matriarchal black family in the 1965 memo infamously known as the Moynihan report. In it, even an espoused white liberal could not help but construct the black family as dangerous, dysfunctional, and in need of government intervention. Rather than understand the legacies and histories of systemic and institutionalized racism, Moynihan blames the supposedly broken black family on the supposedly broken black family. "At the heart of the deterioration of the fabric of Negro society is the deterioration of the Negro family. It is the fundamental source of the weakness of the Negro community at the present time. There is probably no single fact of Negro American life so little understood by whites."[53] Before this determination, Moynihan cites the most substantive treatise available on America's "problematic" Negro, once again, Myrdal's *An American Dilemma*: "What Gunnar Myrdal said . . . remains true today: 'America is free to choose whether the Negro shall remain her liability or become her opportunity.'"[54]

Less than sixty pages into her memoir, this interaction between Halsell and Jim is fueled by desire, anger, and miscommunication, and makes space for this forcible critique of both her and her experiment within its second section. She writes, "I knew that Jim was right in his accusations of whitey. Brotherly love seemed so hopeless. The past so strewn with sins. How rise above them?"[55] However, although Jim challenges Halsell, painting her as an unhelpful, naive, and selfish white liberal satiating guilt and privilege by temporarily flirting with the danger and possibilities of blackness, Halsell rhetorically dismisses his criticisms almost immediately. She is decidedly not "whitey." She continues:

> Then I remembered the beauty of Malcolm X's growth and his rising above hatred of a man because of his color. On his pilgrimage to Mecca in 1964 he discovered he could break bread with a blond, blue-eyed Moslem and be treated as a brother. The trip convinced him that skin color is less important than point of view; that awareness, not pigment, is crucial. Now that it was too late I remembered the final conviction of Malcolm X and wished I had quoted that to Jim: "*You can hate the System*—Malcolm had told the black people in his last days—*but there's no need to hate the person.*"[56]

By invoking an oversimplification of Malcolm's racial maturation, Halsell negates Jim's request to address the systems maintaining racial inequality rather than her own indulgent desire for cross-racial intimacy. Although she never describes Jim as rapacious, she dismisses him as, puzzlingly, an "Afro" and a "black militant," situating him as somehow even more militant than the stereotyped face of black masculine militancy, pre-Mecca Malcolm X.[57] In *Soul Sister*, Jim is too angry to be taken seriously, and Halsell's citation of Malcolm X undermines Jim's frustrations by placing him on the most extreme fringes of "irrational" black separatism. In other words, if Malcolm could change, why couldn't Jim? Their awkward cocktail hour exposes the angst around the place of white liberals, often narrated through the development of a black radical expressive tradition privileging the specific urban geographies of the North. But Halsell, in a hellscape like Harlem, undoes the black protest represented by Jim with her performance of black survival, suffering, and pain.

The next day, after those confrontational cocktails, Halsell awakens to find her feet "swollen into enormous clubs, misshapen and unsightly. Blisters sprout like rampant mushrooms, covering my heels, soles and toes. I try to get out of bed. I cannot walk. I find myself down on my hands and knees on the dirty floor."[58] She seeks emergency medical attention at Harlem Hospital. As she waits too long in the emergency ward, Halsell describes the hospital and its staff as grossly inefficient. When she finally meets her impatient doctor, he scolds her for wasting his precious time, "'*you people*,' [the doctor] lectures me, 'should bathe more often. Your feet are *dirty!*' He says there is nothing wrong with my feet. '*Just* blisters.'"[59] With the privileged position to seek a second opinion, Halsell travels back to Washington, D.C., to receive personal dermatological care from Dr. Kenney. He determines her infected blisters are the consequence of severe sun poisoning and third-degree burns from her time baking black in the tropical sun. After ten prescribed bedridden days, Halsell returns to Harlem to work as a secretary; ironically, in the same hospital where she had previously received substandard health care.

Unsurprisingly, Halsell fails to acknowledge how the privileges of race and class enable her travel and corrective treatment, yet she is eager to imagine her aching body as the corporeal occasion for her communal belonging. She writes, "*I, black woman . . . human, female—ache . . . because we know pain and we welcome pain.*"[60] Although she receives the systemic, substandard health care that often structures what U.S. blackness feels like, Halsell insists it is her now hypersentient black woman body (and not her experience with structural inequality) that enables her representative black suffering.

Halsell visually performs this painful blackness for her readers on the front cover of *Soul Sister*. For the first edition of the memoir, the front flap of the dust jacket features black Halsell complete with an upturned gaze and a decidedly worried expression. Wrinkles furrow her brow, worry or fatigue lines rim the bottom of her eyes, and her parted lips turn downward. She looks desperately imploring, and her disembodied face is shiny from sweat and/or anxiety. This image of black Halsell immediately equates black womanhood with suffering, suggesting a black communal "we" to which she now can lay claim. She imagines the trauma of her hurt feet as her newly acquired ancestral legacy as she writes: "Now it's different. [Negroes] understand me, they are my fellow sufferers."[61] Her black face is "more than bone-weary,"[62] and her imaged black womanhood is based on assumptive templates of pain and fatigue, Griffin-inspired shuffling subservience, and communal martyrdom. In other words, Halsell fantasizes and performs a blackness both enabled and paralyzed by vulnerability. However, when readers turn the book over, they see an opposite image: a white, smiling Halsell. Any discomfort readers might experience after witnessing the transformative effects blackness wrought on Halsell is undermined by the image of her reassuringly happy, white-again face. On that back dust jacket flap, Halsell is restored to herself again and smiles openly and beautifully

Cover of the thirtieth-anniversary edition of Grace Halsell's 1969 book *Soul Sister*.

with a bright, gleaming, and hopeful, rather than despondent, gaze. The thirtieth-anniversary edition of *Soul Sister*, published in 1999 by Crossroads International Publishing, constructs this binary by putting those same images of Halsell's white and black faces on its front cover. The cover is visually striking; it is divided with a white background on the left side and a contrastingly black right side. The Crossroads cover situates Halsell's naturally white face floating on the bottom of the white side of the cover below the boldly black word "SOUL" as black Halsell's sorrowful face hovers above the boldly white word "SISTER." This anniversary edition celebrates Halsell's empathetic racial impersonation with the tagline "The Story of a White Woman Who Turned Herself Black and Went to Live and Work in Harlem and Mississippi."

The visual binary between a pained black Halsell and thriving white Halsell hints at a racial splitting reinforced throughout the narrative. As Halsell situates herself within Harlem's black spaces, her memoir betrays an anxious vacillation between her white interior and her black exterior. Although she previously traveled extensively by her white woman self to places like Lima, Rio de Janeiro, Hong Kong, and New Delhi, she "can't see Harlem the way I've seen other 'foreign' places"[63] because of the intensity of her new racial difference. For example, she describes her fear of Harlem and its residents even after her physical transformation to "caramel." She writes, "Why do I fear entering this black enclave as I have never feared any other place? Because there are signs you don't see, big, lurid signs all over this country. They shout out: you are white, you are a white woman and have no business going into that ghetto—it belongs to *them*. And the rest, *all* the rest, belongs to you."[64] Unlike her previous global journalistic assignments, Halsell's domestic racial schism is palpably reinforced in a narrative scene between her and Longus Moore, the owner of the small diner where she ate dinner before her challenging pseudo-date with Jim Hamilton. For Halsell, Moore's blackness makes a strong impression, and she creepily describes him as "a totally black Negro: not one of the modern pretty boys, but Negroid all the way, the lips, the nose, and the eyes."[65] Recognizing the seriousness of her hurt feet, Moore offers her transportation to that disreputable Harlem Hospital. However, Halsell interprets Moore's help as offensive to her otherwise independently mobile, white woman sensibilities. Facing Moore's frank and compassionate declaration "I will help you," Halsell emotionally crumbles:

> The words are so simple, somehow so sharp-edged—for the good can hurt as much as the bad, sometimes more—that I want to shout, this is not fair! I came here to know you for what you are, you beast, you black, black, black man! And you are ugly to me. You are a nigger. And you feel sorry for me. You are pitying me, you are, Christ in heaven, you are loving me! It's not supposed to be like that! . . . God, how I need you, how I want you.
>
> My face is buried in my hands; the tears are coming. And I feel helpless and stripped naked, stripped bare of those myths I've worn like crown jewels—that white is right, that black is wrong. Moore takes the scales away, he alone, and he does it with four words: *I will help you.*[66]

Halsell is completely undone by Moore's kindness. His compassion challenges her power and position as a "real" white woman, and she despises him for it. Consequently, she wields appallingly racist language about

Moore's blackness and how disgusting it is to feel the upending of supremacy. So, although Halsell wants to experience a personally transformative blackness, clearly she does not want to be seen as helpless or indebted in a way that compromises her privilege. Like the interaction with Jim Hamilton, this intimacy with a Harlem black man disrupts Halsell's version of her intentions.

Both interactions are loaded with desire and fear, and consequently Halsell is besieged by the destabilizing conflict between her temporary black face and permanent white privilege. More than any other impersonator in this genealogy, Halsell articulates a theoretically fruitful, affective racial split. She does not describe love and theft as Eric Lott defines blackface minstrelsy; instead, Halsell's conflicted feelings reveal another important dialectic, one of oppressor and oppressed. As Halsell recognizes her racial bifurcation, she provides a window into the potential empathetic racial impersonation might offer her readers. Rather unintentionally, Halsell feels, and tries to articulate, the difference between privilege and oppression, an uncomfortable affective discovery about race and power.

Taken to its end, Halsell's recognition could model how white liberals might move from complicity with supremacy to real antiracist practice. However, in *Soul Sister*, Halsell's racial splitting is an anxiety most often exposed when race is refracted by gender and sexuality. Rather than sitting in the discomfort of her racial schism, Halsell appoints herself ambassador to and for African American women as "a black woman seated among black women."[67] For example, after moving from the frighteningly mixed Douglas Hotel to the Adam Powell Guest House, a temporary residence exclusively for women, Halsell is finally ensconced amid the very women for whom she purports to speak. At first, she describes the women in the guest house as a community, using language suggestive of her commitment to an idyllic, cross-racial, feminist coalition. She writes, "We are all *women*, with mysterious, unfathomable, tragic-marvelous secrets that in one sense unite us." However, she quickly undercuts this kumbaya moment, finding the homosocial setting of the guest house "alien, depressing, [and] unnatural." She continues, "Yet I know I will know them only in a superficial way. They have lived their lives on one planet, so to speak, and I on another."[68] Here, Halsell's racial discomfort insists that these Harlem women are somehow otherworldly. This is a poignant reminder that Halsell did not find it necessary to consult any black women before becoming one. Her disconnect from the black women at the guest house signals a subconscious awareness that her approximated blackness will not give her the insight or authority she anticipates. By constructing black women as unknowable, Halsell betrays the faulty logics of her project.

Homopanic at the Color Line

As quickly as Halsell realizes she has transformed herself into a black woman only to find she might "know [black women] only in a superficial way," she clues her reader in to what actually undermines her experiment. To ensure that her project remains successful, Halsell displaces her anxieties from the faulty logics of her gendered update of Griffin's empathetic racial transformation to a more acceptable and familiar repository for white anxiety—black sexuality in general and black queerness specifically. She writes, "I have heard among Harlem men that the Guest House has women who make love only with other women."[69] Recalling the queering of Griffin, Halsell locates the intergalactic differences between her and her new "mysterious" housemates at the site of queerness, thus recovering the sanctity of her project. By offering alternative models of black womanhood, the Guest House lesbians unknowingly give Halsell a generic homophobic excuse to avoid authentic cross-racial relationships. Since "women who make love only with other women" are not the women Halsell has come to speak for, she refuses to allow the interlocking nuances of their identities to complicate her relationship to, and/or assumptions of, blackness. Instead, Halsell castigates black queerness, particularly black female masculinity, with the same terror with which she envisions black male sexuality. Consequently, Halsell makes Griffin's epistolary warning—"the threat of rape is widespread"—all the more creepily instructive. Halsell continues, "Now seeing the virile women with muscles like a dockworker's I think that the 'fate worse than death' would be assault by a female."[70] Recasting the doggedly persistent psychic templates of a rapacious black male sexuality with the body of a black stud,[71] Halsell collapses the spectrum of black masculinity on itself. However embodied, black masculinity is always threatening.

For Halsell, queerness is a warped funhouse mirror distorting traditional gender roles. After witnessing the chivalry with which one woman, who Halsell calls "masculine protector-lover," diverted unwanted male attention from her partner, Halsell concludes, "I suddenly see that being a real Negro male—strong, aggressive, leading—and being a real Negro female—feminine, knowing herself lovable and loving—is virtually an impossibility under the rules of white society, rules which for centuries have decreed that a black woman must work like an ox and that a black man must in all instances be submissive to the white master."[72] She continues:

> I go to a "soul food" restaurant. I do not see my usual waitress, who is about forty-five who always wears slacks. She is named Melissa but is always called "Brownie." I overhear the café owner say: "*He* must really have gotten sick, because I know that *he* would have telephoned or been here . . . and *he* has never done this before, *she* must really be sick. . . ."
>
> Confused, I ask the owner, "Do you mean Brownie? You keep saying *he*, then *she*."
>
> "Oh," the owner explains, "*he* is both . . ." And he says it as lightly as he would say, "Oh her name is Melissa but she likes to be called Brownie," without any judgment on his part, but only that the decision is hers and not to be questioned by him or anyone else.
>
> The next morning . . . I see a "man" come in for breakfast. He orders eggs, bacon, and grits and then jumps from his counter stool: "Oh, I forgot my pill!" he calls to a waitress. "I'll be right back!" He lives in the next-door apartment building and is taking pills, I am told, to grow breasts like a woman.
>
> Later he comes in dressed in women's clothes, with an open neckline that shows his bust. Men sitting on the counter stools flirt with him, attempting, in a good-natured, mocking way to make dates.[73]

This lengthy passage is revealing for two reasons. First, it demonstrates Halsell's own preoccupation with black queerness amid a sociopolitical moment witnessing the heroic resistance to constant police harassment by the New York City LGBTQ community in 1969. The resulting series of violent conflicts, collectively called "Stonewall," is a watershed set of resistant acts that many credit as the catalyst for the modern gay and lesbian rights movement, a movement importantly led by genderqueer and trans folks of color. Secondly, this passage reveals how, in *Soul Sister*, black queerness is much more about gender nonconformity than actual same-sex desire. As black lesbians are made legible via the white supremacist pathologies of black male sexuality, the trans and genderqueer bodies in this neighborhood soul food restaurant disrupt Halsell's cisgender and heteronormative assumptions about black authenticity despite the legitimating presence of soul food.

However, it is not simply the presence and performance of gender nonconformity that troubles Halsell but what she views as the nonchalance of its acceptance—the ease with which the café owner's tongue moves between pronouns, and the open flirtations between this transitioning woman and her otherwise heterosexual patrons. Rather than use this moment to help-fully complicate the stereotypes of the black community's supposedly vir-ulent and violent homophobia and transphobia, Halsell anxiously insists that she does not "want to leave the impression that I think there are more homosexuals and lesbians in Harlem than elsewhere. I don't think so." She continues, "What does impress me is the desperate attempt of the people to break from white bondage, to 'find' themselves in the history of mankind."[74] Halsell sees these trans and queer identities as the Moynihanesque conse-quences of racism eroding the stability of the nuclear black family. As an act of desperation, queerness here functions in how Halsell, albeit subcon-sciously, imagines her own new blackness. Both are alternatives potentially moving the oppressed beyond the stifling dictates of white patriarchy. Con-sequently, Halsell's reductive misunderstanding of black queerness inex-tricably links "real" blackness to ideals of cisgender heteronormativity.

Ironically, Halsell pathologizes black gender nonconformity at the same time she negotiates and attempts to disrupt many of the idealized notions of southern white womanhood. Although decidedly a southern woman, Halsell insists she is not a southern belle. Instead, in her 1996 memoir, *In Their Shoes*, she boasts of a paternally encouraged "boyish upbringing": "My father . . . bequeathed me three legacies: the idea of willpower and courage, a motivation to travel and become a full human being who incidentally was female and, perhaps most important, the gift of time. In a sense, he created me by his awareness."[75] Obviously, this incidental girlhood impacted her development as an adult and a woman. It is a tomboy mobility encouraged by her father and reinforced by the legislative gains of second-wave femi-nism and, more explicitly, by her position in the White House during the Johnson administration.

Although Halsell would call Johnson "the worst boss I ever had" since "he saw me as an object which could be alluring but remained a second sex,"[76] her employment in the White House coincided with the passing of the 1964 Civil Rights Act. That legislation stipulated that the "attorney general had to protect citizens against discrimination in voting, education, and public ac-commodations."[77] Effective July 2, 1965, Title VII of that act prohibited dis-crimination based on sex, "theoretically [giving] all women a legal basis to transform their issues into a structured agenda for a new liberation move-ment."[78] Halsell's pursuit of black womanhood shortly thereafter is not a coin-cidence. As Paula Giddings writes, "Black movements are vital to the progress of feminist movements. Feminism has always had the greatest currency in times of Black militancy or immediately thereafter."[79] After traveling globally as a freelance journalist for both foreign and domestic newspapers, Halsell found her work at the White House a mundane alternative to the new freedoms and possibilities readily promised to middle-class white women. She writes, "Walking the corridors of power, looking at portraits of George Washington and Thomas Jefferson and Abraham Lincoln . . . why, I had asked myself, was I lucky enough to be there? What had been my credentials?"[80] Although Halsell questioned her place in the hallowed, male-dominated halls of the White House, she did not question her "need" to become black, or her emulation of Griffin as representative exemplar of that blackness. Her subsequent fashioning of black womanhood in his image makes her pathological rendering of black gender expression and queer sexuality incredibly ironic since she performs black womanhood while relying on the assumptions and stereotypes of a southern white man. In other words, Griffin imagines himself "queen" in order to pass his drag crown to his successor, blurring the lines of race, gender, and sexuality for Princess Grace.

As Halsell continues to negotiate both the constraints and privileges of her gendered empathetic racial impersonation, she is concerned, particularly in the urban landscape of Harlem, about the trappings of class. While she finds queerness a sign of degenerate inauthenticity, Halsell craves the romanticized "realness" of a black working poor, a desire reinforced by her choice to move to Harlem with only twenty dollars. As J. Martin Favor writes, "Class becomes a primary marker of racial difference; to be truly different, one must be authentically folk."[81] Corroborating Favor, Halsell writes, "I now see my job [secretary at Harlem Hospital] as the worst of all possible jobs for my purposes of trying to get an idea of how the mass of black people live. The people with whom I work are good top-level, intelligent, upper-middle-class people, and no different, the middle class being the middle class, from whitey."[82] Halsell's use of "whitey" distances her new black womanhood from both white male privilege and "bourgeois" blackness, reinforcing the value she places on class in her rendering of authentic blackness. "In Halsell's universe," Laura Browder concludes in *Slippery Characters: Ethnic Impersonators and American Identities*, "African Americans who wish to stay authentically black must explicitly commit to an agenda of poverty,"[83] an agenda Halsell attempts not by being simply any black woman but a working-class black woman specifically. After being chastised by other black women in her office for refusing to wear stockings she complained were too expensive to buy, Halsell quits her job. While her "complicit" co-workers enforce middle-class standards of properly feminine workplace decorum, Halsell insists the stockings "[hold] up the standards, the values of the white System."[84] Her insistence reflects the September 7, 1968, demonstrations at the Miss America pageant in Atlantic City, New Jersey, where hundreds of women, led by the feminist organization New York Radical Women, tossed into the "Freedom Trash Can" the accouterments of women's oppression—curlers, high heels, magazines, bras, and stockings. Yet Halsell remains unaware of the irony in her privileged ability to give up a well-paying job on principle. Instead, she rhetorically speaks as one of the "ghetto poor [who] view America's uneven affluence with bitterness" and prepares to leave the "conditions of Negro life in the city, the garbage that isn't picked up, the absentee landlords who refuse to fix the plumbing and eradicate the rats,"[85] for "another world."[86] This other world is the world of her childhood—the South.

Mississippi Goddam

After abandoning Harlem, Halsell continues to shape her black womanhood in Griffin's image, tracing his footsteps by bus after a brief respite at Magens Bay on St. Thomas because "during my final days in Harlem I could see that I was losing some of my hard-earned dark pigment."[87] Properly black again, Halsell then opens the third section of her narrative, "The South," by pausing "in a New Orleans bus station [to] ponder where in the South to begin."[88] It is no coincidence that Halsell would find her black self in the Deep South, since, as Sprigle and Griffin demonstrated before her, crossing the Mason-Dixon line is the hallmark of empathetic racial impersonation. As Griffin reminds her in a letter dated November 6, 1968, "Of course, it is important that you go South."[89] Although the South will stage Halsell's final geography in her cross-racial performance, in many ways it is the psychic beginning of her understanding of black womanhood. Taking the advice of her mentor, Halsell concludes that her experimental blackness must confront both the physical geographies and psychic legacies of the South: "Because I am a creature, so to speak, of 'the Confederacy,' this trip represents an excursion into the past, a reliving of a part of my life, with glimpses into old secrets long buried, yet still vivid and intimidating."[90]

Although Halsell was born and raised in Texas, she faces the South as a black woman with reservation and anxiety. She writes, "My own Southern-ness gives me no comfort" since this return south lacks the protection of white privilege.[91] Yet, she is determined to perform black womanhood in 1969 specifically in Mississippi: "I consider Montgomery and Birmingham,

Alabama, and then choose Jackson, Mississippi, almost, but not quite on impulse. My recollections of Medgar Evers and Governor Ross Barnett and James Meredith make Mississippi at once more challenging and frightening than Alabama. I want to experience firsthand why so many believe it's the most backward state in the Union."[92] Halsell's choice to experience the most frightening South reveals her investment in Dixie terror, a nightmarish rendering of an imagined South whose assumptive and extraordinary racial violence is sought after to necessitate the urgency and profundity of empathetic racial impersonation. Halsell's Dixie terror becomes a Mississippi-specific brand of racism, anticipating historian James C. Cobb's claim that Mississippi is "the most Southern place on earth."[93]

Recognizing Halsell's fears about Mississippi and the ideology of Dixie terror does not undermine how the state often constructed itself as the iconic space of racism. As the setting of the 1955 lynching of fourteen-year-old Emmett Till, the 1963 assassination of Medgar Evers, the voter registration drives during the 1964 Freedom Summer, and the subsequent lynchings of Mississippi Freedom Project workers Andrew Goodman, Michael Schwerner, and James Chaney that same year, Mississippi had become the paradigmatic symbol for the South's need for, and resistance to, the demands of the civil rights movement. According to Leigh Raiford, "'MISSISSIPPI' is best understood as the site of persistent, relentless, and unforgiving racial terror."[94] This reputation, solidified by the Evers assassination, inspired Nina Simone to angrily croon "Mississippi Goddam" in 1964. Punctuated by the refrain "Everybody knows about Mississippi Goddam!" the song became an iconic protest anthem. As the South remains the "national other"[95] and repository for the sins of the rest of the country's racial past, Mississippi is the other's other.

Although Mississippi earned its reputation as the space and locus of racial terror, resistance in Mississippi happened, and black Mississippians persistently and proudly made it home.[96] In 1958, *Ebony* magazine published a short interview with Medgar Evers entitled "Why I Live in Mississippi."[97] In it, he details firsthand experiences with voting discrimination and how white supremacy turned childhood friends into enemies. However, Evers refuses to conclude without reminding *Ebony* readers that Mississippi "is home" and still "part of the United States."[98] Refusing to give up on either his state or the region, Evers emphatically maintains: "I love the South."[99] His violent death in the very place he simultaneously loved but tried to change is a haunting reminder of the tensions between home and vulnerability, community and terror, safety and resistance.

As she rides the bus into Jackson, Mississippi, Halsell does so conscious only of the state's blood-soaked history, uncomfortably describing herself as "a spook among spooks, as the whites sometimes call us niggers."[100] By defining herself and the other southern blacks as "spooks" and "niggers," her vocabulary of racial epithets is equally blood-soaked, reinforcing the Dixie terror she anticipates. Halsell insists she is unequivocally part of a black "us," but upon arriving in Jackson she is alone and without a place to stay. She seeks out a black minister for help, but concerned for his own safety, he refuses to take her in. Knowing "all strangers in the South are suspect,"[101] Halsell despondently writes: "Trudging down a street, I neither know nor care in which direction I'm going. Strangely, I yearn for the rain to drench me. I want the physical discomfort. I hope it will overpower me, distract me from the painful misgivings assailing me."[102] Again, Halsell craves the suffering she figures is an integral part of being a black woman.

Seeing her in the rain, a kind taxi driver takes her to the "all-black Summers hotel." She finds her room bare and unaccommodating, and is intimidated by the fact that she seems to be the only woman staying there. Although she is exhausted from her trip, sleep does not come easily. Mirroring her first night in Harlem, again Halsell is besieged by the encroaching sounds of black men's voices "coming through the thin walls."[103] So on her first full day in Jackson, Halsell gets up to find better accommodations. Although alone, Halsell feels a kinship as she walks the streets, thankfully assuming "all black people speak to me, [and] accept me as their soul sister."[104] Walking until she finds a house with a sign offering a room for rent, Halsell writes:

I muster my courage, rap on the door, and am greeted by a white woman who studies me like an apparition.

"I'd like to see your room," I say. And I couldn't have shocked her more if I'd slapped her.

"I have no room!" She gazes at me incredulously.

"But you put out a sign."

"Why, you *black bitch*!" she shouts, and furiously slams the door.[105]

This is Halsell's first encounter with southern racism. Although she never elaborates on how being called a "black bitch" feels, this moment confirms her commitment to embodying southern black womanhood: "Waiting for a bus to take me back to the hotel, I stand among black women, as cold as I, with more problems than I. I know I must work as they work, immerse myself in their environment, scar myself with their griefs, if I am to end my sense of aloneness, of being on the Outside. I want to stand closer to them, to extract what I can from a physical togetherness."[106] Here Halsell's rhetoric is confusing. While she positions herself as a black woman—part of an "us"— she also simultaneously sees herself as an outsider. Craving a connection to the "authentic" blackness she never found and then denounces in Harlem, Halsell situates the South as the potential place for her searched-for black community and the potential locus of her own southern black womanhood.

Recognizing her own still tenuous blackness, Halsell narrates the difficulty of assimilating into Jackson's black community. For example, on her second evening in Jackson, she meets Floyd, a "young Negro in slacks, turtleneck sweater, [and an] Afro,"[107] who turns out to be a pimp looking for a new girl to work the streets. Instead of immediately turning down his offer, she accompanies him to another bar, where he offers her an opportunity working for his aunt. While neither sex work nor employment with Floyd's family is appealing, Halsell realizes the labor of simply trying to establish herself as a black woman in the South: "I've come from other worlds, and the struggle to enter the Southern black milieu leaves me exhausted."[108] Her sketchy interaction with Floyd helps her understand that she must find employment if she wants to feel a part of Jackson's black community.

Halsell then turns to the State Employment Office the next day, finding employment as a domestic day laborer for a Mrs. Williams. Mrs. Williams is a white woman "in her late forties, wear[ing] blue stretch pants, a blouse and sweater. Her once blondish, now graying, hair is cut too short, too severe. She wears glasses, no makeup, and from the tension in her face, I assume she is a troubled woman."[109] Mrs. Williams's fake hospitality makes Halsell uncomfortable. "When she speaks," she writes, "her tone and drawl are treaclelike, and her sugary intonation of my name makes me wince." She continues, "Her sweet, baby-doll dialect and her feigned defenselessness provide the armor of the Southern woman. Although aware that these weapons are hollow and harmless, I am still vulnerable to them. I am ambivalent. I have one emotion as a white person seeing her and quite another as a black woman seeing her."[110] Halsell feels the uncomfortable bifurcation of empathetic racial impersonation, the binary of oppressor and oppressed. She obviously sees her white southern woman self in Mrs. Williams as well as the power her employer wields over her temporary blackness. During her work in the Williams home, she confronts this white woman's disregard for Halsell's albeit temporarily black humanity. She writes:

While I am "working like a nigger," Mrs. Williams talks on the phone, drinks coffee, smokes cigarettes, and complains to me about being tired. At first, I'd hoped I would be safe in my role as a Negro domestic. Then with some horror I learn that she is not capable of discerning in me anything other than what she assumes me to be, a lowly member in the caste system that perpetuates the easy way some Americans live. I feel sorry for her. . . . I sense that she desperately wants to talk to me, but it can never be as an equal. She looks on me as less than a wholly dignified and developed person.[111]

Back in what Halsell calls "nigger-town," after only temporarily confronting the disrespect black domestics regularly experience while working in white homes, Halsell "feel[s] so degraded, so morally and spiritually depressed" that she wants to tell every black woman she meets, "'Don't do what I did! Don't ever sell yourself that cheap! Don't let it happen to you.' . . . I believe at this moment that my limits have been reached."[112] After claiming to have reached her "limit," Halsell still went back to the employment office to again find similar work scrubbing windows, ironing clothes, and cleaning the oven of a Mrs. Dunlap. Rejecting Mrs. Dunlap's offer of regular work in her home for $6 a day, Halsell decides "to get out of Jackson, to travel around Mississippi, to live with Negroes who will accept me as their loved one, their kin, their soul sister."[113] Once again in search of a connection to the "authentic" black community she desires, Halsell petitions for the protection and guidance of NAACP field director Alex Waites, one of the people she trusts with the secret of her whiteness.

Through Waites, Halsell is introduced not just to a community but also to the realities of community organizing and fieldwork outside of Jackson. While receiving gracious hospitality and over a plate of greasy pork ribs, Halsell hears "several of the most gripping accounts of Klan bombings and lynchings . . . these acts of terror, all in Mississippi, I listen like any interested yet *detached* observer."[114] For the first time in her narrative, Halsell listens to these black Mississippians articulate the threats to their own survival, witnessing what she describes as a "secondhand kind of terror."[115] During this frank truth-telling, Halsell is quickly made to realize the danger her presence puts them in after Winson Hudson, a black woman and the county NAACP president, cautions: "If the Klan find out where you're staying, they'll kill us and you. . . . If there's anything them peckerwoods hate worse than a *nigger* who talks back to them it's a white woman living with the *niggers*."[116] Rather than place this already vulnerable community in further peril, Halsell decides she must continue her racial pilgrimage elsewhere.

Upon reaching the "Delta, an area of rich land and poor people, in the northwest corner of Mississippi" with "towns [that] all seem self-contained, barricaded against strangers, fretful, and lonely,"[117] Halsell suffers the consequences of violating the de facto segregation still lingering after the legal defeat of Jim Crow. Rather than serving as a camouflaged witness to the realities of living black in the Deep South like Ray Sprigle before her, Halsell provokes the status quo. Unlike Sprigle, Halsell is no "good nigger."[118] First, the police are called on her after she asks to use a telephone in the white waiting room at the Greyhound bus station. Then, she attempts to integrate a white congregation in the middle of Sunday morning service. Constructing black resistance through her own agenda, Halsell assumes that the black folks of Indianola want to integrate that white church despite the fact that this was her own idea. She acknowledges that the "militant black teen-age girls"[119] who hesitantly agree to accompany her are "extremely nervous,"[120] so much so that one of them refuses to go. The overwhelming discomfort of the girls, who sit with Halsell as the minister extemporaneously revises his sermon to address the startling and unwelcome presence of black bodies in his church, soon compels them to leave. Here, Halsell is the agitator that conservative southern whites feared. Most important, she is also a bad ally. No one asked Halsell to integrate anything. As she forces these confrontations to incite Dixie terror, Halsell still experiences the conflicting duality of her temporary blackness: "I feel disembodied, a cipher floating in a void. . . . I do not feel a Negro; yet . . . I cannot be my old self, either."[121]

Returning to domestic work, Halsell begins working for the Wheeler family in Clarksdale. On her very first day, she receives passing instructions from a hurried Mrs. Wheeler to "clean the commode, clean the tub, clean the floors, run the sweeper, do the washing, [and] do the ironing" for the abysmally low daily wage of $3.[122] Halsell is then left alone in a two-story colonial only to be surprised when Mr. Wheeler unexpectedly returns. She writes, "I do not look at him directly but keep my eyes to the laundry, yet I sense he is staring at me, and in that moment of silence, I feel he is somehow magnetized."[123] After asking Halsell "usual" questions such as her name and where she's from "in a businesslike manner, almost as if he is appraising a piece of jewelry,"[124] Mr. Wheeler retires to an upstairs bedroom:

Soon from [his mother's] suite comes a thunderous clap . . . and simultaneously he shouts, "Come quick!"

Hurrying upstairs, I walk swiftly into the bedroom. Instantly the door slams behind me and as I turn around I find myself encircled in Wheeler's arms. I am momentarily overwhelmed. He presses his mouth roughly against mine and forces his body against me, muttering hoarsely about his desperate need for "black pussy." He has already unzipped his trousers, indicating he intends few if any preliminaries. His muscles strain against me and he uses his arms like a vise to keep me from breaking away and at the same time force me onto the bed.

"Only take five minutes, only take *five minutes*," he mumbles, partly pleading, partly threatening. "Now quieten down! Just gotta get me some black pussy!"

I try frantically to break his hold but he has my arms pinioned, and we fall awkwardly onto the bed near the headboard. Then he crawls on top of me. I feel myself suffocating from his body weight and panting breath. I wriggle free after some effort and start to run but he jumps after me and pins me against a wall, pushing me practically through the wood-work. I realize he is holding me under a huge and ghastly oil painting of the entire family, in an ornate frame that must weigh a ton. I loose one arm enough to reach up and, with the last of my strength and willpower, I push the large framed picture from its moorings and send it careening down. It grazes the back of Wheeler's head.

His flushed face dissolves from lust into hatred. "You black bitch!" he cries, shaking with anger. More menacingly he adds, his voice lowered to a whisper: "I ought to kill you, you black bitch!"

I suppose I should feel terror-stricken all over again; the lord and master is in a state of mind where nothing might faze him, and where the urge to satisfy himself as a punitive act may be strong. But curiously my feeling is one of utter relief. Then, feeling more contempt than fear: "Go ahead, you coward!" I dare him. "You wouldn't have the nerve!"

He is spared from accepting this challenge by the striking of the grandfather clock in the bedroom. It reminds him apparently that his wife and daughter are due home soon. . . . I imagine he also wants me out of sight before I might be tempted to excite the curiosity of his womenfolk.

I wait for no invitation to leave.[125]

Halsell's blackness triggers Wheeler's fantasy of the lascivious and available Jezebel. In the presence of her black woman body, Wheeler performs an eager lecherousness revealing his part in the well-rehearsed scripts dictating the interactions between white men and black women in the precarious space of the domestic. Halsell writes, "I have heard many Negro maids say that their greatest fear is being in the house alone when the white man comes in. As one bitterly commented, 'They pay you fifteen dollars a week, and then expect to get you too.' "[126] In *Private Lives, Proper Relations: Regulating Black Intimacy*, Candice Jenkins writes, "The vulnerability that African Americans have been subject to at the hands of white racism often *is* the vulnerability of intimacy, not simply because black people have been the objects of white desire, but because black bodies have been assumed always to be excessively proximate and desirous bodies, bodies too readily revealed or exposed, too willing to reveal and expose others."[127] Riché Richardson corroborates Jenkins: "Although white women may have been perceived as the only legitimate victims of rape in the South, the black female body has been more susceptible as the object of sexual brutality by white southern men."[128] The violent consequences of Halsell's assumed blackness expose the very real precariousness of black women, particularly those working and living as domestics in the South.

As Wheeler craves five minutes with a not-so-black pussy, this scene spectacularly reveals the vulnerability of black womanhood while simultaneously mired in the ironies of authenticity, empathy, race, gender, sex, and power. These ironies are not completely lost on Halsell herself: "Now I reflect how I had gone with trembling heart to the ghetto, Harlem, fearful that a big black bogeyman might tear down the paper-thin door separating my 'white' body from his lustful desires. And now it had been a white, not a black, devil whose passions had overwhelmed him."[129] The myth of the black male rapist is inextricably linked to the perceived sexual availability of black women, and Halsell's assault reinforces Angela Davis's assertion in *Women, Race, and Class*: "The fictional image of the Black man as rapist has always strengthened its inseparable companion: the image of the Black woman as chronically promiscuous.... If Black men have their eyes on white women as sexual objects, then Black women must certainly welcome the sexual attentions of white men. Viewed as 'loose women' and whores, Black women's cries of rape would necessarily lack legitimacy."[130]

As Halsell acknowledges her racist assumptions about black masculinity, she articulates a black womanhood constructed in the wake of white masculine rapaciousness, foreshadowed by her decision to affect a blackness that could pass naked. While medical interventions made to her body immediately position Halsell's new blackness in the visual logics of racialization, the spectacle of Halsell's assault and near rape is the generative act of her black womanhood. What makes this scene so incredibly perverse then is that Halsell needs this spectacle of racialized sexual violence for a proper racial belonging. It is a sexual Dixie terror. If Dixie terror for white new black men like Sprigle and Griffin is about putting their masculine bodies in the wake of expected and assumed racial terror like segregation and lynching, for the new black woman, Dixie terror is the anticipation of racialized sexual violence. Even though black sexual violence cuts across race, gender, class, and sexuality, this moment finally cures Halsell of her "secondhand" experiences of black womanhood and racial bifurcation. Halsell's experience of near rape coupled with how she interprets its meaning is deeply unsettling. She writes, "I begin to see the role of the black woman in Wheeler's home objectively," emphatically concluding, "She is me."[131] With uncomfortable paradox and irony, *Soul Sister*'s acknowledgment of the vulnerability of black womanhood is simultaneously an affront to black women.

Can the Darker Sisters Speak?

Rather than reveal the "truth" of her body, Halsell escapes back into whiteness after releasing herself from the grip of her attacker with the literal and symbolic force of bourgeois respectability—the family portrait that undoubtedly witnessed Wheeler's other rapes and attempted rapes. Halsell believes herself to be uniquely resistant, imbued with a legitimacy she assumes is lacking in black women who have survived sexual violence and assault. Knowing she does not need the wages from her temporary domestic work and also knowing that her blackness is only temporary, Halsell challenges her attempted rapist. As she taunts her perpetrator, she does so with a defiance she assumes most black women in similar situations would not have the economic opportunity to display: "Traditionally, if the Negro woman wants to keep a job, she all too frequently has to submit to the white man's desires."[132] Halsell continues, "Suppose the black woman in [Wheeler's] frenzied embrace had been a mother of hungry children, waiting for her to bring them food. Could she have resisted his advances? Run from home without collecting *any* money for her day's labor?"[133] She asks, "If I had been a black married woman, could I have told my Negro husband: 'Wheeler tried to rape me?' Then what? What could one black man have done against the entire System? Would one black man have the nerve to take a gun and shoot the white man?"[134] The anticipated answer to these rhetorical questions is supposed to be a resounding "no" since Halsell is unable to imagine a scenario where neither a black woman nor her fantasied husband is able to resist. However, in *At the Dark End of the Street: Black Women, Rape and Resistance—A New History of the Civil Rights Movement from Rosa Parks to the Rise of Black Power*, Danielle McGuire reminds, "Rumors about the mistreatment and rape of *black* women by *white* men started plenty of brawls throughout the South, too."[135]

How Halsell constructs her uniquely resistant black womanhood is inextricably linked to how she constructs the South. Washed in the wild fantasies of Dixie terror and sexual Dixie terror specifically, Halsell's Mississippi is one of "big houses" and "lords and masters"—the antipode of *Soul Sister*'s Harlem. This is certainly not the same Mississippi staging the Mississippi Democratic Freedom Party or Stokely Carmichael's first call for black power. Here, the South is a premodern space severed from industrialization, the gains of the civil rights movement, and burgeoning black power. For example, Halsell describes the incident with Wheeler as a "centuries-old bedroom scene," citing the sexual legacy of slavery as her rhetorical and narrative framework.[136] In this South, Halsell imagines her black woman body from overworked domestic to atypically heroic antebellum house slave.

To be seen as heroic, Halsell must create a false history that obscures black women, their stories, and their particular resistance to sexual violence. Otherwise, *Soul Sister* is rendered either merely duplicitous or completely unnecessary. What *Soul Sister* must refuse then is any acknowledgment of those histories since the grim tales about the threat of sexual violence against black women both historically and currently cannot be told in any full and accurate detail without recognition of how black women narrate, understand, resist, and still survive in the face of it. Although the stories of sexual violence experienced by black women are never easily told or even believed,[137] the African American literary canon offers testimony explicitly challenging Halsell's dangerous and spurious representation of herself as a uniquely resistant black woman. In *Incidents in the Life of a Slave Girl*, Harriet Jacobs revealed the perilous conditions of black women and girls under slavery back in 1861. She writes, "The slave girl is reared in an atmosphere of licentiousness and fear. The lash and the foul talk of her master and his sons are her teachers."[138] Jacobs bemoans how the South's peculiar institution denies black women the opportunity to attain or maintain the feminine respectability already presumed the birthright of middle-class white women. Writing within the confines of nineteenth-century propriety and

under the pseudonym Linda Brent, Jacobs details the "trials of girlhood"[139]—
the physical, emotional, and psychosexual abuse she received from her
master, Dr. Flint. She writes, "[Flint] came every day; and I was subjected
to such insults as no pen can describe. I would not describe them if I could;
they were too low, too revolting."[140] Writers such as Frances Harper, June
Jordan, Maya Angelou, Gayl Jones, Alice Walker, and Toni Morrison do
the cultural labor of fully representing the stark complexities of black
women's survival, vulnerability, and resistance to sexual violence. They un-
flinchingly fill the suggestive and provocative silences left by Jacobs and
ignored by Halsell.

Introducing the African American literary canon as a counterpoint to
Halsell's narrative makes her claims about representative black womanhood
much more spurious. At the beginning of her narrative, Halsell writes, "It
seemed to me I was in a good position to notice all the fetters binding my
darker sisters."[141] Throughout *Soul Sister*, Halsell appropriates blackness as
a representative mouthpiece for black women, seeking to testify on their
behalf with prescience, unique insight, and perspective. Although black
women in the United States have been articulating their own intersec-
tionality since Sojourner Truth queried "Ar'n't I a Woman?" Halsell's presumptive representation does not acknowledge or even imagine how black
women can and often do speak for themselves. The same year *Soul Sister* hit
bookstore shelves, so did Maya Angelou's *I Know Why the Caged Bird Sings*;
and notably, 1970 saw the publication of a number of eventually canonical
texts written by black women, including Toni Morrison's *The Bluest Eye*,
Toni Cade Bambara's edited anthology *The Black Woman*, and Alice Walker's *The Third Life of Grange Copeland*. Halsell's presumption also fails to
consider the historical restrictions on, and denial of, access to women of
color by the publishing industry, the same restrictions that prompted Au-
dre Lorde to tell Barbara Smith in 1980: "We really need to do something
about publishing."[142]

When *Soul Sister* hit the market, the mainstream white press, including
Publisher's Weekly and *Life* magazine, lauded it as "unforgettable . . . most
moving" and "a vital book," respectively.[143] Even *Ebony* featured a six-page
spread on Halsell and *Soul Sister* in its December 1969 issue, "Black Christ-
mas." However, *Ebony*'s readers expressed concerns with Halsell's blackness,
Soul Sister, and the magazine's choice to advertise either. Since its founding
in 1945 by publisher John H. Johnson, *Ebony* magazine had focused on African American achievement by narrating, reporting on, and imaging black
life in its pages. Along the way, *Ebony* shaped black middle-class taste and

Sketches of Grace Halsell as a black woman in the December 1969 issue of *Ebony*.

accompanying discourses about racial uplift and black respectability. Situated among stories about black marines, black stunt men in Hollywood, and the anniversary of the attack on Pearl Harbor, "I Lived Six Months as a Black Woman" was published with Halsell's byline. The six-page spread included lengthy excerpts of the most titillating passages from *Soul Sister* along with twelve photographs of white Halsell ranging from images of the author sitting with President Lyndon B. Johnson, posing with John Howard Griffin and his wife, strutting down a street in Washington, D.C., and being interviewed by Barbara Walters and Hugh Downs for NBC's *Today* show. The article also included four pencil sketches of Halsell—all while black. These four images include Halsell walking the streets of Harlem, having a drink with angry Jim Hamilton, tirelessly working as a domestic worker in Mississippi, and being assaulted by Wheeler. They provide a visual archive of her temporary black womanhood in the absence of corroborating photography, and these images feel reminiscent of the sketches commissioned in a closed courtroom. In sum, pencil-black Halsell approximates the black experience black *Ebony* readers already experience.

And *Ebony* readers responded. "Now that Grace Halsell . . . has lived six months as a black woman, SO WHAT?" Eugene Lewis angrily writes, "I share totally the feelings of Jim Hamilton about whites who turn black to 'do their thing.' We (black people) don't need experiences like Miss Halsell's. We know, and for a long time have known, 'what it is like to be black.' The time has passed when we needed to make white Americans understand."[144] Similarly, Jane Fort Morrison demands Halsell "relinquish all indirect as well as direct proceeds of her experience to the blacks from whose tragic condition she benefits. These proceeds could go to the Delta Ministry of Greenville, Miss., so that they at least begin to help correct the condition of blacks in the state she visited."[145] The editorial choice to include *Soul Sister* so prominently in *Ebony* coupled with this pushback reveals a tension around the supposed values of the magazine's presumably respectable, middle-class readership and the critics voicing their concern about Halsell's pseudo-blackness. As Alfred F. Brown writes:

> Merely getting a suntan and going to Harlem or the South is not sufficient to evoke black thought and feeling.
>
> Your article of the last month about Grace Halsell was the promotion of a highly questionable undertaking. What is to be gained from her "experiences" other than profit to her? So she found out that black people are human! What else is new?
>
> Miss Halsell stated: "She also made another discovery: the pain and shame of being black in a culture where the esthetic ideal is white." Well, we're about through the "pain and shame" stage (or hadn't you noticed?). . . .
>
> Shame! Shame![146]

Echoing Jim Hamilton, critical *Ebony* readers like Brown found Halsell's blackness shameful because of her assumptive timing.

Halsell's memoir is also featured in the black newspaper the *Chicago Defender*. Positioned deep in the issue, below the prominent Janus faces of white and black Halsell from the dust jacket of *Soul Sister*, the article positively quotes Halsell's friend, the then-mayor of Fayette, Mississippi, Charles Evers: "I think 'Soul Sister' is the most factual treatment of black women by southern white men."[147] However, the *Defender* visually undermines this recommendation with a picture of Halsell sandwiched between two reporters framed by the caption: "Not a Book You Would Need to Read." Halsell provided the language of the caption when she sheepishly admitted to the reporters her book was not intended for them. Despite her presumed authority on the black experience, Halsell knows *Soul Sister* is ultimately for white folks.

Still, thirty years later, in the epilogue for *Soul Sister*, Halsell maintains the validity of her impersonation. Although she admits she couldn't "do it again," she is glad she did, "because . . . I am [now] black as well as white."[148] Halsell recalls her time in the South: "The emotions I harbored belonged to two persons: a black woman and a white woman. I was cast in a twin, paradoxical role of oppressor and oppressed. I was a vessel of sorts for two personalities, two sets of eyes, two bodies."[149] Although Halsell writes about her racial duality in this retrospective, she stubbornly concludes, "Nothing prevents me from feeling spiritually black."[150] Despite once feeling the tension between oppressor and oppressed, Halsell claims this questionable "spiritual blackness" as a permanent change to her identity.

Sexing Myrdal

Even with the vacillation in her "knowing" about blackness and the critiques of her project, Halsell's self-constructed authority still allowed her to offer her conclusions on the root cause of U.S. race relations. After her harrowing confrontation with Wheeler, Halsell concludes, "Sex is what's important, it's the root of all our racial frustrations (and a few more besides!), and the basis for three centuries of lies."[151] Halsell's conclusions were not confined to the logics of *Soul Sister* but also set the stage for her pseudo-sociological study *Black/White Sex*. Published in 1972, *Black/White Sex* culls a series of interviews taken from individuals involved in various sexual escapades traipsing back and forth across the black/white binary. By interrogating the taboos behind interracial desire, Halsell insists that the myths and consequences of cross-racial sex, and not structural inequalities and institutional racism, are the foundation of hundreds of years of black disenfranchisement. Excising the structural realities of U.S. race relations, as we have seen, is the calling card of the postwar liberalism defined by Gunnar Myrdal.

Halsell assumed that the argument put forth in *Black/White Sex* was the missing piece to Gunnar Myrdal's conclusions in *An American Dilemma* about how to remedy racial injustice. Whereas Myrdal insisted the remedy to the "Negro problem" was in the heart of the white American, Halsell posited that the rapacious sexual dynamic she experienced as a black woman with white men was the central feature of America's racial problem. Or, as she writes, "The white man created the taboos about blackness and then fell prey to them, desiring the flesh not in spite of but *because* it is black."[152] Halsell was so hell-bent on this idea that she asked Myrdal himself to write the introduction to *Black/White Sex*. In an August 7, 1971, letter to Myrdal, Halsell writes, "I am familiar with your studies and find your books invaluable.... I would like so very much if you could write the introduction for this new book."[153] To her surprise, he refused. "I have read your new book," Myrdal replies in an October 26 letter. He continues, "Let me first give you the negative answer that I am not prepared to write a preface."[154] Although Myrdal politely excuses himself from Halsell's request by suggesting he was too busy with the never-completed follow-up to *An American Dilemma*, Myrdal questions the importance Halsell places on interracial sex: "I would like to discuss with you what role sexual complex really plays in race relations in the United States. Your book is full of insight. Nevertheless I question the importance of this factor."[155] Clearly, when Gunnar Myrdal wrote that *"the moral struggle goes on within people and not only between them"*[156] he was not speaking of the clandestine, taboo desires and sex acts Halsell freely describes. For Myrdal to sell his particular brand of palatable liberalism, he must do his best to disavow the cross-racial sexual desire and sexual violence leading to miscegenation and the supposed collapse of the black/white binary. Or, as he writes, "Even a liberal-minded Northerner of cosmopolitan culture and with a minimum of conventional blinds will, in nine cases out of ten, express a definite feeling against amalgamation.... He may sometimes hold a philosophical view that in centuries to come amalgamation is bound to happen and might become the solution. But he will be inclined to look on it as an inevitable deterioration."[157] Myrdal rejects any suspicion that his prescriptive cure for U.S. race relations might sacrifice racial purity by displacing amalgamation, the apocalyptic consequence of interracial, heterosexual sex, onto the dystopian fantasies of an unforeseen national future. So although Halsell's self-miscegenated body is helpfully distracting, turning heads from the increasingly fraught shift from the accommodationist civil rights movement to the more separatist black power movement, reassuring readers that postwar liberalism is still a viable political option, Myrdal's refusal signals how Halsell's scenes of subjection cannot fully service liberalism's needs. Despite Myrdal's rejection of Halsell's request in 1971, she still commits to the validity of empathetic racial impersonation. After her blackness in 1969, Halsell went on to become a Navajo woman, publishing *Bessie Yellowhair* in 1973. She then feigned noncitizenship and crossed the U.S.-Mexico border multiple times as an undocumented Mexican migrant worker for *The Illegals* in 1978.

These subsequent racial impersonations, coupled with her bestselling narrative as a black woman, should have solidified Halsell's place alongside her more memorable mentor, John Howard Griffin. However, her frankness about the sexual violence experienced by black women at the hands of white men ensured that she could not meet the tastes of a white liberal readership. Consequently, Halsell disappeared from the annals of empathetic racial impersonation, even though she made a career out of walking in the shoes of many "others." So, when in 1980 John Howard Griffin died of diabetes complications, rumors abounded that he had died from skin cancer resulting from his racial masquerade. Ironically, in 2000, it was Halsell who died from a tragically long battle with multiple myeloma, a cancer presumably resulting from her six-month martyrdom to the "quick and difficult baptism into the life and times of a black woman."[158]

Warning: blackness can be fatal.

CHAPTER FOUR

Empathy TV

Family and Racial Intimacy on Black.White.

Black.White. premiered Wednesday, March 8, 2006, at 10 P.M. (EST) on the Fox Entertainment Group cable network FX. Advertised as a "true" conversation about race in the United States, *Black.White.* provided audiences the opportunity to watch an experiment in empathetic racial impersonation on a scale never before attempted. Instead of one individual heroically crossing the line, the show featured two "typical" American families—the born-black Sparkses and the born-white Wurgels—"swapping" races. Enabled by the transformative power of Hollywood makeup, prosthetics, and digital technologies, the born-black Sparkses (Brian, Renee, and son Nick) and the born-white Wurgels (Bruno, Carmen, and daughter Rose) became white and black, respectively. For six weeks, the families not only performed versions of each-otherness but also lived together in Los Angeles, California, processing and discussing their experiences under the hypersurveillance that is now the hallmark of "reality" television. This chapter attends to how *Black.White.* moves the genealogy of empathetic racial impersonation from the theatrical stage, newspaper, trade books, and film to the visual logics of television. This shift reveals an investment in empathetic racial impersonation at a moment dominated by the changing discourses about race and race relations in the twenty-first century.

Racial Impersonation in the Interim

Before fully considering *Black.White.*'s contribution to this genealogy, attention must first be paid to the large genre and chronological leaps between Grace Halsell's empathetic racial impersonation in Harlem and the South in 1969 and the Wurgels' and Sparkses' impersonations in 2006. After Halsell's *Soul Sister*, empathetic racial impersonation seemed to all but disappear. However, it is empathy, and not racial impersonation, that fell immediately from view. Racial impersonation, a long-entrenched hallmark of how Americans perform and practice identity through appropriations of blackness, from blackface minstrelsy in the mid-nineteenth century to hip-hop culture into the twenty-first, is an important corollary to this particular genealogy. Racial impersonation continued to dominate our racial, legal, and popular culture landscapes during this apparent disappearance.

Ultimately, after 1969, racial impersonation morphed according to the needs of a post–civil rights, post-soul sociopolitical moment across primarily visual media. Ray Sprigle's 1948 newspaper articles and 1949 memoir, alongside both Griffin's and Halsell's journalistic, memoir-style trade publications, allowed readers to imagine empathetic racial impersonation through the poignancy of the written word. Although *Sepia* magazine readers could visualize Griffin's transformation through Don Rutledge's photographs, the 1964 film adaptation of *Black Like Me* provides the most immediate bridge from the readerly logics of memoir to the visuality of film.[1] Along with *Finian's Rainbow*, the cinematic *Black Like Me* is the most exemplary visual bridge for empathetic racial impersonation; its traces are undoubtedly felt and are often satirized in the important corollaries to this genealogy. For example, in 1970, Melvin Van Peebles's comic film *Watermelon Man* lampooned the premise of *Black Like Me* by portraying the racial transformation of its protagonist, Jeff Gerber, played by black actor Godfrey Cambridge. Gerber inexplicably changes from a white, comfortably bigoted insurance salesman to a militant black man. *Watermelon Man* satirizes Griffin's fear of seeing his white family while temporarily black by staging Gerber's change from white to black in front of his most judgmental audience—his white wife and children. His wife, Althea, played by Estelle Parsons, helped Jeff's desperate attempts to turn white again with milk baths, a Plaster of Paris–like treatment for his face and arms, and falsely encouraging platitudes about the temporariness of his blackness. However, Althea refused to have their regularly scheduled Wednesday night sex while Gerber's skin remained black. Unlike John Howard Griffin, Gerber never recovered his whiteness, and the couple permanently separated after Jeff's blackness uncovered the always already lurking racism of his neighbors, who unselfishly pooled their money to buy out the Gerber family home and drive the family from the neighborhood. Interestingly, *Watermelon Man* used a black actor in whiteface for the first few scenes of the film. Therefore, Gerber's unconventional racial impersonation—his sudden blackness—was actually a return to the actor's real black body.

In another corollary to the genealogy of empathetic racial impersonation, Hollywood put out *Soul Man*, a 1986 teen comedy that was a failed take on affirmative action, starring C. Thomas Howell as an entitled and affluent trust-fund baby, Mark Watson. Cocky, spoiled, and overly self-assured, Watson wrongly assumes his father will continue to fund both his education and his irresponsibility, until his father decides to spur along Watson's manhood by insisting on his son's financial independence. After Watson realizes he needs $53,979 to cover three years of tuition, fees, and living expenses, he panics, quickly confronting the stigma of being the son of the newly "stingy" upper class. His parents make too much for Watson to file for financial aid, and he does not have the credit history to qualify for a bank loan. Desperate to matriculate and apparently having no other options, Watson applies for the Henry Q. Bouchard Memorial Scholarship for the most qualified black Harvard Law student from Los Angeles and wins. Watson then offensively "becomes" black to gain entrance into Harvard Law School on that scholarship, an impersonation he would have to uphold for at least three years. Watson performed an egregious neo-blackface on the silver screen for the assumptive benefits of affirmative action.

As in *Soul Man*, when Hollywood tried to imagine racial impersonation on the big screen, it often lacked logic as well as empathy. For example, in 1990, *Heart Condition*, the critically and commercially panned film starring Denzel Washington and Bob Hoskins, was an interracial buddy film—the kind made famous in the early 1980s. Unlike Eddie Murphy and Nick Nolte's 1982 film *48 Hours*, *Heart Condition* reimagined the buddy film with a convoluted plot: an unhealthy and racist white cop in need of a heart transplant receives a heart from the very lawyer he despises, a black man who then goes on to haunt him throughout the film. Similarly, the 1995 film *White Man's Burden*, starring John Travolta and Harry Belafonte, portrayed an alternate racial reality where the logics of white supremacy are inverted to make black folks America's dominant race.

These cinematic renderings are corollaries to this genealogy of empathetic racial impersonation, proving how racial impersonation always haunts our racial and cultural imaginaries. While films like *Soul Man*, *Heart Condition*, and *White Man's Burden* tangentially bridge the gaps between Sprigle, Griffin, Halsell, and *Black.White.*, a young, white University of Maryland college student named Joshua Solomon represents the closest example of empathetic racial impersonation in this interim period. In 1994, Solomon medically dyed his skin to become a black man after, unsurprisingly, reading Griffin's *Black Like Me* in his Springbrook High School library. He "sat there all day reading it, oblivious to everything else, to the end of the school day. Then and there I decided that sometime soon I too would become black. It's as simple as this—I wanted to know what it was like."[2] Growing up in Silver Spring, Maryland, Solomon insisted he "always had a lot of black friends. Whenever something went down, they always said it was racism . . . they blamed everything on color."[3] Solomon allegedly "sympathized with my friends, and . . . wanted to support them, but secretly, inside, I'd always felt that many black people used racism as a crutch, an excuse."[4] Originally conceived as a semester-long experiment for which he had temporarily dropped out of school, Solomon did not set out on an empathetic pursuit; he sought to discredit the stories of his hyperbolic black "friends."

To facilitate his skeptical blackness, Solomon consulted Halsell's doctor, Aaron B. Lerner. Solomon took the vitiligo corrective medication Psorlen, until he was "reddish-brown" and, in "someone'[s]" opinion, "looked Haitian."[5] He then shaved his head, tanned, and had his brother, Jon, rub "theatrical skin stain over my head to even the color."[6] Although Solomon never mentions Halsell, he details his experiment in a column for the *Washington Post*. That article, "Skin Deep; Reliving 'Black Like Me': My Own Journey into the Heart of Race-Conscious America," eerily reads like a truncated version of Griffin's memoir complete with meeting the reflection of his new black face: "When [Jon] finished," Solomon writes, "I looked in the mirror. It was scary. I wasn't me anymore. I was black."[7] In the familiar footsteps of Sprigle, Griffin, and Halsell, Solomon heads south. Following the prescription for empathetic racial impersonation, Solomon anticipates Dixie terror—even in 1994.

Wearing the preppy clothes he usually wore to class at the University of Maryland, and with $1500 cash in the pocket of his khakis, Solomon first travels by plane to Atlanta, and describes the discomfort he felt when white people routinely avoided his gaze. He then traveled by bus to Gainesville, Georgia, the closest he could get to his ultimate destination, Forsyth County, where he would live because "no blacks live there." He writes, "Following the rape of a young white girl in 1912, two black men were convicted. Several lynchings were recorded following the verdict; the accused were eventually hanged. Using force and intimidation, the white community drove all black residents from the county. The 1990 census statistics on Forsyth County today show 'N/A' under all categories for black people."[8] Although Solomon sought to experience daily life in Forsyth as a black man decades after its most famous instance of racial terror, he still found resistance to his plan. For example, a "light-skinned black man" who Solomon says called him "'brother' and asked where I was going," cautioned him: "'Man!' [the black man] said shocked, 'You don't want to go to Forsyth. They got old ways down there, the lynching mentality. You should stay in the city.'"[9] However, Solomon insisted, "I'm sure it isn't so bad. . . . Things have changed a lot don't you think?" The anonymous black man is both resigned and skeptical: "'Okay, okay, man, it's your hide,' he said, backing away from me. 'Be safe, brother, be safe.'" Although he ignored the warning, Solomon describes soon feeling "alone," "confused and angry about the intense emotions that petty indignities stirred in me" during his time in Gainesville. He encountered dirty looks; a conversation between strangers that stopped too abruptly when he passed; an interaction with a white police officer that made him recall the iconic 1991 beating of Rodney King; and a white woman who, over a plate of barbecue chicken, casually told him, "You [black folks] ruin everything."[10] Solomon called these moments the "drip-drop of indifference and fear from the white people I had encountered." All too quickly, Solomon "was sick of being black. I couldn't take it anymore," he writes. "I wanted to throw up." He continues, "Enough is enough, I thought. I didn't need to be hit over the head with a baseball bat to understand what was going on here. Usually, I'd made friends pretty easily. I was nice to them and they were nice to me. Now people acted like they hated me. Nothing changed but the color of my skin."[11] Racially nauseous, Joshua called his "mother and told her I was finished with my journey . . . I started to cry."[12] Even though Dixie terror is presumably lessened for Solomon's empathetic racial impersonation in the very late twentieth century, he exposes the vulnerabilities of empathetic racial impersonation and its privileges, or as he writes, "I could return home to my comfortable world. I could wait for my skin to turn white again."[13]

Although Solomon was only black for days, it was enough blackness for a *Washington Post* column as well as an appearance on *The Oprah Show*. On a February 1995 episode, Oprah Winfrey lauded Joshua's "remarkable" decision to take "some potentially life-threatening pills to change his skin color from white to black." She continued, "What he experienced as a black man was chilling. So chilling, in fact, that after just one week of being black, he abruptly called off the experiment and went home to let the medicine wear off."[14] Solomon retraced his steps as a briefly young black man in the South, re-creating his empathetic racial impersonation for Oprah's audience of predominately middle-class, white women. Solomon narrated how he looked like a "typical black teenager . . . with a bald head," recalling how white people regarded him with suspicion and fear as he walked the streets while black. He concluded, "Perhaps we haven't come as far as we thought." Oprah was more than sympathetic to Solomon's apparent bravery and impersonating plight: "Over the years I've done at least a hundred shows on racism," she tells her studio and television audiences, "and it's so hard to convey what that, having that happen to you, being treated like a suspect every day of your life, what that does to your personal psyche." Solomon agrees: "Right. Well ya know, that's the hardest part. Whites receive this primo badge of respect. I walk into a room regardless of how much money I have in my pocket, there's a certain level of respect that I get from folks. . . . The first thing I realized when I was black was, it's gone. You don't get any of that. . . . White people get this respect and black people constantly trying prove that they deserve it or are worthy of it."[15] This moment of empathetic racial impersonation firmly sutures Sprigle's, Griffin's, and Halsell's experiments with blackness to the more recent version of it in *Black.White.*

Race in the New Millennium

When *Black.White.* premiered in 2006, America was obsessed with race. Hip-hop had revolutionized the entire landscape of popular culture, moving far beyond its origins in the black, brown, and urban spaces of the South Bronx while simultaneously negotiating the consequences of its association with supposedly innate criminality, violence, homophobia, and misogyny. Hip-hop became a global, commercialized brand dictating and shaping literary, cinematic, television, and sartorial taste. The allure of hip-hop was different from previous cultural fads. It was not simply a soundtrack for a generation searching to define and narrate their angst, nor did it enable a youthful introduction to consumer culture like the American automobile or rock 'n' roll had for earlier generations. Instead, through the innovative sampling of its rhythm and blues, funk, and soul predecessors, hip-hop became accessible and relatable across multiple generations and consumers. Hip-hop more than just crossed over, and its resonance and popularity was feared, celebrated, and lamented. Recognizing how the globalization of hip-hop also made certain performances of blackness accessible, hip-hop not only had a significant hand in prepping the nation to see a black face in the Oval Office but also provided the financial infrastructure, publicity, and audience to present and support that black face as a viable political option.

On July 27, 2004, that relatively unknown black face, Barack Obama, was an Illinois state senator who burst onto the national political stage after delivering what might be his most impactful speech—the keynote address at the Democratic National Convention in Boston, Massachusetts. In it, he articulated an audacious hope for his country, urging an ethos of collectivity to unite the divisions between red, blue, and purple America. Enamored by his eloquence and inspired by the exceptionality of his background, pundits began whispering about the real possibility of a black man in the White House: "I have seen the first black president," gushed MSNBC pundit Chris Matthews.[16]

But then, in August 2005, Hurricane Katrina made landfall, and the hopeful, postracial America Obama represented in 2004 was swept under by Katrina's wind and water. Even before the water receded, Katrina revealed unclaimed and/or missing bodies as well as destroyed and hastily abandoned neighborhoods. The rest of the country was quickly schooled in a code of death and survival emblazoned the X—the graffiti of volunteers and members of the National Guard on buildings and homes throughout Gulf Coast cities like New Orleans. During the relentless 24-hour news coverage, the country was trained to be hopeful for a "o" in the bottom quadrant of the X, although "o" signified many unknowable possibilities. Maybe someone or many survived here, or maybe someone or many were among the stranded "lucky" refugees taking shelter elsewhere. However, that hoped-for "o," meaning no dead bodies found, was also sprayed on buildings even when the right quadrant of the "X" read "NE"—or "not entered." More disturbing was when instead of "o," a "1" or even a "2" was present, numbers publicly announcing the number of dead bodies found inside. As the country learned to interpret this code, it also learned about the precarious and vulnerable communities along the Gulf Coast, quickly realizing how the "X" translated the deaths of black, brown, and working-class bodies. As a disaster both natural and unnatural, Katrina, and its aftermath, impacted the national psyche in profound ways. The stark visuals of stranded black bodies desperately awaiting rescue from the rooftops of flooded homes not only uncomfortably challenged what it meant to be an American but also exposed an unreliable government. As racist narratives emerged to pathologize those in-crisis black bodies as criminals and looters rather than survivors in the attempt to render horrific images of racial and class subjection palatable, many of these stranded confronted their misrepresentation. They defiantly waved American flags both to attract the attention of relief workers and to unflaggingly remind us they were still here. They demonstrated their citizenship, showing allegiance to their country, while also reminding their country of its duty to help its citizens in need. Those watching and reading about Katrina far from rising or receding floodwaters faced the grim reality that there are many Americans and many Americas—some much more vulnerable than others. So when hip-hop producer turned artist and mogul Kanye West stunned his co-host, comedian Mike Myers, during a live telethon to raise money for Hurricane Katrina relief with the unscripted declaration "George Bush doesn't care about black people," his comment was just one of many instances highlighting the racial, regional, and class disparities Katrina's winds, rains, and levee breeches laid bare.[17]

America's early twenty-first-century obsession with race was, and still is, indexed by popular culture. Obama represented a historically impossible possibility—America's readiness for and/or resistance to a black family in power in the White House. Conversely, Katrina demonstrated how, even in the twenty-first century, it can never be safely assumed that black bodies are ever guaranteed all the rights and privileges of U.S. citizenship, government intervention on behalf of their survival, or fair, nuanced, and even accurate representation. Billed as a conscious effort to provoke a national conversation about twenty-first-century American race relations, *Black.White.* is undoubtedly part of this tempest in the national racial imagination.

Race, Family, and Reality Television

The genre of reality television, often dismissed as a cheaply produced, lowbrow form of trashy entertainment, moved from a fad to an overwhelmingly successful staple of television programming early in the 2000s. In *Reality TV: Remaking Television Culture*, editors Susan Murray and Laurie Ouellette define reality television as "an unabashedly commercial genre united less by aesthetic rules or certainties than by the fusion of popular entertainment with a self-conscious claim to the discourse of the real."[18] But reality, like beauty, is in the eye of the beholder. Despite the genre's explicit claims to "realness," reality television is often heavily scripted, produced, and edited in ways similar to traditional programming. Its success, what Leigh Edwards calls its "triumph" in American television, is largely predicated on approximations of the real, including an audience willing to suspend disbelief, the accepted hypersurveillance and renouncement of privacy by cast members, and the interaction fostered and encouraged between cast and audience beyond the show in the pressurized spaces of social media.

As Mark P. Orbe writes, "Sweeping generalizations fail to acknowledge the great diversity with this ever expanding genre."[19] Although recognized by its often shorter programming seasons, the broad umbrella of reality television includes seemingly disparate shows including celebrity family sitcoms like VH1's *T.I and Tiny*, MTV's *The Osbournes*, and E's *Keeping Up with the Kardashians*; not yet celebrity families like TLC's *Jon and Kate Plus 8* and *19 Kids and Counting*; forced-intimacy docusoaps like MTV's *The Real World* and *The Jersey Shore*; relationship docusoaps like the franchises of Bravo's *Real Housewives* and VH1's *Love and Hip Hop*; competitive talent searches like CW's *America's Next Top Model* and Fox's *American Idol*; career-testing competitions like Bravo's *Top Chef* and NBC's *The Apprentice* and *The Celebrity Apprentice*; and rush to the altar dating competitions like ABC's *The Bachelor* and *The Bachelorette*, and VH1's *Flavor of Love*.

Black.White. intervenes in this panoply of options with a subgenre called, oxymoronically, serious reality television. The show's co-producer, R. J. Cutler, Harvard educated and University of Southern California trained, initially established his career as a film documentarian with *The War Room* (1993) before making his move to the smaller screen as both a director and producer. Blending documentary filmmaking and the generic constraints and conceits of reality television, Cutler's programming vision aims to create thoughtful and provocative television positioned against more popular representatives of the reality genre such as CBS's long-running, multiple Emmy-winning competitive reality, *Survivor*. Championing the idealized notions of a rugged American spirit of individuality, sacrifice, and competition, *Survivor* seeks to render recognizably caricatured "types" unfamiliar through their confrontation with unfamiliar environments. As a social experiment, *Black.White.*'s unfamiliar environment is new skin.

However, *Black.White.* is not exclusively "serious," since the reality show finds its closest subcategorical kinship with what could be called the family switch, a popular genre typified by ABC's syndicated show *Wife Swap*. First broadcast in 2004, the predictable script of both *Wife Swap* and its 2012 spin-off, *Celebrity Wife Swap*, features two families with seemingly nothing in common. The families are typically unabashed about their seemingly irreconcilable differences on everything from child rearing to class aspirations, and from leisure to religion and gender norms. Ultimately, *Wife Swap* traffics in and reinforces the myth of the heteronormative American nuclear family since the very conceit and title of the show mandates that each family have a *wife* to swap. The genre of the family switch reminds us how anxieties around ideals of the family have always been a preoccupation of television in general and reality television specifically. As Edwards argues in *The Triumph of Reality Television: The Revolution in American Television*, "Reality TV becomes a cultural site at which contemporary family politics are being negotiated."[20] Ultimately, *Black.White.* signifies America's obsession with race as well as family.

Similar to *Wife Swap*, *Black.White.* begins with the heteronormative nuclear family. As Cutler admits, the casting team sought established, middle-class, educated, liberal families that could mirror each other throughout the show's "experiments."[21] He purposefully searched for families, confirming, "As much as this was about race it would also be about families. . . . I just felt like family was an interesting thing to explore—how race affects relationships [and] culture. . . . [T]he guts of the show were the relationships among the family members." With that in mind, Cutler sought two families other than the "clichéd . . . redneck racist and the black militant. I wanted open minded, open hearted, progressive thinking people . . . who saw themselves as socially liberal." Rather than put diametrically opposed individuals in a house with little hope of reconciliation, Cutler wanted to show a more nuanced depiction of twenty-first-century American race relations by imaging two families with "progressive points of view [and] not the most reactionary point of view." He continues, "People have deep rooted, complicated, strong feelings about race in this country regardless of how progressive they may or may not be."[22] By constructing each family as moderate, typical, and representative, their physical embodiment of racial difference presumably becomes all the more legible.

The idea of "typical" is important here. The born-white Wurgels— Bruno, Carmen, and daughter Rose—introduce themselves in the first episode as a "typical, white, American family . . . from Santa Monica." They are presented as a nuclear family sanctioned by the legal, economic, and social privileges of state-recognized marriage. However, off-screen they are a blended family. Carmen and Bruno are unmarried, and Rose is not Bruno's biological daughter. Since statistically blended families represent a much more accurate representation of how this country practices kinship, the decision to reconstruct *this* family as always "the Wurgels"—even though Bruno, Carmen, and Rose all have different last names—betrays the show's problematic investment in representing an imagined ideal of what the "American family" should look like. In addition, Bruno is singularly presented on the show as a substitute teacher when he has a rather extensive acting résumé under the name "Bruno Marcotulli," with film and television acting credits that include *Moon in Scorpio* (1987), *Spy Hard* (1996), and *One Tough Bastard* (1996). Similarly, daughter Rose, also known as Rose Bloomfield, was featured in the 2004 film *The Princess Diaries 2: Royal Engagement*. Although most of the family is in the business of Hollywood, the Wurgels are charged with representing the average, white American family.

Conversely, the born-black Sparkses—Brian, Renee, and son Nick—represent "typical" African Americanness but are not at all connected with the business of Hollywood. The Sparkses are portrayed as specifically "from Atlanta," and this spatial specificity is presented without any acknowledgment of how new southern metropolitan spaces like Atlanta nuance and impact their blackness. Atlanta holds a dominant place in the black imagination as exemplary of a cosmopolitan, class-aspirational blackness. Through the musical oeuvres of rappers Ludacris, T.I., and Outkast; the reality television of the *Real Housewives of Atlanta*, *Married to Medicine*, and *Love and Hip Hop Atlanta*; scripted comedies like *Atlanta*; and films like *ATL*, popular culture has often conflated Atlanta with this kind of blackness. Subsequently, Atlanta often stages the tensions, anxieties, and possibilities of the changing understandings and redefinitions of blackness, indexing the realities and consequences of reverse migration since the Great Migration. Although Atlanta dominates the image of this reversal, this southern homecoming includes primarily urban cities like Houston, Washington, D.C., New Orleans, and Raleigh-Durham as a new, geographically located narrative of racial uplift. To this end, the born-black patriarch on the show, Brian, shows off his integrated, middle-class Atlanta neighborhood to *Black.White.* audiences in the first episode. As he points out his white, Vietnamese, and Mexican neighbors, he gleefully brags, "We're just like the UN, baby."[23] Brian's integrated class comfort was seemingly unavailable to him while growing up in Michigan. A self-described light-skinned black man with green eyes who was born and raised in Michigan, Brian shares the intraracial indictments suffered because of his presumed insufficient blackness: "It was tough," he admits. "I had to fight the darker-skinned blacks because I was too light, and then I had to fight the whites because I was too dark."[24] Brian's honesty about communal belonging, cultural acceptance, and the alienation of not being regarded black enough by some and too black by others never complicates his position on the show as the representative patriarch of authentic black masculinity.

Even before the Sparkses and Wurgels swap races, *Black.White.* is clearly invested in the transformative potential of cross-racial empathy through the particularities of the myths, anxieties, and ideals of the American family. Ultimately, by focusing on "typical" families while masking how rigorously constructed their typicality actually is, the show reinforces how empathetic racial impersonation is often about how that potential is performed in the context of interpersonal relationships rather than institutionalized difference and structural inequality. This familial strategy is strikingly different from the experiences of empathetically crossing the line undertaken by Sprigle, Griffin, and Halsell—*individual* investigations into blackness. For example, Griffin left home and family to complete his sojourn into blackness, and Halsell, a single woman, sought blackness to transform herself specifically. These singular experiences translate well for the generic conceits of the memoir. However, as Edwards makes plain, since the televisual medium is already deeply invested in representing various types of families through logics of commercialization, mediation, coerced intimacy, and hypersurveillance, families are best suited to meet the generic and representational demands of reality television's take on empathetic racial impersonation. Audiences, Cutler implied, needed to *see* the visual transformation of each cast member to fully understand their potential for racial growth. Also, as we will see, the often covert regimes of twenty-first-century racism, rather than the spectacles of racial terror animating Sprigle, Griffin, and Halsell, were better caught by *Black.White.*'s ever-present camera, and its roughly 2500 hours of footage.

Beginning in August 2005, for six weeks, the white Wurgels and black Sparkses lived together in a house in the San Fernando Valley of Los Angeles. In the now recognizable style of MTV's *The Real World*, they lived under the omnipresent gaze of both handheld and mounted cameras while individual "confessionals" supplemented the footage. The narrative beat of each episode largely revolved around the tension between the two families in the house—the uncomfortable and revealing quirkiness of strangers living together—and how each cast member navigates various social settings in and around L.A. The series opens with a dizzying and scattered set of introductions. The show's first minutes quickly introduce the cast to its viewing audience both with and without makeup through digitally constructed Polaroids spliced between scenes of each cast member sitting in the makeup chair showing off their new skins. The show then stages the moment when those new skins are introduced to their original families for the first time. Even before we see the Wurgels and Sparkses meet each other in their shared house, we briefly see born-black Brian golfing as a new white man, and born-white Rose walking the streets of South Central L.A. as a black girl. When the families do meet, twelve minutes into the first episode, born-black Brian confesses his hope that the Wurgels are "clean," and Rose, acknowledging her parents have never spent time with black people, fears her parents "might say the wrong thing."[25] As cameras follow the families, they document the Wurgels' and Sparkses' attempts to broker interpersonal relationships and understand the consequences of their constantly changing racial identities while navigating the triumphs and pitfalls of twenty-first-century race relations. Ultimately, *Black.White.* is a far too ambitious project that feels uneven, incomplete, maddening, and often quite boring.

Making Up Race

Unlike *Wife Swap*, whose hook is to destabilize participating families by introducing the threat of an ideologically opposed mommy, *Black.White.* upsets the stability of the show's families by technologically and cosmetically usurping and destabilizing our familiar assumptions about racial classification. What makes *Black.White.* so provocative, particularly in this genealogy of empathetic performance, is its visuality. Or, as Cutler states, makeup is "the heart and soul of the show."[26] The show's makeup team was comprised of ten artists, led by Keith VanderLaan, Brian Sipe, and Will Huff. VanderLaan, makeup effects creator, is known for his work on films like *Pirates of the Caribbean: The Curse of the Black Pearl* (2003) and *Apocalypto* (2006). Brian Sipe, the show's special makeup designer, is well known in Hollywood as a result of his collaborations with VanderLaan on *Pirates of the Caribbean* and with Huff on *The Curious Case of Benjamin Button* (2008), as well as his ability to turn comedian Martin Lawrence into a thick, ballsy, black woman for *Big Momma's House 2* (2006) and changing the Wayans brothers into *White Chicks* in 2004. Will Huff, *Black.White.*'s key makeup artist, also worked with Sipe on *White Chicks* and was special makeup effects artist on *Nutty Professor 2: The Klumps* (2000).

For *Black.White.*, the cast and crew endured a yearlong process of digital design. That year included a six-week series of polymer head castings, repeated pigment tests on the skin, and traditional methods of Hollywood cosmetics such as prosthetic features and stereotypically racialized hair. Cutler and his team understood the importance of makeup to this social experiment. They recognized the difficulty in constructing new racial personas that could simultaneously be read legibly by television audiences while also remaining undetectable to the individuals interacting face to face with the cast's new white and black bodies. Unlike the theatrically contoured blackface mask exaggerating the artifice of blackness through caricature, the cast of *Black.White.* must pass. Every day, each cast member sat through a lengthy and grueling reracialization process in the makeup chair, as well as the return to an "authentic" racial self at the end of the day when the makeup was removed. Unlike Halsell, Griffin, and Solomon, who embodied a

LIVING IN EACH OTHER'S SKIN

Born-white Rose "becoming" black in the makeup chair for *Black.White.*

medically induced blackness that had to fade rather than be washed away, the Sparkses' and Wurgels' transformations were only temporary, Hollywood-style cosmetics. Although the makeup had to sell on the street and the small screen, the racial transformation for both families was only topical.

Before the show could be fully greenlit as a viable programming option for the network, FX executives had to buy its racial transformations, both literally and figuratively. After the initial rounds of casting interviews, white daughter Rose and black father Brian were chosen as representative members of each family, and each underwent six trying months of makeup testing before being scrutinized by FX executives. Out of the entire cast, Rose spent the most time in the makeup and stylist chairs. In order to look black, her skin was painted four different shades of brown and three shades of red, as well as shades of blue and yellow. Each layer was applied in a carefully predetermined order and with a specified thickness. Nose and dental prosthetics, colored contacts, and a hairstyle made from her own colored and crimped tresses along with an artificial hairpiece supplemented the effects of Rose's technicolor black skin. Stylists then outfitted her with the right type of teenaged black girl clothing. The result was a white-turned-black

Born-white Carmen Wurgel without makeup in *Black.White.* (left) and after her black transformation in the opening credits (right).

girl who the show's executives, producers, castmates, and later audiences could accept as "real." After the six months of scrutiny and trials, executives bought the cast transformations and guaranteed Cutler and his team a full production commitment and financial support. In fact, the makeup was so impressive that the team won a 2006 Primetime Emmy Award for "Outstanding Makeup for a Series (Non-Prosthetic)." Race is an experience of being, performance, and persona, but this tedious process reminds how, in the domain of the visual, it is also imagined, constructed, and fashioned. It should also be noted that Rose's real skin reacted so negatively to her impersonation that the crew had to provide calming and restorative facials for her once a week. Faking black is hard.[27]

Rose was certainly not the only one who found it difficult to adjust to her new black body. In the DVD audio commentary, born-white Carmen admits she did not envision herself as the same black woman the makeup team imagined, expressing dissatisfaction in how her teeny weeny afro represented her as simultaneously both "militant" and "a little country."[28] Instead, Carmen imagined her new black identity through her own vision of beautiful black womanhood—the actress turned iconic sex symbol, Bo Derek. Made most popular by the poster advertising her role in the 1979 film *10*, Bo Derek's famous gold swimsuit and white-woman cornrows dominated Carmen's fantasy of what appropriated black womanhood should look like. She laments the makeup team "didn't let me keep the braids" tried during testing, continuing: "I wish I could've looked a little more attractive."[29] After *Black.White.* aired, Carmen anecdotally related her friends' discontent: "Whoa, Carmen!" she mimicked her friends, "Don't ever turn black!"[30] Both Carmen and her friends could only imagine black beauty through appropriated, stereotyped, stylistic mimicry—even as Carmen attempted to become a black woman. This representational conceit would haunt her participation throughout the show's six episodes.

Carmen was not the only one haunted by stereotypes of race and beauty. According to makeup artists Sipe and VanderLaan in the DVD commentary, born-black matriarch Renee was the most "difficult person to transform" because of the "great, luscious lips" the team had to "minimize."[31] After seeing her new, white self, Renee admitted she "didn't like the way I looked . . . because, to me, I thought I looked a lot older."[32] Because of the fabricated wrinkles around her eyes and mouth, Renee imagined her white self as "Barbara White," "an average middle-age, white, female who was happily married and had a teenage son." Frankly, Barbara was not the white woman Renee expected to be: "I imagined myself to be a long, blonde hair[ed], white woman. . . . I had this image of a tennis mom."[33] Renee coveted the long, blonde hair that for so many is the emblem of white feminine beauty. Both matriarchs' honest reactions are instructive—they remind us how palatable and culturally endorsed notions of beauty are aligned with whiteness.

Unsurprisingly, Bruno and Brian both escape these gendered pressures to be beautiful. Instead, they attempt to position their new bodies as representative of respectively proper, racialized masculinity. For example, Bruno modeled himself after America's iconic image of black fatherhood: "My initial reaction was I kind of looked a little bit like Bill Cosby," he states. "Thrilled" by his new blackness, Bruno recalls going to the bathroom "as soon as I could" to get "to know my new friend and ma[ke] lots of funny faces."[34] Bruno's confrontation with his new blackness is strikingly dissimilar to how Griffin narrates seeing himself black for the first time, even though both stage their moment of racial impersonation in the private space of the bathroom. Griffin writes, "The transformation was total and shocking. I expected to see myself disguised, but this was something else. I was imprisoned in the flesh of an utter stranger, an unsympathetic one with whom I felt no kinship."[35] Here, the difference is about tone and anticipation. Whereas Griffin feared the consequences of his black male body through the logics of Dixie terror and segregation, Bruno channeled the friendly, comic image of America's black patriarch.

With "funny faces" and letting his "imagination . . . fly,"[36] Bruno delights in the possibilities his new persona affords. For Bruno, becoming black is play rather than a daunting exercise in anticipated racial violence.

Importantly, Bruno does not see himself as Shaft, Superfly, or even more updated tropes of hip-hop masculinity. Instead, he insists on cultivating his persona through the particular brand of black masculinity's most successful representational crossover. Before the allegations that he raped a number of women became public, Cosby was heralded as America's favorite dad. In the wake of his widely successful sitcom, *The Cosby Show*, Bill Cosby was not just any black father; he was a commercially palatable and didactic patriarch, enabled by the sociopolitical realities of what Nelson George refers to, in the subtitle of his book *Post-Soul Nation*, as the "Explosive, Contradictory, Triumphant, and Tragic 1980's." As the Cosby family stood as an exemplary model of black respectability combating Reaganist representations of crack babies and black welfare queens, Bill Cosby safely wore sweaters rather than threatening leather jackets. While Bruno casts himself in Cosby's image, he also cloaks himself in the controversially conservative rhetoric of Cosby's now infamous "Pound Cake speech" delivered at an NAACP ceremony commemorating the fiftieth anniversary of the Supreme Court's 1954 *Brown v. Board of Education* decision. In 2004, Cosby demands, "We've [presumably educated, respectable, middle and upper class black folk] got to take the neighborhood back" from the "knuckleheads" killing each other over a piece of pound cake, refusing to learn proper English, and eschewing the educational opportunities afforded by *Brown*.[37] Rife with stereotypes about hip-hop's interpretation of black masculinity, Cosby's speech placed the responsibility for racial, communal, and neighborhood safety squarely on the shoulders of what he saw as dangerously ignorant, working-class black parents. Although audiences of *Black.White.* might not be privy to the Cosby-aspirational logics Bruno espouses in his DVD commentary, or Renee's and Carmen's confessions about whiteness and beauty, those interviews inform how each family interprets, performs, and "becomes" their respective approximations of twenty-first-century whiteness and blackness.

While *Black.White.* stages each cast member's reaction to their own changing race in the mirror and the makeup chair, the show also dramatically stages the shock of racial transformation for their loved ones. Not only does *Black.White.*'s audience witness each cast member's racial transformation, they also witness how each individual is seen and interpreted by those they know and love. The first episode of *Black.White.* captures the unscripted reactions of the cast's racial transformation, otherwise known as the show's emotional appeal. For example, when newly black Carmen first sees newly black Bruno, they mutually express an overwhelming attraction for each other, musically underscored by smooth R&B. "Oh my God! Bruno!" Carmen exclaims. A spliced interview underscores the intimacy of their racial reintroduction: "It's nice," Carmen reflects, "I love black. I mean visually, and somehow, heart wise, there's a warmth." Cutting back to the moment of their unveiling reveals Bruno clasping hands with Carmen, pronouncing, "You're beautiful," as she gleefully and cheekily responds, "Thank you. You look like a really nice man." With tears streaming down his face, Bruno gushingly stares into Carmen's contacts, "It's just really beautiful. I just feel like I'm in love with this woman. It's beautiful."[38] Bruno's insistence on his partner's beautiful blackness lovingly challenges Carmen's personal anxieties about not being an attractive black woman. The Wurgels' desire for each other is uncomfortable, especially since Bruno says "it's" beautiful and not "she's" beautiful. Their unchecked desire for even an impersonated blackness finds root in dangerous stereotypes about the innate seduction and sexual availability of black bodies, the very type of disturbing cross-racial intimacy Halsell argues is the very basis of American racism after her encounter with the rapacious Wheeler.

Contrastingly, the Sparkses' reaction is very different from the Wurgels'. Seeing each other "white" provokes mixed reactions of awe and mostly humor. Both Brian and Renee laugh boisterously when they see each other, giggling uncontrollably until Renee sheepishly admits to her newly white husband, "You can't take this the wrong way because remember, we're in makeup, but I mean, you don't look *anything* like a guy I would be *any way* attracted to." "Come on white girl, come on white girl," Brian teases, pulling Renee in for a less than enthusiastic kiss: "I don't want to," Renee counters, insisting on "just a peck."[39] As the Sparkses' hesitancy about their new bodies challenges the Wurgels' desire and attraction to blackness, Brian and Renee also reveal their own stereotypes about the supposed awkwardness and ugliness of whiteness.

White Like Me

Whiteface does not hold place in the nation's cultural memory or psyche like the histories and legacies of blackface and/or blackface minstrelsy. However, in *Whiting Up: Whiteface Minstrels and Stage Europeans in African American Performance*, Marvin McAllister excavates the history of whiteface minstrelsy as a "coherent and sustained performance tradition," defining it as an "extra-theatrical, social performance in which people of African descent appropriate white-identified gestures, vocabulary, dialects, dress, or social entitlements,"[40] beginning in the nineteenth century and continuing into the twenty-first. He writes, "The earliest whiteface minstrels . . . offered an alternative brand of cross-racial play generally devoid of the need to denigrate white bodies."[41] He later adds, "Whiteface minstrels . . . have succeeded where blackface minstrelsy failed precisely because these acts reject a top-down, exclusionary performance model."[42] Unlike Eric Lott's theorization of blackface as a dialectic of "love and theft," an ultimately perverse caricature of blackness used to denigrate black bodies in the service of both whiteness and its corollary ideals of American citizenship, whiteface comments on and often satirizes racial privilege from below.

Unlike the performances of whiteface promenading through the streets of nineteenth-century New York and Charleston described by McAllister, the Sparkses' whiteness is reminiscent of more recent iterations of whiteface, which arguably reached its apotheosis more than two decades before *Black.White.* In the December 15, 1984, *Saturday Night Live* sketch "White Like Me," comic Eddie Murphy cheekily recalls Griffin's memoir *Black Like Me.*[43] In the sketch, Murphy muses: "Ya know, a lot of people talk about racial prejudice, and some people have gone so far as to say that there are actually two Americas: one black and one white. But talk is cheap. So I decided to look into the problem myself, firsthand. To go underground and actually experience America—as a white man." Like the producers of *Black. White.*, Murphy "[hired] the best makeup people in the business," recognizing, "If I was going to pass as a white man everything had to be perfect." As the skit progresses, we see again and again how everything did *not* have to be perfect for Eddie Murphy to pass as "Mr. White." Murphy's "Mr. White" is a comic exaggeration of white masculinity. He is cartoonish— outfitted with implausible makeup and a full, broom-like mustache. Murphy also explains that he "studied for my role very carefully [by watching] lots of *Dynasty*" while reminding himself "to keep my butt real tight when I walk." He practices the cadence and phonetics of an exaggeratedly "proper" white diction by "[reading] a whole bunch of Hallmark cards. . . . Finally, I was ready." As the *SNL* studio audience laughs, tension builds. If the sketch had stopped there, it would be exemplary of theatrical whiteface minstrelsy; however, the sketch continues as the people he encounters throughout Manhattan corroborate Murphy's white persona without question. During the sketch, "Mr. White" tries to pay for his newspaper but is told by the white shopkeeper to take it without charge. He realizes with surprise: "When white people are alone, they give things to each other for free." Later, as he rides a city bus after the only visibly black man disembarks, the bus driver puts on music as the white passengers relax and begin to dance. A woman pulls out a platter of cocktails, serving the riders until she unabashedly plops herself on Eddie's white lap. If that was not comedy enough, later, "Mr. White" receives a generous bank loan despite his overwhelming lack of creditworthiness. Eddie Murphy as "Mr. White" has seen enough.

Murphy's whiteface performance reveals an exaggerated and parodied white privilege. When not in the assumed presence of black folks, white folks were not strategizing methods of racial discrimination or even thinking about black people. Instead, generous white men in positions of economic, institutional, and commercial power were just eager to celebrate the otherwise arbitrary privileges of whiteness, thereby maintaining white supremacy. Out of makeup and again recognizably black, Murphy tells the audience: "So what did I learn from all of this? Well, I learned that we still have a very long way to go in this country before all men are truly equal," he warns, "But I'll tell you something, I got a lot of friends, and we've got a lot of makeup. So the next time you're hugging up with some really super groovy white guy, or you meet a really great, super keen white chick, don't be too sure. They might be black." Like the rest of the sketch, Murphy's humorous warning is instructive. First, his training in plausible white masculinity, learned from consuming the detritus of consumer and popular culture, reveals just how much cross-racial performance is mired in stereotype. And while "Mr. White's" adventures in whiteness are hyperbolic, Murphy's vision of unchecked and unregulated racial privilege indicates something very uncomfortable about the often invisible truth of white supremacy, particularly when supremacy conspires to guarantee the financial comfort of a few at the expense of most. Tellingly, Murphy does not imagine a white world obsessed with how to exact racial terror, discrimination, or oppression. Instead, he imagines how the structures of race and power insidiously exist to perpetuate the status quo without any need for overt repressive strategies.[44]

As Eddie Murphy channels the classed and racial hyperbole of *Dynasty* and the sappy, lyrical verse of Hallmark cards, the "White Like Me" sketch can be easily characterized as "white people be like" comedy, a form of whiteface minstrelsy rooted in perceived racial difference. Media scholar Bambi Haggins typifies this observational humor as a lowbrow subgenre of black comedy popularized through programs like Russell Simmons's *Def*

Comedy Jam. For decades, this reductive brand of humor, rooted in the performance of social perceptions, circulated in stand-up comedy clubs, recorded albums, and taped "live" performances. These comedic comparisons appear in the repertoire of nearly every black comic from Eddie Murphy to Monique to Katt Williams."[45] In *Laughing Mad: The Black Comic Persona in Post-Soul Cinema*, Haggins identifies Eddie Murphy as the

> first "successful" post-soul comic. . . . Murphy presented black humor for media babies—across lines of race, class, and color. Yet one might argue that by failing to engage in direct sociocultural critique, Murphy's comic persona rebelled against one form of containment while engaging in an unproblematic standoff with another. As the unqualified star of the show in his *SNL* days, Murphy brought black humor and sensibility to a series in which it had previously only played an ancillary role . . . like . . . the ideological work done with Murphy's short film, "White Like Me," provided a problematic televisual text that engaged popular conceptions about the experience of blackness by calling into question the experience of whiteness.[46]

Haggins contextualizes "White Like Me" as "arguably Murphy's most overtly political televisual sketch on *SNL*"[47] while also noting its airing a year after Murphy officially left the late-night cast. Rather than celebrate Murphy's satirical send-up of Griffin and, by extension, the genealogy of empathetic racial impersonation more generally, Haggins calls the sketch "absurdist" with "its resonance . . . somewhat shallow. In an era when the realities of racial inequity, particularly in relationship to black access to the era's financial bounty, which had not managed to trickle down to those with credit histories that were much more economically viable than Mr. White's, the notion of racial masquerade may have very well seemed like the only option. However, the 'solution' in this mockumentary on disparity, while clearly offered with tongue firmly wedged in cheek, is still rooted in individual action and initiative."[48] Ultimately, this seemingly progressive, "white people be like" humor instructs the Sparkses' interpretative performance of whiteness throughout *Black.White.*

For example, Brian renames himself, importantly in the shadow of Murphy (and not Griffin), as "Brian White," affecting the persona of a white man who overpronounces his words, says "awesome" a lot, gives approval with a corny thumbs-up, and delights in hobbies like "building computers, fixing things with [his] hands," and golf.[49] If Brian was a post-soul black comic like Murphy, his persona, "Brian White," easily maps on top of Murphy's *SNL* sketch as Mr. White. Although this stereotyped kind of "white people be like" humor and impersonation might be seen as lowbrow, it is necessary to understand the cultural work and value of whiteface to discourses of race, representation, and empathy. Or as McAllister provocatively asks: "What if whiting up could resolve racism?"[50]

In the first episode of *Black.White.*, whiting up is given the same power as empathetic blackness in the show's overall effort to confront race and racism. However, at the end of the first day of the project, the responsibility for teaching a methodology of racial impersonation rests on the born-black Sparks family. As Brian narrates, "First thing we had to do was teach each other how to pass as members of the other race," while Bruno insists, "We're gonna help each other walk the walk and talk the talk."[51] Over their first communal dinner, the Sparkses clearly assume their role as instructors on how to be black. Carmen is taught not to be too "curious," as they assume white folks are stereotypically inclined to be, while Bruno practices how he imagines black men walk, "with a little bit of roll,"[52] for the Sparkses' approval. Both Brian and Renee cosign his performance. Brian then shows Bruno how to appropriately hug another black man—with clasped fists between their bodies—ensuring there is no hint of homoeroticism in their friendly touching.

After their blackness tutorial, Carmen asks: "Were we supposed to coach you all [about how to be white]?" Renee admits: "She doesn't have to do that. Because I know how to adapt and get along with white people because that's something that I learned to do. Because white people were the ones I had to deal with when I had to interview for a job or anything, you know? I know how to communicate with them to get what I want." Brian bolsters Renee's claim: "We interact with whites. Daily. Black culture has to conform to white society to make it."[53] In *Acting White?: Rethinking Race in "Post-Racial" America*, Devon W. Carbado and Mitu Gulati define the racial performance Renee and Brian deem necessary to twenty-first-century black life as a "double-bind." It is a theorization predicated on W. E. B. Du Bois's foundational understanding of the black experience as a "double consciousness," the bifurcation of black experience behind the veil. The Sparkses articulate this "double-bind" through the language of persona and performance, perfectly mirroring the anxieties about race produced and scripted by the dictates of reality television. Carbado and Gulati write:

> Being an African American in a predominately white institution is like being an actor on stage. There are roles one has to perform,

storylines one is expected to follow, and dramas and subplots one should avoid at all cost. Being an African American in a predominately white institution is like playing a small but visible part in a racially specific script. The main characters are white. There are one or two blacks in supporting roles. Survival is always in question. The central conflict is to demonstrate that one is black enough from the perspective of the supporting cast and white enough from the perspective of the main characters. The "double bind" racial performance is hard and risky. Failure is always just around the corner. And there is no acting school in which to enroll to rehearse the part.[54]

As tokens, the Sparkses understand how representation works in predominately white spaces, and they insist that being black already includes the skillful negotiation of those racial demands. They reveal the synecdochical nature of blackness—the white supremacist logic mandating individual minorities stand in for a racial whole. Although synecdoche is a literary term explaining how one can colloquially ask for another's "hand in marriage" when the obvious implication is to marry the entire person, that literary concept can be repurposed to describe particular anxieties around how blackness is both experienced and represented. For example, recognizing how entrenched stereotypes of innately black criminality always already pathologize all black bodies, particularly black men, one might hope that a crime gaining news coverage does not have even the assumption of a black perpetrator. Racial synecdoche animates a deep groan, an uncomfortable racial knowing—that when anyone black is accused of doing something wrong, all black folks are indicted in the crime. It is the recognition that any black person can and often will dictate how *I*, as a black person, will be seen and encountered. This is how the synecdochical nature of blackness works; it is a racist logic mirroring and motivating the "salvific wish," a desire bound up with ideas and ideals of racial uplift located at the heart of black respectability politics.[55] The salvific wish mandates a refusal to air racial "dirty laundry" in an effort to put forward the most palatable, communal black face. For example, the salvific wish demands that black men pull their pants up and stop wearing grey hoodies to avoid the hypersurveillance and aggression of the police and their vigilantes, even though Marin Luther King Jr. was arrested and killed while wearing a suit.

These representational anxieties haunt the Sparkses on *Black.White*. Their refusal to accept any advice about being white reveals the tension between whiteface and the performative practice of "code-switching," what Dwight Conquergood defines as a "commonplace ethnographic term used to describe the complex shifts minority people deftly and continuously negotiate between the communication styles of dominant culture and subculture."[56] For the Sparkses, their whiteness is merely the physical manifestation of the interpretive masking and code-switching already mastered to successfully navigate all-white spaces and institutions. They imagine their whiteness as fundamentally different from the Wurgels' temporary blackness. However, as Carbado and Gulati suggest with the provocative question mark in the title of *Acting White?*, the supposedly unmarked category of whiteness should not be assumed to be so easily accessible. Like blackness, whiteness is a racial category both constructed and performed, and code-switching is far from innate.

Although Brian and Renee confidently perform their whiteness, ironically their son, Nick, reveals how code-switching must be learned. That the Sparkses are a "typical black family" delighting in their mastery of the dangerous precariousness of tokenism and assimilation is an important part of *Black.White.*'s supposedly innovative racial experimentation. The Sparkses are a specific kind of black family—one where the mere presence of a black father challenges notions of a fractured nuclear family pathologized as dangerously matriarchic by Moynihan. As demonstrated, *Black.White.* is deeply invested in the middle-class structure of nuclear, heteronormative families with mommies, daddies, and obedient children. However, whereas Brian celebrates his successful navigation of post–civil rights race relations, his own son is revealed to be woefully ignorant about the realities and consequences of black masculinity specifically and race and racism in general.

At the time of filming, Nick is sixteen and seemingly oblivious to the consequences of being held back in both the sixth and eighth grades, as well as his expulsion from eighth grade for holding a knife for his best friend at school. Nick is vocally disinterested in the show's social experiment, insisting that although his father talks about the differences between white and black people, his generation does not see color. It is a rhetoric often taught as the idealized version of cross-racial interaction for a new and purportedly racism-free generation of millennials, reinforced by the myth of Obama's postracial age—the lauded cross-racial ethos of color blindness. Nick's nonchalant perspective reveals how the rhetoric of color blindness seduces both black and white youth, cushioning them in a logic that renders racism as only something from "back in the day." "As long as you're cool with us, we're cool with you,"[57] Nick states. He goes on, "I don't pay attention to racism no way. I'm not the type of person to sit there and try to pay attention to it or really care about it. My parents—they experience it. I don't. I'm just out there doing what I have to do and enjoying my day basically."[58] Even when his parents ask him point-blank if he knows what racism is, Nick casually shrugs. Consequently, Nick refuses to modify his affect, including his speech, manner, and interests, for the project. Instead, he insists he is just going to "do me."[59]

For *Black.White.*, Nick's disinterest becomes representative of the supposed failures of young black masculinity, a failure largely blamed on the glorification of violence and superficial excesses of hip-hop culture. As Rose judges, "I think Nick is a perfect example of many different black stereotypes incarnate—rap videos, baggy clothes, inarticulate. That is something that, like, Nick takes pride in."[60] And, on the show, Nick is punished for it. For example, his parents publicly reprimand Nick for his decision to spend $150 on a gaudy watch, a frivolous choice since he is unemployed. If his parents represent how to reap the benefits of the civil rights movement, Nick epitomizes both the "thug"[61] and the endangered black man—presumably only suitable for a life in and on the streets he imitates.

That Nick comes to represent the dangers of hip-hop is complicated by the show's co-producer, rapper turned mogul Ice Cube. Led by Cutler, the production team not only sought palatable families for this experiment but also a black co-producer to serve as an alibi. O'Shea "Ice Cube" Jackson is most recognized for his work in the controversially political, Compton-based musical collective N.W.A. (Niggaz With Attitude), which also includes hip-hop legends Dr. Dre and Easy-E. N.W.A. is still widely and rightfully considered one of the most prescient and important collaborations in gangsta rap, and one of the most formative and influential groups in hip-hop history. After breaking with N.W.A. and launching a solo career in 1989, Ice Cube went on to establish a formidable cross-media brand that in 2006 included production, writing, and acting credits in music, television, and film, giving him a cultlike status as the leading role in numerous black films, including *Boyz N the Hood*, *Higher Learning*, the *Friday* trilogy, and the controversial *Barbershop* films.[62] Despite Ice Cube's extensive résumé, the tangible marker of his involvement is the show's theme song, "Race Card," performed by him and produced by Warren G. During the opening credits and against a montage introducing the cast, Ice Cube's recognizable lyricism and phrasing frames the show: "Please don't believe the hype/ Every thing in the world ain't black and white."[63] The song sonically sutures the concerns of the show to hip-hop.

Hip-hop continues to be a persistent theme in Nick's narrative arc, reinforced by the show's decision to enroll newly white Nick in an etiquette class. Unaware that Nick was really black, his upper crust, Bel Air etiquette class becomes suspicious of his whiteness after visiting the shared Sparks-Wurgels home. While riffling through his room, his classmates discover too many trappings of hip-hop youth, like "bling bling"[64] and a DVD library featuring films such as *Barbershop*, *The Player's Club*, and *Next Friday*.[65] Caught by the overwhelming blackness of his interests, Nick is all but forced to out himself and then is peer pressured to show the unpainted skin on his legs as proof. He is then positioned in front of the mirror and asked to "be black" by excited white kids who try on his fitted hats and do-rags and then awkwardly mimic phrases like "keepin' it real." After "being black," those same kids offer Nick advice on how to more successfully perform convincing white boyhood, focusing mostly on how he needs to "articulate your words." Later, two of those same boys tell very unfunny racist jokes, casually bandying about the word "nigger" in front of the outed black but still temporarily white Nick. He insists he is not offended, even as one of his uncomfortable white girl classmates begs the boys to stop using *that* word.[66]

Subsequently, Nick's parents are angered that his nonchalance effectively excused the boys' racist language, and they express their disappointed realization that Nick is completely ignorant about the seriousness of race and racism: "I'm so ashamed of you right now,"[67] Brian sighs. Since learning how to fine-tune their performance of whiteness fails to interest Renee and Brian, their desperate recuperation of their son becomes the driving motivation for the family's continued participation on the show. Recuperating Nick takes the Sparkses to a black barbershop for a lecture about the history of the word "nigger," a working-class neighborhood tour led by a former gang member who confidently diagnoses Nick with "street poison,"[68] and L.A.'s Museum of Tolerance. Here, understanding racism falls on the shoulders of people of color. Nick's angst and rebellion does not get coded as the typical obliviousness of teenaged American boyhood, nor is he given the ignorance excuse afforded to the unfunny white boys. Nick is to blame for not properly disciplining his similarly oblivious white peers and bears all corrective responsibility; consequently, his parents blame him also. Born-black Brian resigns, "I've been so focused on trying to get Bruno and Carmen to understand what racism is all about when I should've been spending all the time to get Nicholas to understand what it's about."[69] As we will see, Nick's storyline unwittingly excuses born-white Bruno's racial myopia. In other words, if the exemplary and representative Sparkses' own kid doesn't "get it,"[70] how could Bruno?

Looking for It

In the very first episode, born-white Bruno states his motive for being on the show, to "poke into the issue of race and see if any flames would emerge."[71] And Bruno definitely wants "flames," disturbing moments of overt racism he can then dismiss as merely oversensitive black reactions to a white person's "bad day."[72] While he describes "being black [as] a subtle thing,"[73] he repeatedly voices the hope that his black masculinity will be authenticated through racist epithets. In the first episode, both families meet with a moderator to "talk about the idea of racism"[74] before swapping races for segregated focus groups. Bruno speaks first: "It'll be interesting, and I'm sure it'll happen, where I'll be in black, and I'll get some attitude from some prick white guy, and I won't have all the history of resentment that a black man has, and I'll be able to fuck with him. Just, ya know, mentally spar with him. He goes, 'Hey nigger!' I won't get angry, I'll just kind of smile to myself and go, 'Wow, why'd you say that?'" Then, as a voiceover, born-black Brian narrates what he does not say in the moment: "When I hear the 'N-word' my jaws clench up. It resonates with me ... the word still gets me. It's powerful." Back around the focus group table, Brian challenges Bruno: "No one is going to straight, strictly, come up, you know, and say 'hey nigger!' or anything like that because that kind of racism is really not there today. Now it's more we won't get the positions that we're qualified for, or we won't get the service that everybody else get[s]."[75] He then explains how Bruno, Rose, and Carmen will get more out of the empathetic conceit of *Black.White.* because they will finally experience the "day to day, small"[76] discriminations he did.

When Bruno leaves the makeup trailer as a black man for the all-black focus group, he consciously ignores what Brian earlier tried to teach him about racism. Instead, he offers his brazen misunderstanding of racial discrimination. Seated at a conference table full of black folks, Bruno sits dismissively as each speaks intimately about race. One black man painfully recalled being talked *at*, like a boy instead of a man, and another black woman lamented how she doesn't "think there's any way we will ever be considered equal."[77] After these testimonies, the group moderator prompts: "There's a lot of controversy about the 'N-word,' and who can use it, and whether it should be used at all. Who has experienced an intentional attempt to disrespect you by using that term?"[78] Without waiting to hear from any of the actual black people in the group, black Bruno immediately responds: "Yeah, I used to work as a doorman at a disco, you know. And if somebody came up intoxicated and didn't have the right dress on, you know, they'd say, 'Come on, nigger.' And it was a lot more hostile than that. And I just, you know, [said to myself], 'Mm-hmmm. Yeah, that's right. I'm a nigger.' It just wouldn't affect me. That would be the end of the conflict. Just like that!—'cause I wouldn't give it the power." Even with Brian and Renee watching through a two-way mirror, Bruno constructs a disturbing fake scenario, playing out this weird, imaginary memory of the rhetorical violence he anticipates as a black man. In a confessional aside, he continues: "The only reason why people call you derogatory names is so that they can inflame you. If you don't empower the people that call you the 'N-word' by getting upset, you win, and the idiot that just called you that doesn't have any power."[79] Switching places, Brian and Renee approach their all-white focus group differently. Rather than participate as Bruno had done, they sit back and see what white folks had to say when people of color were not in the room. One of the things they heard was a young white man, Matthew, anxiously confess that he was taught to wipe his hand after shaking a black person's. Sitting next to Matthew, and in white makeup, Renee and Brian are both speechless. Carmen and Bruno watch everything through the two-way mirror. However, the whole experience teaches Bruno nothing.

Driving back to the house, Bruno again tells Carmen, "I look forward to having someone say, 'Hey, nigger!' You know, 'You're a son of a bitch. I hate you, nigger.' And expecting me to get all freaked out about it, and I just look at 'em and go, 'Gee, why are you calling me that?'" He scoffs, "and that would be the end of it!" Bruno obsessively repeats his perverse fantasy about a charged confrontation that proves racism can be diffused by simply not reacting. Bruno conjures up moments of rhetorical violence he can charmingly handle in the space of his own imagination, without, as he describes it, the "history of resentment that a black man has."[80] Insisting "I'll be able to fuck with"[81] any racist, Bruno's gleeful anticipation of the word "nigger" dismisses Brian's wisdom and ignores how race and power work. For Bruno, racism is exclusively limited to an unabashed racist obnoxiously and publicly brandishing "nigger."

With racism as the central tension of almost every interaction between the two fathers, Brian is consistently frustrated that Bruno "tries to make light of my experiences of racism."[82] For example, when originally black Brian and in makeup Bruno are out shopping, they encounter two white women who hurriedly step out of the way to avoid them on the sidewalk. "Did you see that? She looked and ran over," Brian asks Bruno, to which Bruno replies "I didn't see that." As Brian tries to explain how the women fearfully moved out of the way, Bruno forcefully counters: "She had to. They were taking up the whole sidewalk.... They had to give it up." "It's the *way* she did it," Brian insists.[83] Here is a scenario refracted by two deeply opposed perspectives. Brian interprets the white women as fearfully refusing to either acknowledge or be near him, and Bruno sees white women politely giving two black men ample space on the sidewalk: "I experience that all the time, Brian. That's not super unique."[84] Even as Brian tries to teach Bruno how to recognize and interpret social interactions while temporarily black, back on the bus, Bruno attempts to school forty-year-old Brian on walking while black. He concludes, "I think from your reaction today, you're looking for [discrimination]." As Brian continuously points out racist microaggressions, Bruno insists these are normal social interactions, arguing that an "open heart," coupled with an ethic of individual responsibility, will defend against racism. Bruno positions himself as *Black. White.*'s "good nigger." Not only does he insidiously hope to be called a "nigger" only to casually dismiss the historical and painful legacy the word connotes with unaffected nonchalance, but also Bruno's mimicking of Bill Cosby reinforces how he interacts with the world while "in black," as he calls it. For Bruno, only bad niggers encounter discrimination. Good niggers—upstanding, responsible, assimilating black men—receive the racial goodwill he purports to perform throughout the project. After one episode, Bruno arrogantly concludes that he receives the same treatment as a black man that he gets as a white man. Consequently, Bruno even undermines the testimonies of the black people he lives with, blaming tender and wounded people of color for dwelling in the past and playing the race card. Racism only becomes legible if and when those in power can easily see it. According to Bruno, anything else is resentfully "looking for it"[85] and can be dismissed with the callous notion that discrimination is only imaginary, until a white person corroborates it.

Bruno would assuredly diagnose Brian as suffering from what John L. Jackson calls "racial paranoia," the "distrustful conjecture about purposeful race-based maliciousness and the 'benign neglect' of racial indifference."[86] Jackson uses two exemplary moments in the twenty-first-century American racial imagination to theorize and contextualize racial paranoia: Dave

Chappelle's controversial decision to walk away from his lucrative and wildly popular sketch comedy show, *Chappelle's Show*, after deducing that one of his crewmembers was laughing *at* him instead of *with* him in 2005; and the persistent rumor that the levee breaches in the wake of Katrina's landfall were an intentional sacrifice of the black and working-class neighborhoods of New Orleans to protect the city's tourism industry. Jackson's theory of racial paranoia explicates why Bruno might have difficulty recognizing covert racism. He writes, "When racism was explicit, obvious, and legal, there was little need to be paranoid about it. For the most part, what blacks saw was what they got."[87] Here, Jackson bolsters Renee's somewhat surprising, but far from unique, admission: "I think it would be better to have it like it was back in the day, because you know what you're dealing with." *Black.White.* uncovers a very real but nuanced problem in empathetic racial impersonation after the most egregious forms of segregation in America have been seemingly overcome: how do you teach someone without a lifetime's experience of being black to recognize microaggression? In *Microaggressions in Everyday Life*, Derald Wing Sue defines microaggressions as "the brief and commonplace daily verbal, behavioral, and environmental indignities, whether intentional or unintentional, that communicate hostile, derogatory, or negative racial . . . slights and insults to the target person or group."[88] Brian confidently insists he knows the difference between someone having a bad day and microaggressions. As Brian insists, black folks are capable of an intuitive, racial knowing, an epistemology of encountered racism often felt bodily—through anxiety and stress in the moment to the long-term racial stress of trauma, hypertension, heart disease, and death.

However, on *Black.White.*, racial intuition is not just experienced by the born-black Sparkses. Importantly, the only time Bruno admits to "feeling racism" is when his temporarily black body walks through the all-black space of L.A.'s Leimert Park with still-white Carmen. He interprets what he feels as a hostile energy reacting to his blackness moving through the park with a white woman: "I'll tell you what I feel. I feel racism." Bruno's voice narrates the scene: "I was very uncomfortable at Leimert Park where those very angry people—and they were angry people, you know, just bitter, self-pitying people, uh that, you know, definitely didn't like us being there."[89] Approximating the spurious language of reverse racism, Bruno finally feels an anger and hostility he concludes must be racism. These competing racial intuitions, Bruno's feelings of reverse racism, and Brian's forty years of discrimination and microaggressions cement an impenetrable wall between Bruno and Brian.

On the Failures of Racial Intimacy

On *Black.White.*, the possibility for racial transformation is coded by gender. While Bruno defiantly insists he "represent[s] the black race well,"[90] Brian celebrates his skillful mastery of his new persona as the golf-loving bartender "Brian White," and Nick is rather disinterested. Carmen, Rose, and Renee are left to navigate the precarious domain of empathetic racial impersonation. From the very first episode, the personalities of Renee and Carmen clash. Without the forced interaction of the show, these two women would undoubtedly never encounter each other, let alone build a lasting friendship. At the beginning of episode two, Renee and Carmen meet with a linguistic coach to teach them racialized vernacular. During the exercise, Carmen playfully exclaims, "Yo, bitch!" extemporaneously performing the intimacy between two black women comfortable using that word. Renee is immediately offended, stunned by Carmen's overly assumptive code-switching: "You just don't call another woman you don't know a bitch," she chastises. Carmen apologizes and assures Renee she was only reading from the prepared list of black vocabulary. Now forever guarded, Renee reads and interprets the rest of their interactions through that one moment of admittedly misguided lingual slippage and wounding. Bitchgate comes up repeatedly throughout the show and is only the first in a series of moments where Carmen is seemingly unable to control her words or anticipate how her language might be misinterpreted.

Carmen is again on the hot seat at the beginning of episode three, after she called the co-director of Rose's black poetry class a "beautiful black creature." When later confronted about her choice of words, Carmen bristles from the critique. "It was not about being politically fucking correct," she angrily defends herself, suggesting the space of shared poetry invited unfiltered reflection. "And it was not about choosing my goddamn fucking words!" She continues, "I don't wanna have to *choose my words*! I want my heart to be seen and read. And that's where I need to come from. If I have to walk on eggshells again, I can't do it. I can't exist in a world like that. And I was coming from *total love*. If you misinterpreted it, that is on you." She then confesses, "I'm having a hard time right now—liking them [the Sparkses], frankly."[91] After the confrontation, Carmen seeks a black best friend to teach her about the "politics in the community, some of the church ways, [and] some of the black history."[92] She finds that friend in a black woman named Deanna, moderator of a community town hall about issues in the black community like the representation of women in hip-hop. Later, she meets Deanna at the Oran Z Pan African Black Facts and Wax Museum, where she acknowledges her lack of education about black history. She diagnoses herself as "suffer[ing] from whiteness."[93]

After building a friendship with Deanna, Carmen's racial consciousness begins to evolve. For example, she and Bruno go on a date to line dance at the Cowboy Palace Saloon, a country bar decorated with a proudly displayed Confederate flag. As the only visibly black bodies in the place, Carmen asks for a coffee at the bar but is told to wait for Bruno to get out of the bathroom so he can pay before she is served; she is confused and offended by their inhospitable refusal. Throughout the segment, cameras catch the all-white patrons scrutinizing the couple as they dance. Carmen admits she has never experienced this hypervisibility as a white woman. Back in the car, Carmen explains how she is beginning to notice "a nuance of a sense of how that would be as a human being—to actually feel there are places, consistently, that I'm not welcome. Just due to my *me*—me—my—*me*, my flesh, my body, my beingness is not welcome. It's regarded with hate. That's deep. And that would be more challenging to deal with than just 'get over it.' It still makes me very sad. How would that be to live with? How would that be to have to even hesitate or think when I go to say 'Hi' to somebody that they might look away or might have to be [re]strained because of . . . ," she trails off before finding the right vocabulary. She then concludes: "That would be sad."[94] Rather than affirm Carmen's burgeoning racial intuition, Bruno dismisses her: "You can wallow in it, or you can move on with your life." Like Brian, Carmen tries to get Bruno to get "it." After admitting how painful it was to be the "best player"[95] on his high school basketball team but still be shut out from playing by a group of black teammates, Bruno insists "it" was something he got over, and subsequently "it" was something black folks had to get over as well. Bruno conflates the orchestrated inability to touch that *one* basketball on that *one* team that *one* time back in high school with hundreds of years of racial oppression. After that conversation, Carmen begins to realize how this project is not just about the intimacy of cross-racial interaction with the Sparkses but also about the growing discordance between her and her partner. Despite Carmen's disconnect from both the Sparkses and Bruno and the budding friendship between her and Deanna, Carmen's "hard time" in the project ultimately lies in the tensions between the misinterpretation of her language and her intention. This tension is portrayed as the very problem preventing cross-racial miscommunication. After yet another rehashing of Bitchgate between the four adults, Bruno states, "This difference in the races is based on just this type of thing [miscommunication and misinterpretation]. . . . Forget it. It's never gonna go anywhere."[96] By misrepresenting cross-racial empathy as simply a failure of communication, *Black. White.* dangerously traffics in, and perpetuates the logics of, interpersonal and transformative racial intimacy.

The show invests much of its transformative hope on the Wurgels' daughter, Rose, who one critic referred to as "a guilty liberal on training wheels."[97] Rose quickly becomes the voice of reason on the show. She is the only one who dives headfirst into the opportunity of the project, calling out her own stereotypical thinking and deeply wanting to connect with the others she encounters while black. Even Renee applauds Rose for "actually making an effort to learn what it is to be black."[98] The majority of Rose's storyline revolves around how she negotiates the pressures of her all-black slam poetry class. Rose attempts to physically perform black teenaged girlhood while at the same time being anxious about the authenticity of her poetry. The poetry class is portrayed as an honest and raw space where black youths narrate various experiences of blackness—from having a father in jail and young love to the intraracial pressures of heteronormative black masculinity. From her first workshop, Rose is both impressed and intimidated; she is overwhelmed by emotions that eventually force her to come out to her peers as a white girl in black makeup in episode two. Although Nick, Renee, and Carmen all reveal their real races to various people throughout the series, only Rose experiences anything but shocked acceptance. When black Rose outs herself to the poetry class participants, her peers first comfort her with validations of her bravery and express hope for her experimental opportunity. Only one poet, Chaz, retorts: "I feel like throwing up. And right now, looking at you, I am disgusted. I'm afraid, 'cause I cannot see you. I cannot see who you are. You have not shed one tear in apologizing to me. Not one . . . So cry, so I can see part of your white skin, because I don't know who you are."[99] This is the most intense reaction to Rose's self-exposure voiced by any of the workshop participants, and the rest of the poets chastise Chaz for being too harsh. However, Rose is appreciative and humble in the face of Chaz's anger, expressing her vulnerability as a new black girl seeking to learn.

Rose's truth provides the opportunity for her to be chaperoned through blackness. Eager to have her experience a taste of black life, the poetry class takes her on as a project. For example, in episode four, Rose accompanies one of her new friends to a salon in order to experience the lengthy process of managing black hair. She also later applies for jobs with classmate

LaToya in the boutiques dotting Rose's familiar hometown of Santa Monica. Feeling dismissed and unwelcome in the same shops and on the very same streets she once confidently inhabited as a white girl shakes Rose: "I felt like an outsider in a place that I've been so many times."[100] Even Carmen recognizes the difference: "What I detected in their faces and in their turning their heads away was fear. I can see how over time—Wow, that would either empower the hell out of me or make me lose it."[101]

Later, over dinner with her class, she excitedly shares what she learned as a black Rose: "I realize, there *is* something to being black. There is such a kinship and a brotherhood that is literally, like, instilled. One of my truisms about being white is I do not know where I come from. You guys have such a root in where you're from."[102] Earlier in the same episode, Rose reveals to Renee that she feels the white American family has been fractured by an epidemic of divorce. So, when Rose concludes that black folks know "where they're from," she idealizes a nuclear black family structure markedly anti-Moynihan. Rose's peers clamor to challenge her conclusions by invoking the history of slavery. One young woman begins, "White people—they have this whole idea of the melting pot. . . . Everybody blends in. Unfortunately, African Americans don't have that same immigrant mentality because we didn't come by choice. So when I hear somebody say that . . . you don't understand what black is. Because we don't know where we come from."[103] Another poet chimes in, "All I have is basically what was fed to me by slave owners back then. I mean my last name wouldn't have been this. . . . I don't know what my name would've been had, you know, I had that culture that was mine."[104] The poets' Afrocentrism confronts white ethnocentrism and the pressures of assimilation, revealing a nostalgic desire for a racial home before the encounter of the Atlantic slave trade. It is a comforting fantasy but also undermines the thriving communities comprising African America and is an example of the intraracial anxieties *Black. White.*'s simplified typicality cannot fully address.

As Rose trots out her conclusive thesis on black culture in a room full of black people who know she is only temporarily black, she impressively remains open to their critiques of her racial assumptions. Toward the end of that same episode, Rose processes her classmates' critiques in an intensely gendered, melodramatic scene between her and her mother. This moment is presented as Rose's racial epiphany and serves as the emotional climax of *Black.White.* As tears stream down her face, Rose laments the limits of the cast's collective impersonation, and her own personal frustrations about being temporarily black:

I didn't feel like I was part of the group. Even though I've been as much a part of that group as each person in there. Honest to God, I don't feel like people are clicking with me. And I understand it, but, like, I'm not . . . I'm not black. *I'm not black.* You can't *act* black. You *are black.* There are just some things you can't be a part of if you're not a part of it. And for some reason, like just before this project, I didn't understand that, you know, why people couldn't get along in ways, and I realize, like, you can have a black best friend if you're white, but you meet in a middle ground. I don't have that history. And as much as, like, white me can feel like it's history—it's not just history. It's what you grow up with. . . . It is who they are. . . . It taught me. . . . And that is the one crazy piece to this project—that you become invisible. You're somewhat into that world but you're, like, flirting with the boundary because you're not black and they'll feel it.[105]

Her mother sympathetically agrees, "[It's] simply entrance into a conversation I wouldn't have entrance to, but it's not assuming that I'm gonna understand what it *is* to be black."[106] "No," Rose affirms, "it's *real.*"[107] This is the emotional climax of *Black.White.*'s experiment not only because it is one of the show's most honestly intimate conversations about race, privilege, and white guilt but also because the rest of the series and the already tense relationships between the two families quickly devolve after this scene. The Sparkses confront the nigger-bandying etiquette class participants, Bruno shows his parody of hip-hop music in his obnoxiously offensive video "Midlife Rap," and a therapist is brought in to help the families communicate. Of course, much more important than the narrative arc and structure of the show are the painful conclusions Rose and Carmen confront. Tellingly, this moment is not between two people speaking across the chasms and binaries of race but between two liberal, white women—mother and daughter. Here, racial consciousness is staged as labor undertaken in the context of family. Even for the Sparkses, understanding racism and its consequences is located in the generational space between father and son.

Both Rose and Carmen come away from this project with a profound sense of alienation. They feel a wall—one built by history, suspicion, paranoia, stereotype, and assumptions they conclude are nearly impossible to either penetrate or scale. The forced intimacy of *Black.White.*'s constructed reality never fosters the types of connection and friendship it hopes to celebrate. For example, during the two-family therapy session, Carmen frustratingly admits, "We've all agreed to participate in a project, from my perception, geared toward healing misunderstanding, not resurrecting it and maintaining it."[108] Ultimately, *Black.White.* uncomfortably and unintentionally bumps against the limit of cross-racial empathy, a limit found at the level of racial intimacy. As much as Bruno wants it to be, *Black.White.* is not about racial violence. The lack of this recognizable spectacle challenges not only Bruno's racial assumptions but also the realities of reality TV. Quietly clutched purses, coincidentally missing job applications, and fearfully averted eyes are difficult to capture even with the hypersurveillance of reality television cameras. The precious nuances of racial intimacy are instead about the banal, the everyday, and the covert, what Sharon Patricia Holland calls "the erotic life of racism." She writes, "It is not difficult to see that proximity and familiarity can create the conditions to overcome racist practice. Or do they? What if proximity and familiarity don't create a level playing field of difference, but instead replicate the terms upon which difference is articulated and therefore maintained? What if our coming together (all the time) is the thing that we continue *not* to see as the lie of nonrelation and difference rolls off our tongues each time we say who we are and where we come from?"[109] This is *Black.White.*'s crisis—the crisis of racial intimacy. Holland's conclusion, entitled "Racism's Last Word," provides the theoretical scaffolding to understand that crisis. She writes, "This concluding chapter is an experimental exploration of the intimacy upon which *everyday* racism relies. . . . [It] is not focused upon egregious or spectacular acts of racist violence, but instead investigates the more quotidian acts of racism—the kind that separate (and simultaneously conjoin) black and white in family genealogies, the sort created by a simple touch or a word uttered between 'blood strangers.' "[110] Holland's reading of the erotic life of racism offers a way to understand not only *Black.White.* but also the whole of this genealogy. So as Carmen wrongly presumes a cross-racial friendship excusing the too soon playfulness of one word, and Rose presupposes a monolithic black kinship unaware of how everything, including class, colorism, sexuality, and region, impacts the complex multiplicity of black experience, *Black.White.* leaves us with blood strangers who are wounded and defensive. Through Holland, the show uncovers the core thematic deception at the heart of all of these empathetic racial impersonations—the deception of intimacy. Ultimately, temporarily walking in another's skin does not guarantee racial knowing; in fact, it impedes it.

In the final episode, each cast member shares their therapeutic homework, letters about what they learned. With no one vulnerable enough to admit change much less transformation, the letters are disappointing and bleak. As viewers, we are left with the sense that, although the makeup was successful, cross-racial intimacy failed. Proximity failed. In the penultimate scene featuring both families, Brian attempts to turn this palpable discomfort and hopelessness into something: "So while we are all sitting here, how do we make it better?"[111]

No one speaks.

The six-part series of *Black.White.* could end here. In fact, this chapter could end here—dystopically—without a viable answer to Brian's echoing and lingering question. For the sake of a more hopeful and satisfying televisual conclusion, and the health of the national sociopolitical and psychic racial imaginary, *Black.White.* awkwardly ends with a giant group hug. As the two families sway in unison, Rose's voice narrates: "Until you open your mind and your ears to other people's words and experiences, you can't make a difference. If you've got it in you to accept and forgive and move and learn . . . beautiful. You're changing the world."[112] Even in its closing moments, *Black.White.* puts the onus on the individual, the interpersonal, and the family.

Warning: intimacy is not enough.

Epilogue
The Last Soul Sister

It was the pause heard 'round the world.

In the summer of 2015, a video went viral—starting the clock on a relentless fifteen minutes of fame. During an interview with the ABC affiliate KXLY4, Rachel Dolezal failed to answer a seemingly straightforward question from reporter Jeff Humphrey: "Are you African American?" Rather than answering right away, Rachel paused for three very long, very awkward seconds before responding with her now infamously bemused quip: "I don't understand the question."[1] She then abruptly walked away.

Nodding to Grace Halsell's 1969 memoir of life as a black woman for six months, Rachel Dolezal is this book's last soul sister. However strange her story, Dolezal is the appropriate conclusion to this genealogy of empathetic racial impersonation. As a white woman self-identifying as black, Dolezal demonstrates how a well-versed, liberal white woman attempts to renounce her biological claims to whiteness and white privilege under the alibis of good intentions, empathy, allyship, activism, and familial intimacy. The very reason Dolezal hit a cultural nerve is the same reason she challenges this genealogy of empathetic racial impersonation. Dolezal refuses the temporary blackness of others in this genealogy, and her racial stubbornness exposes our deepest fears about blackness, impersonation, performance, and authenticity. Throughout this book, I have detailed how Billboard Rawkins was only magically black for a few days, Sprigle, Griffin, and the Wurgels for weeks, and Halsell for months. What coheres them is their turning back to white again, but Dolezal remains steadfast in the permanence of her racial change. Unlike the rest of these impersonators who return to whiteness, Dolezal stretches this genealogy to its absurd conclusion: "It's not a costume.... It's not something that I can put on and take off anymore."[2] Ultimately, this epilogue brings together the thematic concerns of *Black for a Day* through the framework of Dolezal.

Rachel Dolezal's pause is the gap between self-identification and the policing of racial authenticity. The uncut version of the interview revealed how Dolezal, then president of the Spokane, Washington, chapter of the National Association for the Advancement of Colored People (NAACP),

Rachel Dolezal during the viral KXLY interview.

was ambushed.[3] The interview originally focused on her latest hate crime allegation, a suspicious piece of mail placed in her PO box without canceled stamp or barcode. It then turned to Humphrey questioning her credibility regarding that allegation and others (including death threats, hung nooses, swastikas, and lynching photographs) made between 2008 and 2010, during her time as the education director of the Human Rights Education Institute in Coeur d'Alene, Idaho. After insinuating that Dolezal herself fabricated those crimes, Humphrey then confronted Dolezal about her alleged dad, born-black Albert Wilkerson. "Is this your dad?" he asked. She responded, "Yes."

Just as quickly, we discovered that Rachel was not telling the fullest version of the truth. Although Wilkerson might have been her "dad" in a chosen family kind of way, he was not her biological father and called their relationship "a good acquaintance."[4] The damning KXLY4 footage bolstered a *Coeur d'Alene Press* story exposing Dolezal to its Pacific Northwestern readers. The official story is that veteran reporter Jeff Selle first began investigating her after questioning the legitimacy of the hate crime allegations.[5] Unofficially, anonymous posts in the online comments of the paper insisting Dolezal was born white and that the hate allegations were false began appearing at least five years earlier. When Dolezal resigned from the Human Rights Education Institute in 2010, she cited "issues of fairness and equity," hinting that discrimination might have been the root cause of her failure to receive the promotion to executive director.[6] As readers discussed her resignation in the comments section of the article "Dolezal Resigns from HREI," a user with the handle "Inorderto" interrupted the thread:

> Unfortunately Rachel will need to make her discrimination claims based on something other than race. Knowing her, and being disgusted with her attempts to attract attention to racial provocation and/or threats, I feel the need to comment on her latest attempt at publicity and alleged racial discrimination . . . given that she is in no way African American, Hispanic, Chinese, Native American, or any other nationality she falsely claims. She is a native to Montana, her parents are very white, and although her siblings are mixed, she in fact, has German roots and anyone who looks at her and disregards the extensions and fake tan can see that.

Less than an hour and a half later, online reader "I'm just sayin'" corroborated:

> Yep . . . Inorderto has stated the facts accurately. Rachel is 100% caucasion [sic], white as the driven snow. Two lovely white parents, four lovely white grandparents, German decent [sic]. I was surprised when articles referred to her as "black." There are way too many people who know that is simply not true. I suppose she did this because of her bi-racial son, even though he knows she's white. She has adopted African-American, multiracial siblings. I would have to say she does like to be the center of attention . . . which she could accomplish easily wthrough [sic] her art, even though she focuses on controversy. It just seems rather hypocritical to try to pass oneself off as black to "fight for the cause." Her efforts would be more fruitful if she was only honest. I'm not even sure exactly what cause she's been fighting for. Racism exists only in the eye of the accuser.

The motivations behind these comments are as suspicious as their laudatory claims to a multigenerational, "lovely" whiteness, and the crude dismissal of the realities of race and racism. When "I'm just sayin'" exposes Dolezal's less than "fruitful" dishonesty, the commenter further sutures her to this genealogy of empathetic racial impersonation. Reminiscent of Rose in *Black.White.*, "I'm just sayin'" uncovers the failure of Dolezal's empathy. The comment trolling of "I'm just sayin'" and "Inorderto" foreshadowed one of the biggest viral stories of 2015. On June 11, the *Coeur d'Alene Press* published "Black Like Me?: Civil Rights Activist's Ethnicity Questioned," complete with four images: the first features Dolezal chairing a meeting of the Spokane Police Ombudsman Commission; the second is Rachel as a child—freckled, blonde, and smiling; the third is on her May 2000 wedding day posing with her now ex-husband, adopted siblings Ezra, Izaiah, Esther, and Zachariah, parents, and grandparents, Peggy and Herman; and the last is an image of Rachel posing with former sibling and now adopted son Izaiah, and Albert Wilkerson. Wanting to escape the "physiological, emotional, [and] mental"[7] abuse suffered during his upbringing, Izaiah encouraged Dolezal to present herself as his biological mother: "'I got you,' Rachel told him . . . [knowing] the agreement meant [she] would have to alter her look more often. 'I knew, internally, that that also meant I had to monitor my experience a bit more because he's not even mixed.'"[8] The first and fourth photographs were taken from Facebook, but the two older images were provided courtesy of Larry and Ruthanne, Dolezal's biological parents, who helped Jeff Selle and Maureen Dolan "out" their daughter. "It is very disturbing that she has become so dishonest," Ruthanne told the reporters.[9] With birth certificates and photographic evidence, Dolezal's estranged parents framed themselves as unimpeachably and impeccably white, similar to their portrayal in the reports by the anonymous whistleblowers online.

When the Dolezal story broke, the social and traditional media responses can only be described as a frenzy, growing more salacious and bizarre as details emerged. For example, *The Smoking Gun* reported that, under her married last name, Moore, Dolezal sued Howard University specifically as a white woman. Working on her Master of Fine Art degree and pregnant with her son Franklin, Dolezal "claimed discrimination based on race, pregnancy, family responsibilities and gender, as well as retaliation. . . ." She alleged that University officials ". . . (a) blocked her appointment to a teaching assistantship during the Fall semester of 2001, (b) rejected her application for an instructorship following completion of her graduate studies, and (c) denied her scholarship aid while a student."[10] The lawsuit was eventually dismissed. In another, far more uncomfortable example, we learned Rachel's older, biological brother, Joshua, had been accused of the molestation of a younger family member. Rachel was a witness in the pending case against him, but only a month after she had been outed, a Denver, Colorado, court dismissed the charges before she or the victim could testify.

If Rachel Dolezal's biological whiteness was used to destroy her credibility and detract from her capacity as a witness, as she has often alleged,[11] it sickeningly seems to have worked. The fallout came swiftly. Days after the story broke, she resigned as president of the Spokane NAACP, citing the "unexpected firestorm" caused by the exposure of her racial impersonation. In a lengthy post on the chapter's Facebook page addressed to its Executive Committee and NAACP members, Dolezal stepped down while maintaining her commitment to activism and the eradication of racism. She writes, "Please know I will never stop fighting for human rights and will do everything in my power to help and assist, whether it means stepping up or stepping down, because this is not about me. It's about justice. This is not me quitting; this is a continuum."[12] Eastern Washington University, where Dolezal taught as a part-time instructor in the Africana Studies Department, severed their affiliation by not renewing her quarter-to-quarter contract. To complete the trifecta of professional disgrace, the Spokane City Council voted unanimously to remove Dolezal from her seat on the Police Ombudsman Commission.

In the midst of the "viciously inhumane"[13] firestorm, Dolezal launched a defensive, televisual media blitz from an appearance on the *Today Show* with Matt Lauer to a full-episode sitdown with professor and former MS-NBC talk show host Melissa Harris-Perry. While she narrated varying and sometimes competing versions of herself and upbringing for each audience, on one point Dolezal was frustratingly consistent: she identified as black. For example, during a live morning interview, Lauer pressed Dolezal with a number of questions, including: "Are you an African American woman?" and "When did you start deceiving people?"[14] Expectedly, Dolezal balked at the line of questioning and then described how the national media unevenly portrayed her racial identity as first "transracial," "biracial," and then "black" when documenting the harassment she suffered as a social justice worker in northern Idaho. Although these claims about her racial identity are also described in unedited video interviews with Dolezal on the experience of black womanhood conducted in 2014 by EWU student Lauren Campbell, there is no evidence to suggest that the national news referred to her racial identity in this way. In fact, the national news never carried the story of her alleged hate crimes. Although Dolezal *was* mentioned in a February 15, 2010, *New York Times* article about the Tea Party's backlash to Obama's presidency in Idaho, there she was identified as "multiracial."[15] In that same *Today Show* interview, Dolezal insisted Albert Wilkerson was her "dad," not necessarily her father, and that her lawsuit against Howard University was a strategic act of self-identification and "survival." She ended her interview with Lauer by repeating the words of one of her sons: "Mom, racially you're human and culturally you're black."[16]

Although the mainstream media contributed to the hysteria around Dolezal, the frenzy would not have existed without social media. Memes, hashtags, Vine parodies, and clickbait thinkpieces rained down to critique and comment on the national identity crisis Rachel inspired. The response is part of what Jon Ronson calls our current sociocultural moment—a "renaissance of public shaming."[17] In *So You've Been Publicly Shamed*, Ronson writes, "With social media, we've created a stage for constant artificial high drama. Every day a new person emerges as a magnificent hero or a sickening villain."[18] Although pop star Rihanna called Dolezal "a bit of a hero,"[19] she was largely in the minority. The overwhelming response, particularly from online black communities, criticized and shamed Dolezal with large doses of skepticism about her blackness. Almost immediately after the story broke, the hashtag #AskRachel relentlessly began trending on both Twitter and Instagram. The hashtag, a barrage of rhetorical questions testing Rachel's racial authenticity, featured mostly multiple-choice questions on black popular culture and often-stereotypical aspects about growing up black. For example, accompanying a screenshot image of a grieving Florida Evans from *Good Times*, Black Twitter "asked Rachel" if Florida was exclaiming: "A. Man! Man! Man!; B. Damn! Damn! Damn!; C. Lawd! Lawd! Lawd!; or D. All of the above." (Hint: the answer is "B.") Folks also asked Rachel: how many fights prompted the Fresh Prince's mom to relocate him from Philly to Bel-Air?; how long did her church service typically last?; and to complete Tupac, Biggie, Soulja Boy, and Boosie's hip-hop lyrics. Even Larry Wilmore, host of the *Nightly Show* on Comedy Central, got in on the act. "A boat is leaving from Africa," he queried, "were your ancestors above deck or below deck?"[20]

Through tweeted and retweeted "Ain't Jemima" and "Straight Outta Melanin" memes, we not only debated the validity of Dolezal's blackness but also laughed. The summer of 2015 was one of crisis in the black community, an overwhelming and painful season of black death. While still grieving over the senseless murders of 2014—Michael Brown, John Crawford, Ezell Ford, and the young Tamir Rice, to name only a few—we faced swelling numbers of unarmed black youth murdered by the spurious authority of the police. We saw the video of Walter Scott's horrific murder by Officer Michael Slager in South Carolina and heard the twisted justification of Freddie Gray's death while in the custody of the Baltimore police. The narrative about black death was all too familiar. In sum, black folks were constructed as always already criminal, monstrous, and deserving of assassination. As false evidence conspired to render black bodies inhuman, we emphatically protested that black lives mattered.

As blackness was strategically conflated with death, I took a break and scrolled through my Instagram and Twitter feeds, laughing out loud in communal solidarity. #AskRachel became a welcome distraction in the midst of mourning and resistance. Although the questions and references were paradoxically all too familiar and simultaneously all too obscure, they offered a brief respite from my grieving protest. Yes, my grandmother also owns that same white-speckled black pot. And, yes, I spent far too much time in a salon chair pretending my scalp was not burning. As Gene Demby writes, "It was nice to be able to sit in all of that for an evening, to spit-take and blast out tweets full of tear-streaked emojis and 'DEAD. JUST DEAD' with thousands of others. This was the *other* part of the story we need to tell ourselves about ourselves. Sometimes it's important to remind ourselves that blackness isn't just a parade of calamities and disadvantage."[21] For a moment, blackness meant more than just vulnerability to the lies of supposedly fearful cops and vigilantes. It was what Torraine Walker called the black community's "family reunion"[22]—a needed moment of catharsis.

Unfortunately, this cathartic reunion did not last long. On June 17, 2015, domestic terrorist Dylann Storm Roof tried to mount a race war by entering the Emanuel African Methodist Episcopal Church, a historic black church in Charleston, South Carolina, by murdering nine of its constituents, including its senior pastor and state senator, Clementa Carlos "Clem" Pinckney. Roof turned his loophole-obtained handgun on his unknowing victims after praying with them during their regularly scheduled Wednesday Bible study. The lightheartedness of #AskRachel quickly turned to anger. For example, actress Tracee Ellis Ross told the *Hollywood Reporter*, "[Dolezal is] just not that funny now after what happened in Charleston. The day those people were murdered, it stopped being a funny story."[23] Echoing Ross, Black Twitter collectively demanded to know if Dolezal would still self-identify as black in the aftermath of this assault, even suggesting Roof would ignore Dolezal as a potential racial target.

Constructing Blackness

In the face of unrelenting ridicule and anger after Charleston, Dolezal still insisted on her self-miscegenated blackness. Defiantly challenging her parents, Dolezal's claim to blackness remains deliberately and carefully crafted. Admittedly, she has weaved a narrative of self-identity emboldened by the alibi of "creative nonfiction,"[24] and the Dolezals collectively agree on very few facts. We know Rachel Anne Dolezal was born white at home in 1977, and is the oldest daughter in a family with one biologically older brother and four younger, black adopted siblings. She attended Belhaven University (then College) in Jackson, Mississippi, and continued her education at Howard University, graduating in 2002 with a Master of Fine Art degree. With a portfolio full of mixed-media artwork featuring primarily black subjects, Dolezal moved to Idaho with her family, establishing herself there as an artist, activist, and educator. After divorcing her husband in 2004 because of domestic violence, and resigning from the North Idaho Human Rights Education Institute, Dolezal moved to Spokane, Washington, an overwhelmingly white part of the Pacific Northwest with less than a 2 percent black population. She taught Africana studies at Eastern Washington University, served as the faculty advisor of the Black Student Union, presided over the city's chapter of the NAACP, and served as chair of the Office of Police Ombudsman.

Dolezal's creative nonfiction is most evident in her February 5, 2015, interview with Eastern Washington University's student paper, the *Easterner*. Dolezal told interviewer Shawntelle Moncy that she was born in a tepee with Jesus Christ as witness to her birth, and how her family hunted food with bows and arrows because her mother believed in "living off the land."[25] She also confessed a painful story of being beaten with a baboon whip "similar to what was used as whips during slavery,"[26] a horrifying punishment doled out according to skin color.

Skin color is a major element of Dolezal's childhood story, and she often recounts her self-birth into blackness by recalling how she drew self-portraits with the brown crayon rather than the peach one. "Since I was four . . . all of my portraits were with the brown crayon. Brown crayon, black hair,"[27] she told Campbell. Throughout the scandal, Dolezal repeated her crayon story, later elaborating: "In terms of drawing myself, my self-portrait, I instinctively felt my skin color was brown. That looked better in the picture, Rachel says, adding, The peach crayons did not look—I don't know. They didn't resonate with me. When I got to kindergarten, there were no black kids in the class. Everybody was drawing these white-looking faces, and you learn about peer pressure, [that] you don't do [the wrong color]. I remember people saying, 'Look, this isn't your skin color.'"[28] Although chastised by teachers for her resistance to the symbolic whiteness of the peach crayon, Dolezal's narrative of consistently choosing the brown crayon is the origin story of her constructed blackness.

Dolezal's brown crayonhood is only the beginning of her often inconsistent racial identity. Her story moved from crayons to hair. Dolezal weaves a tender story about how her hair journey began when she learned to braid her adopted younger black sister's hair as a teenager. Inspired by, and envious of, the beauty of Esther's black hair, Dolezal describes her time as an undergraduate student in Jackson, Mississippi, when her silky, blonde hair was first snatched into braids. She then felt truly accepted and celebrated as a black woman. "I noticed that it did change how people perceived me" . . . "[black folks in Mississippi were] like, 'oh, she's down.' Because it went from 'Rachel . . . looks white' to . . . when I got braids, it was just like . . . smiles . . . [My hair] felt like an affirmation of 'black is beautiful.'"[29] Hair for Dolezal was a visual marker of her commitment to blackness and the vehicle for her acceptance into a black community. Robin Thede, the satirical "Black Emergency Technician" on the *Nightly Show*, joked "[Rachel] cracked the holy grail of black secrets—black women's hair . . . [It's] even secret to black men."[30] Ultimately, Dolezal understands the political and aesthetic power of black women's hair. As Kobena Mercer articulates in "Black Hair/Style Politics," "black people's hair has been historically *devalued* as the most visible stigmata of blackness, second only to skin."[31] Although Dolezal admitted to Lauer, "I certainly don't stay out of the sun,"[32] for her, adopting styles associated with black hair was a choice of the "prettier" option. Hiding her coveted blonde hair under a myriad of black hairstyles was Rachel's way of confronting centuries of white supremacist aesthetic ideals.[33] Not only did she sport the look and style of black women's hair, she also *does* black hair, often for black children adopted by white families. Identifying as a braider, Dolezal describes her stylist work as "healing."[34] As Mercer describes doing black hair, "The agency of human hands—is valued in its own right as a mark of both invention and tradition, and aesthetic skills are deployed within a complex economy of symbolic codes in which communal subjects recreate themselves."[35] After losing all of her professional associations in the wake of scandal, at the writing of this epilogue, Dolezal now supports her family by doing hair out of her house. Admittedly, it is a very black way to make ends meet.

As the story broke, speculation swirled about Dolezal's hair. "What's up with your hair?"[36] Harris-Perry asked Dolezal, and tabloid talk show host Wendy Williams, mimicking black gay slang, claimed Dolezal was giving "hair realness."[37] The fascination with Dolezal's hair simultaneously questioned how a white woman could appropriate black hair while celebrating her commitment to it. Thinkpieces featured images of Dolezal rocking traditionally black styles from naturally curly wigs, weaves, twist-outs, cloth-wrapped high buns, and floor-length, blonde faux-locs to chestnut brown box braids. The same folks who questioned Dolezal's racial authenticity could not help but celebrate her hair choices. For example, *Jezebel* writer Kara Brown collated images of Dolezal's varying hairstyles for an article entitled "Rachel Dolezal Definitely Nailed the Hair, I'll Give Her That."[38] She writes, "Of the many pressing questions raised by the Rachel Dolezal circus that was wrapped in a trainwreck and dipped in a forest fire, one of the things that stands out most for me is: How did she get her hair so on point? Black people come in all shades, but clearly Rachel knew: Those spray tans would not be enough. The hair—she had to nail the hair—and boy did she."[39] Dolezal nailed her hair to fashion her own black identity; she knew getting her hair "right" enabled aesthetic acceptance into black womanhood.

Along with her brown crayon and hair, as an adjunct Africana Studies professor, Dolezal bolstered her blackness with carefully crafted, academic language about race and identity. She studied how to talk about the complicated contours of race and black womanhood, defensively thwarting speculations that her blackness had anything to do with blackface: "I have huge issues with blackface," she told Lauer. "This is not some freak, *Birth of a Nation*, mockery, blackface performance. This is on a very real, connected level how I've actually had to go there with the experience—not just the visible representation."[40] Trumping visuality and biology, experience is foundational to Dolezal's blackness. For example, take this exchange between Dolezal and Melissa Harris-Perry:

HARRIS-PERRY: Are you black?

DOLEZAL: Yes.

HARRIS-PERRY: What do you mean when you say that? What does it mean to you to assume the mantle, the identity, of blackness?

DOLEZAL: Well, it means several things. First of all it means that I've really "gone there" with the experience in terms of being a mother of two black sons and really owning what it means to experience and live black. . . . Another aspect would be, from a very young age, [I] felt, I don't know if it's a spiritual, visceral, just very instinctual connection with "black is beautiful," ya know, just the black experience and wanting to celebrate that, . . . This is not been something that is just a casual, you know, come and go, sort of identity, you know, or an identity crisis or something, that's going to fade away.[41]

Unlike her unacknowledged white-turned-black-woman role predecessor, Grace Halsell, Dolezal insists on her blackness by focusing on her ability to own the black experience above and beyond temporary black imperson-ation. Dolezal's narrative of her black experience is mainly twofold. First, she identifies primarily as a mother, specifically of black sons. She describes herself as a teen mom who raised her younger siblings in the neglectful ab-sence of her parents. In the predominately white geography of the Pacific Northwest, Dolezal felt the need to perform unquestionably black moth-erhood. This desire intensified when Dolezal became the legal guardian of her former sibling Izaiah, who sued Larry and Ruthanne for emancipation in 2010 at the age of 16. Legally, "getting Izaiah"[42] added another layer to the construction of her blackness.

The other layer of Dolezal's stubborn blackness is far more complicated than motherhood. During a gotcha interview with the four women of color co-hosts of the daytime talk show *The Real*, Dolezal smugly describes her experiences with the police who, without prompting, "mark 'black' on [her] traffic tickets."[43] These interactions with the police rang hollow with the show's co-hosts and audience. Dolezal has a suspicious history of hate crimes against her in both Idaho and Washington. Although each incident was re-ported to the police, none of the allegations seemed credible enough to fully investigate. Still, before she was outed, Dolezal boasted about these hate crimes and used them as the last line of her various social media and professional biographies. Dolezal's hate crimes punctuate the legitimacy of her constructed racial identity, and her narrative of invented racial terror reinforces the Dixie terror Sprigle, Griffin, Halsell, and Solomon sought during their impersonations. Whereas each traveled south to put themselves in the assumedly probable path of racial terror, Dolezal created a mythol-ogy of racial harassment north and west of the Mason-Dixon. More than her black sons, impeccably coiffed hair, and penchant for tanning, her tales of terror are how Dolezal attempts to pass what Adrian Piper, in "Passing for White, Passing for Black," calls the "Suffering Test."[44] As a black woman often assumed to be white, Piper describes her awkward social encounters with people questioning her racial authenticity, curious individuals demand-ing racial proof her body could not provide. According to Piper, the "Suf-fering Test" is administered most often by other black people, similar to the lines of questioning motivating #AskRachel. Piper writes, "And I have sometimes met blacks socially who, as a condition of social acceptance of me, require me to prove my blackness by passing the Suffering Test. They recount at length their recent experiences of racism and then wait expec-tantly, skeptically, for me to match theirs with mine. . . . I would share some equally nightmarish experience along similar lines."[45] As with Piper, shared suffering is the foundational premise of black communal belonging. However, unlike Piper, who is "really" black, Dolezal's constructed history of hate crimes reveals how she, like many of the other empathetic racial impersonators in this genealogy, forecloses any real possibility for true antiracist work. Similar to Halsell, Dolezal is a failed white ally, using overdetermined black experiences to overshadow structural inequality.

Although her falsified hate crimes fail to pass the "Suffering Test," Dolezal defined her blackness based on feeling and pain. "I definitely am not white," she told Savannah Guthrie in an interview, "Nothing about being white describes who I am."[46] While nothing about whiteness describes Dolezal, she spins a narrative of well-researched, experiential blackness: "It's taken my entire life to negotiate how I identify, and I've done a lot of research and a lot of studying."[47] She insists, "I don't know spiritually and metaphysically how this goes, but I do know that from my earliest memories I have awareness and connection with the black experience, and that's never left me."[48] In yet another interview, she claims, "Sometimes how we feel is more powerful than how we're born."[49] Dolezal's self-definition of blackness is the epitome of white privilege.

The Stubborn Blackness of Rachel Dolezal

In "Rachel Dolezal's True Lies," Allison Samuels concludes, "Dolezal's claim on black womanhood still seems non-negotiable."[50] In our racial imaginary, Dolezal's nonnegotiable blackness is inconceivable since, as Greg Tate describes, white folks historically take everything but the burden.[51] Consequently, Dolezal's stubborn blackness is so confounding that some dismiss her as mentally ill. Others assume her blackness results from a crude "dick too bomb" argument steeped in the myth of the transformative power of black virility. Dolezal would even be a curiosity to Adrian Piper. Dispelling accusations she would impersonate blackness for the benefits of affirmative action, Piper writes, "It's an extraordinary idea, when you think about it; as though someone would willingly shoulder the stigma of being black in a racist society for the sake of a little extra professional consideration that guarantees nothing but suspicions of foul play and accusations of cheating."[52] Dolezal did and, stubbornly, still does.

Academic discourse has undoubtedly enabled Dolezal's blackness. Nowhere is this more evident than in the language and argument about transracial identity. Adding volume to the cacophonous crescendo about Dolezal, Caitlyn Jenner, Olympic gold medalist and reality television star, appeared on the front cover of *Vanity Fair* for the first authorized photographs of her very public transition.[53] Discussions about Jenner became a way to reverse theorize transracial identity. On social media, mostly transphobic memes questioned our collective capacity to accept Caitlyn and not Rachel. Although "transracial" seemed to be a new term to name an individual born racially "wrong," Michael Awkward used the term in his 1995 book *Negotiating Difference: Race, Gender, and the Politics of Positionality*. Awkward identifies "transraciality" in texts "such as memoirs, novels, and films by John Howard Griffin, Grace Halsell, George Schuyler, Eddie Murphy, and Melvin van Peebles.... The plots of such narratives can conclude with an endorsement of black militancy ... or in the articulation of better-informed pleas for racial understanding that characterize Griffin's and Halsell's texts."[54] Despite Awkward's early usage of the term and social media's misuse of it, transracial has a concrete definition naming the placement of a child of one race with the family of another, like Dolezal's younger siblings.

Although Dolezal might feel instinctively black, I refuse to consider her transracial because its theorization easily falls apart. Transracial is exclusively one-directional—from white to black. In its (il)logics, blackness becomes the space of racial play, performance, and affect, whereas whiteness does not. American whiteness remains pristinely unimpeachable. If a person of color felt an instinctive or spiritual connection to whiteness, that feeling would never fully guarantee the protection of white privilege. Even with a consideration of the long and understandable histories of racial passing from black to white, a tenuous and precarious option for black and brown folks seeking to escape the consequences of violence, stereotype, racial synecdoche, terror, surveillance, and/or suspicion, this option is not equally available to all. If the police stopped a person of color, their stubborn insistence, "I identify as white," would never be a viable alibi. Consequently, it is dangerous to collapse the nuanced categories of gender identity onto the realities of race and racism. Although Dolezal might disagree, rhetorically rejecting an association with the history of white supremacy and how whiteness functions will never remove her from white privilege, regardless of her hair, skin, study, and sons. Rather, her insistence on a self-constructed blackness is mired in the self-righteousness of privilege.

Ultimately, Dolezal exercises her assumed, white American birthright— to define and redefine herself, Gatsby-style. It is an exercise that pokes holes in my conclusion that "once you go black you do go back," as Joe yelled at the *Finian's Rainbow* cast party, and solidifies Dolezal's place at the end of this genealogy as its last soul sister. Dolezal reminds us how blackness can be seductive, provocatively indexing a rather wonderful idea about blackness. Blackness, even in its vulnerability, pain, and suffering, is an identity worth performing and pursuing. In a strange way, this one white woman's commitment to what blackness means in our *not* postracial moment reinforces, nearly paradoxically, how much *I* love being black.

Loving my blackness allows me to return to bell hooks's and Leslie Jamison's definitions of empathy. Again, hooks concludes, "To make one's self vulnerable to the seduction of difference, to seek an encounter with the Other, does not require that one relinquish forever one's mainstream positionality,"[55] and Jamison questions what is "gift and invasion."[56] Selfishly, I want to close this book by cleaving to the idea that recognizing another person's pain is possible, and visiting the landscapes of difference can be meaningful and rich. Although this genealogy of empathetic racial impersonation has often meant power, privilege, and stereotype, it also teaches us about the process and hazards of racialization, and the naive but sincere search for cross-racial understanding. Although this genealogy about walking in someone's skin exposes the limits of empathetic racial impersonation, these racial stunts also demonstrate how identity is shifting and contingent. We must continue to crave an epistemology of empathy. As we demand that black lives matter, we do so in the face of ghosts. There are so many names that will never become politically charged hashtags because we will never know their names. However, those we know and those we do not implore us to turn empathy into systemic and necessary change.

To do so, we must admit blackness is an identity those without biology or papers might want. We must admit blackness is as expanding, variegated, and mercurial as Dolezal's confounding stubbornness. And ultimately, we must admit that, although blackness is co-opted, impersonated, mocked, mimicked, and appropriated, it has also changed the entire world—from music, hair, literature, and style to Diaspora, belonging, magic, slang, and the Oval Office.

Warning: black is beautiful.

Notes

Introduction

1. Peterson, "I Was a Teenage Negro!," 35.

2. Gubar, *Racechanges*, 5.

3. Although Oscar Hammerstein and Richard Rodgers are the most well-remembered writers of American musical theater, Harburg wrote the song "Over the Rainbow" for *The Wizard of Oz*.

4. *Finian's Rainbow* would be Astaire's last role as a dancing lead.

5. Isherwood, "A Pot of Sunny Gold," C1. The 2009 revival starred Cheyenne Jackson and Kate Baldwin and was directed and choreographed by Warren Carlyle.

6. Woody Mahoney is a "union organizer" and a recognizable homage to folk musician Woody Guthrie.

7. Harburg and Saidy, *Finian's Rainbow*, act 1, scene 5, 83–84. Emphasis in original.

8. Ibid., act 2, scene 2, 110–111.

9. Ibid., 111.

10. This would not have been true if Harburg had mounted the original version of the musical. In it, Rawkins is nearly lynched for raping a white woman after having consensual sex with his wife. It is a scene briefly reminiscent of George Schuyler's 1931 speculative and satirical novel, *Black No More*, which features the lynching of two white supremacists in blackface. One can easily speculate why Rawkins's near lynching might have been unpalatable to postwar audiences.

11. Harburg and Saidy, *Finian's Rainbow*, act 2, scene 2, 112. Emphasis in original.

12. Ibid., 114.

13. Ibid.

14. "Oh, Dem Golden Slippers" was a popular song performed in blackface. James A. Bland wrote it in 1879.

15. Harburg and Saidy, *Finian's Rainbow*, act 2, scene 3, 121.

16. Ibid., act 2, scene 4, 136.

17. Ibid., 138. Emphasis in original.

18. Ibid., 139.

19. Ibid.

20. Kennedy, "Radio and Television Report."

21. hooks, "Eating the Other," 367.

22. Ibid.

23. Jamison, *The Empathy Exams*, 6. Emphasis in original.

24. Ibid., 5.

25. Jackson, *Gunnar Myrdal and America's Conscience*, 35.

26. Gunnar Myrdal, quoted in Jackson, *Gunnar Myrdal and America's Conscience*, 86.

27. Myrdal, *An American Dilemma*, 8.

28. Ibid., 24.

29. Chafe, "Race in America," 164.

30. Myrdal, *An American Dilemma*, lxxvii.

31. Ibid.

32. Ibid., lxxix. Emphasis in original.

33. Several scholars make this claim. See Jackson, *Gunnar Myrdal and America's Conscience*; Lewis, *W. E. B. Du Bois 1919–1963*; and Singh, *Black Is a Country*.

34. Jackson, *Gunnar Myrdal and America's Conscience*, 231.

35. Ibid., 247. Jackson sees Wright's 1945 semi-autobiography, *Black Boy*, as that very reflection on the black psyche.

36. Before becoming a bestselling novel, Hobson's story was first serialized in *Cosmopolitan* in 1946, the same year Harburg wrote *Finian's Rainbow*.

37. Harburg and Meyerson, *Who Put the Rainbow in "The Wizard of Oz,"* 223.

38. Peterson, "I Was a Teenage Negro!," 49–50.

39. Harburg and Saidy, *Finian's Rainbow*, 116.

40. Halberstam, *The Queer Art of Failure*, 2.

41. Ibid.

Chapter One

1. Sprigle, *In the Land of Jim Crow*, 18.

2. Sprigle, "I Was a Negro in the South for 30 Days," August 9, 1948, 1.

3. Ibid. Emphasis in original.

4. Ibid.

5. "The Press: Meat Makes News," *Time*, 1.

6. Steigerwald, "Sprigle's Secret Journey." http://old.post-gazette.com/sprigle/Sprigleintroduction.asp.

7. Ibid.

8. Sprigle, "I Was a Negro in the South for 30 Days," August 10, 1948, 1.

9. Ibid.

10. Sprigle, *In the Land of Jim Crow*, 21.

11. Sprigle, "I Was a Negro in the South for 30 Days," August 10, 1948, 2.

12. Sprigle, *In the Land of Jim Crow*, 3.

13. Ibid., 21.

14. Ibid., 10.

15. Sprigle, "I Was a Negro in the South for 30 Days," August 10, 1948, 1.

16. Kennedy, "Racial Passing," 1145.

17. Ibid.

18. Hobbs, *A Chosen Exile*, 4–5.

19. Ibid., 6.

20. See Chesnutt's short story "Mars Jeems Nightmare" in *The Conjure Stories*; Craft and Craft's slave narrative *Running a Thousand Miles to Freedom*; Jacobs's *Incidents in the Life of a Slave Girl*; Dunbar's poem "We Wear the Mask" in *Selected Poems*; Johnson's *Autobiography of an Ex-Colored Man*; Schuyler's *Black No More*; and Hughes's "Who's Passing for Who?" For the treatment of passing by white authors, see Cho-

pin's short story "Desiree's Baby"; Hurst's novel *Imitation of Life*; Lewis's novel *Kingsblood Royal*; and Twain's novel *Pudd'nhead Wilson*.

21. See Broyard, *One Drop*; and Derricotte, *The Black Notebooks*.

22. Sandweiss, *Passing Strange*, 9.

23. Ibid., 7. Emphasis in original.

24. Ibid., 8. Emphasis in original.

25. Sprigle, *In the Land of Jim Crow*, 9.

26. Ironically, Natchez, Mississippi, was the birthplace of Richard Wright.

27. Cox, *Dreaming of Dixie*, 155.

28. Baker and Nelson, "Violence, the Body, and 'The South,'" 233.

29. Sprigle, "I Was a Negro in the South for 30 Days," August 9, 1948, 1.

30. Ibid., August 11, 1948, 1.

31. Ibid.

32. Ibid.

33. Ibid., 2.

34. Ibid., 1–2.

35. Sprigle, "I Was a Negro in the South for 30 Days," August 9, 1948, 1.

36. Sprigle, *In the Land of Jim Crow*, 1.

37. Ibid., 198.

38. For example, colloquial definitions of the South on websites like Wikipedia do not recognize either Texas or Florida as part of "the South." However, according to the United States Census Bureau, the South includes Texas, Florida, and even Delaware. Culturally, the South can be defined as the place where the sugar is in the tea and not in the grits.

39. Emmett, "I Wish I Was in Dixie's Land."

40. Sprigle, *In the Land of Jim Crow*, 103.

41. Sprigle, "I Was a Negro in the South for 30 Days," August 14, 1948, 1.

42. Ibid., August 11, 1948, 1.

43. Hartman, *Scenes of Subjection*, 3.

44. Ibid.

45. Ibid., 5.

46. Harris, *The Scary Mason-Dixon Line*, 2.

47. Ibid.

48. Baldwin, *No Name in the Street*, 68.

49. Wright, *Black Boy*, 7–8.

50. Sprigle, "I Was a Negro in the South for 30 Days," August 9, 1948, 2. Emphasis in original.

51. Ibid.

52. Ibid.

53. Ibid.

54. Recognizing that Marion, Indiana, is the site of one of the most famous lynchings and iconic photographs in U.S. history, it is important to note that Marion is not in the South. There is a way in which this image is assumed to be the South and in specific histories often stands for southern racial terror.

55. Baker and Nelson, "Violence, the Body, and 'The South,'" 235.

56. Steigerwald, "Sprigle's Secret Journey," 2.

57. Sprigle, "I Was a Negro in the South for 30 Days," August 9, 1948, 1.

58. Sprigle, *In the Land of Jim Crow*, 5–6.

59. Ibid., 5.

60. White, "I Investigate Lynchings."

61. Sprigle, "I Was a Negro in the South for 30 Days," August 9, 1948, 1.

62. Ibid.

63. Ibid.

64. Sprigle, *In the Land of Jim Crow*, 111–112.

65. Holloway, *Jim Crow Wisdom*, 74.

66. Sprigle, *In the Land of Jim Crow*, 112.

67. Ibid.

68. Sprigle, "I Was a Negro in the South for 30 Days," August 24, 1948, 1.

69. Ibid., August 11, 1948, 2.

70. Ibid.

71. Ibid.

72. Ibid.

73. Sprigle, "I Was a Negro in the South for 30 Days," August 13, 1948, 2.

74. Ibid., 2.

75. Sprigle, "I Was a Negro in the South for 30 Days," August 9, 1948, 1.

76. Ibid., September 1, 1948, 2.

77. Ibid.

78. *In the Land of Jim Crow*, 212.

79. Ibid., 9.

80. Sprigle, "I Was a Negro in the South for 30 Days," August 11, 1948, 2.

81. "Oreo" is an intraracist epithet used most often by African Americans to describe black folks who are supposedly black on the outside and white on the inside. It is a way to shame those called "oreo" by suggesting they are racially inauthentic. "Oreo" usually accompanies charges of "acting white" or "talking white."

82. Kennedy, "Reporter Posing as Negro," 1. Kennedy became famous for his 1940s infiltration and chronicling of the Ku Klux Klan. For more, see Kennedy's *The Klan Unmasked* and *Southern Exposure*. Kennedy's story of his time in the Ku Klux Klan came under fire in 2006 with Stephen J. Dubner and Steven D. Levitt's *New York Times* magazine column "Hoodwinked." In *Freakonomics*, Dubner and Levitt nearly retracted their chapter on Kennedy's passing as a white supremacist, questioning Kennedy's methods and story. Even in the midst of this controversy, Kennedy still can be considered Sprigle's white liberal foil. Although his infiltration was exaggerated, his exposé of the KKK demonstrates how white privilege can be used to challenge the consequences of white supremacy and power since his efforts helped to enact real and substantive change.

83. Sprigle, *In the Land of Jim Crow*, 112.

84. Ibid.

85. Sprigle, "I Was a Negro in the South for 30 Days," August 16, 1948, 1.

86. Ibid., 2.

87. Ibid.

88. Ibid.

89. Sprigle, "I Was a Negro in the South for 30 Days," August 17, 1948, 1.

90. Ibid., 2.

91. Ibid., 1.

92. Sprigle, *In the Land of Jim Crow*, 39.

93. Sprigle, "I Was a Negro in the South for 30 Days," August 17, 1948, 1.

94. Ibid., 2.

95. Sprigle, "I Was a Negro in the South for 30 Days," August 20, 1948, 1.

96. Ibid.

97. Ibid., 2.

98. Ibid., 1.

99. Sprigle, *In the Land of Jim Crow*, 8.

100. Sprigle, "I Was a Negro in the South for 30 Days," August 13, 1948, 1.

101. Ibid., 1–2.

102. Sprigle, *In the Land of Jim Crow*, 43.

103. Sprigle, "I Was a Negro in the South for 30 Days," August 11, 1948, 1.

104. Sprigle, *In the Land of Jim Crow*, 1.

105. Baldwin, "Stranger in the Village," in *Notes of a Native Son*, 167.

106. Morrison, *Playing in the Dark*, 38. Emphasis in original.

107. Ibid., 5.

108. Ibid., 38.

109. Savage, *Broadcasting Freedom*, 238.

110. Ibid.

111. Ibid.

112. Ibid., 241.

113. Sprigle, "I Was a Negro in the South for 30 Days," August 11, 1948, 2.

114. Ibid.

115. Roosevelt, "My Day," 1.

116. Roosevelt, "If I Were a Negro," 8.

117. Holloway, *Jim Crow Wisdom*, 57.

118. Ibid., 58.

119. Neal, *New Black Man*, 1.

120. Sprigle, "I Was a Negro in the South for 30 Days," September 1, 1948, 1.

121. Berlant, "Poor Eliza," 299–300.

122. Stowe, *Uncle Tom's Cabin*, 12.

123. Baldwin, "Everybody's Protest Novel," 16.

124. Ibid., 14.

125. Ibid.

126. Ibid., 16.

127. Ibid. Baldwin does not just generically describe the protest novel but also lays the theoretical groundwork for my genealogy. He cites Hobson's postwar tolerance text, *The Gentleman's Agreement*, to further his point.

128. Ibid., 14.

129. Ibid.

130. Berlant, "Poor Eliza," 297.

131. Ibid. Emphasis in original.

132. Myrdal, *An American Dilemma*, lxxix.

133. Singh, *Black Is a Country*, 147–148. Emphasis in original.

134. See Singh, *Black Is a Country*; and Jackson, *Gunnar Myrdal and America's Conscience*.

135. Sprigle, *In the Land of Jim Crow*, vii–viii.

136. Baldwin, "Everybody's Protest Novel," 18.

137. Myrdal, *An American Dilemma*, 2:1024.

138. Ibid., 1021–1022. Emphasis in original.

139. Berlant, "Poor Eliza," 297.

140. Sprigle, "I Was a Negro in the South for 30 Days," August 25, 1948, 1.

141. Ibid.

142. Ibid.

143. Ibid., 2.

144. Ibid., 1.

145. Sprigle, "I Was a Negro in the South for 30 Days," August 31, 1948, 1.

146. Ibid., 1.

147. Ibid.

148. Ibid.

149. Sprigle, "I Was a Negro in the South for 30 Days," September 1, 1948, 2.

150. "No Help to Our Cause," 1.

151. Sprigle, "I Was a Negro in the South for 30 Days," August 31, 1948, 1.

152. Ibid., September 1, 1948, 1.

153. Ibid.

154. Ibid.

155. hooks, "Eating the Other," 367.

Chapter Two

1. Griffin, *Black Like Me*, 5.

2. Griffin, *Journal*, 982.

3. Ibid., 988.

4. Quoted in Bonazzi, *Man in the Mirror*, 4.

5. Ibid., 6.

6. Ibid.

7. Griffin, *A Time to Be Human*, 1.

8. Ibid.

9. McLaurin, *Separate Pasts*, 30–31.

10. Griffin, *A Time to Be Human*, 7.

11. Bonazzi, *Man in the Mirror*, 10.

12. Ibid., 17.

13. Quoted in Bonazzi, *Man in the Mirror*, 22.

14. Ibid., 17.

15. Griffin, *Scattered Shadows*, 217.

16. Griffin, *A Time to Be Human*, 20.

17. Ibid.

18. Ibid.

19. Ibid.

20. Ibid.

21. Ibid., 21. Emphasis in original.

22. Ibid.

23. Griffin, *Journal*, 982. Emphasis in original.

24. Ibid., 983.

25. Griffin, *A Time to Be Human*, 22.

26. Griffin, "Journey into Shame," April, 12.

27. Griffin, *Black Like Me*, 7.

28. Pittenger, *Class Unknown*, 159.

29. Ibid., 159–160.

30. "Soul on Ink," 118.

31. Ibid., 114.

32. Ibid., 116.

33. Griffin, *Journal*, 982–983.

34. Griffin, *Black Like Me*, 10.

35. Sprigle, "I Was a Negro in the South for 30 Days," August 11, 1948, 2.

36. Griffin, *Journal*, 984–985. Emphasis in original.

37. Griffin, "White Man," 18.

38. Griffin, "Journey into Shame," April, 12.

39. Ibid., 14.

40. Ibid.

41. Griffin, *Black Like Me*, 15.

42. Ibid.

43. Ibid., 12.

44. Ibid., 15.

45. Ibid., 14.

46. Griffin, "Journey into Shame," April, 4.

47. Griffin, *Black Like Me*, 139.

48. Ibid., 140.

49. Griffin, "Journey into Shame," April, 12.

50. Ibid.

51. Griffin, *Black Like Me*, 72.

52. Ibid.

53. Griffin, "Journey into Shame," April, 17.

54. E. V. G., "Letter to the Editor," 6.

55. Smith, "Letter to the Editor," 6.

56. Trapp, "Letter to the Editor," 6.

57. Griffin, *Scattered Shadows*, 10.

58. Griffin, *The Church and the Black Man*, 1.

59. Ibid. Emphasis in original.

60. Ibid.

61. Ibid., 37.

62. Ibid., 39.

63. Griffin, *Black Like Me*, 156–157.

64. Griffin "White Man Who Turned Black Is Praised and Damned," October, 18.

65. *Black Like Me*, directed by Carl Lerner, DVD. Emphasis in original.

66. "$273,000 Budget," 3.

67. Stewart, "James Whitmore Brings Humor," 1.

68. Peper, "*Black Like Me* Hits Hard," n.p.

69. Scott, "'Black' Was Shot Undercover," A–27.

70. Ibid.

71. Ibid.

72. Ibid.

73. Ibid.

74. Heffernan, *Ghouls, Gimmicks, and Gold*, 206.

75. Griffin, *Black Like Me*, 46.

76. Crowther, "James Whitmore Stars," 42.

77. Ibid.

78. Griffin, *Black Like Me*, 47.

79. Peper, "*Black Like Me* Hits Hard," n.p.

80. *Black Like Me*, directed by Carl Lerner, DVD.

81. Ibid.

82. Ibid.

83. Ibid.

84. Baldwin, "Black Like Who?," 128.

85. *Black Like Me*, directed by Carl Lerner, DVD.

86. Peper, "*Black Like Me* Hits Hard," n.p.

87. For more on Sprigle and "good niggerhood," see chapter 1.

88. Wald, *Crossing the Line*, 156.

89. Griffin, *Black Like Me*, 85.

90. This language is indebted to Eve Sedgwick's groundbreaking *Between Men: English Literature and Homosocial Desire*.

91. Stewart, "James Whitmore Brings Humor," 1.

92. Bonazzi, *Reluctant Activist*, 1.

Chapter Three

1. Halsell, "I Lived Six Months as a Black Woman," 130.

2. Halsell, *Soul Sister*, 13.

3. Ibid., 11.

4. Halsell, *In Their Shoes*, 32.

5. Halsell, *Soul Sister*, 11.

6. Ibid., 9.

7. Ibid., 9.

8. Ibid.

9. Nemiroff, *To Be Young, Gifted and Black*, 256–257. Emphasis in original.

10. Horton, *Race and the Making of American Liberalism*, 185.

11. Halsell, *Soul Sister*, 15.

12. Griffin, Letter to Grace Halsell, March 22, 1968.

13. Halsell, Letter to John Howard Griffin, March 29, 1968.

14. Griffin, Letter to Robert Gutwillig, May 23, 1968.

15. Halsell, Letter to John Howard Griffin, March 20, 1978.

16. Halsell, Letter to John Howard Griffin, April 19, 1968.

17. Griffin, Letter to Grace Halsell, April 20, 1968.

18. Jackson, *Real Black*, 17.

19. Ibid. Emphasis in original.

20. Wald, *Crossing the Line*, 158.

21. Ibid., 156.

22. For more on Griffin's queer encounters, see chapter 2.

23. Halsell, *Soul Sister*, 11–12.

24. Griffin, Letter to Robert Gutwillig, May 23, 1968.

25. Griffin's racial myopia works on multiple registers. Griffin began to lose his sight after an injury sustained in World War II. He regained it in 1957.

26. Griffin, Letter to Grace Halsell, April 20, 1968.

27. Griffin, *Black Like Me*, 68.

28. Halsell, *Soul Sister*, 50. Emphasis in original.

29. Ibid., 51.

30. Ibid., 50.

31. Richardson, *Black Masculinity and the U.S. South*, 3–4.

32. Ibid., 36.

33. Its most iconic sufferer, Michael Jackson, made vitiligo famous. In fact, in an unpublished piece entitled "I Turned Myself 'Black'—and Michael Jackson Turns 'White,'" Halsell situates Jackson's attempts to offset the visual disruption vitiligo had wrought on his once deeply brown skin against her own racial impersonation. In it, Halsell conflates Jackson's turn to medical depigmentation to deal with his disability with her own temporary blackness.

34. Halsell, Letter to Robert Stolar, September 2, 1968.

35. Halsell, Letter to Aaron Lerner, November 13, 1968. Emphasis in original.

36. Halsell, *Soul Sister*, 46. Emphasis in original.

37. Ibid., 49.

38. Ibid.

39. Ibid., 13.

40. Ibid., 51.

41. Ibid., 50–51. Emphasis in original.

42. Ibid., 50.

43. Ibid., 60–61.

44. Ibid., 50.

45. Ibid. Emphasis in original.

46. Ibid., 51.

47. Ibid., 52.

48. Ibid., 53.

49. Ibid., 54.

50. Ibid. Emphasis in original.

51. Ibid., 57.

52. Ibid., 58–60. Emphasis in original.

53. Moynihan, "The Negro Family."

54. Ibid.

55. Halsell, *Soul Sister*, 60.

56. Ibid. Emphasis in original.

57. Ibid.

58. Ibid., 61–62.

59. Ibid., 66. Emphasis in original.

60. Ibid., 46. Emphasis in original.

61. Ibid., 70.

62. Ibid., 144.

63. Ibid., 53.

64. Ibid., 51. Emphasis in original.

65. Ibid., 63.

66. Ibid., 63–64. Emphasis in original.

67. Ibid., 74.

68. Ibid., 78. Emphasis in original.

69. Ibid.

70. Ibid.

71. I purposefully use "stud" here instead of "butch" or "lesbian butch" to call attention to its colloquial use in the African American lesbian community as an alternative that names the unique specificity of black lesbian masculinity while also highlighting its historical connection to black male masculinity, which further complicates this moment.

72. Halsell, *Soul Sister*, 79.

73. Ibid., 79–80. Emphasis in original.

74. Ibid., 80.

75. Halsell, *In Their Shoes*, 11.

76. Ibid., 114.

77. Taylor, "Black Feminist Theory and Praxis," 242.

78. Ibid.

79. Giddings, *When and Where I Enter*, 340.

80. Halsell, *In Their Shoes*, 124.

81. Favor, *Authentic Blackness*, 10.

82. Halsell, *Soul Sister*, 114.

83. Browder, *Slippery Characters*, 220.

84. Halsell, *Soul Sister*, 116.

85. Ibid., 119.

86. Ibid., 123.

87. Ibid.

88. Ibid., 127.

89. Griffin, Letter to Grace Halsell, November 6, 1968.

90. Halsell, *Soul Sister*, 127.

91. Ibid.

92. Ibid.

93. Cobb, *The Most Southern Place on Earth*, 2.

94. Raiford, "Come Let Us Build a World Together," 1151.

95. For more, see Baker and Nelson's article "Violence, The Body, and 'The South.'"

96. The incredible history of black resistance in Mississippi is recovered and chronicled in Umoja, *We Will Shoot Back*.

97. Evers, "Why I Live in Mississippi," 66.

98. Ibid.

99. Ibid.

100. Halsell, *Soul Sister*, 127.

101. Ibid., 131.

102. Ibid.

103. Ibid., 132.

104. Ibid.

105. Ibid., 132–133. Emphasis in original.

106. Ibid., 133.

107. Ibid.

108. Ibid., 136.

109. Ibid., 141.

110. Ibid., 142.

111. Ibid., 143.

112. Ibid., 144.

113. Ibid., 150.

114. Ibid., 153. Emphasis in original.

115. Ibid., 157.

116. Ibid., 155. Emphasis in original.

117. Ibid., 166.

118. For more on Ray Sprigle and "good niggerhood," see chapter 1.

119. Ibid., 183.

120. Ibid., 184.

121. Ibid., 192.

122. Ibid., 194.

123. Ibid., 195–196.

124. Ibid., 196.

125. Ibid., 196–197. Emphasis in original.

126. Ibid., 198.

127. Jenkins, *Private Lives, Proper Relations*, 19–20. Emphasis in original.

128. Richardson, *Black Masculinity and the U.S. South*, 59.

129. Halsell, *Soul Sister*, 202.

130. Davis, *Women, Race and Class*, 182.

131. Halsell, *Soul Sister*, 201.

132. Ibid., 199.

133. Ibid., 202. Emphasis in original.

134. Ibid., 199.

135. McGuire, *At the Dark End of the Street*, 27. Emphasis in original.

136. Halsell, *Soul Sister*, 203.

137. For more, see Pierce-Baker, *Surviving the Silence*.

138. Jacobs, *Incidents in the Life of a Slave Girl*, 49.

139. Ibid., 26.

140. Ibid., 79.

141. Halsell, *Soul Sister*, 12.

142. Smith, "A Press of Our Own," 153.

143. Halsell, *Soul Sister*, back cover.

144. Lewis, "Letter to the Editor," 10. Emphasis in original.

145. Morrison, "Letter to the Editor," 10.

146. Brown, "Letter to the Editor," 18 and 20.

147. "To Suffer as a Black," 22.

148. Halsell, *Soul Sister*, 207.

149. Ibid., 206.

150. Ibid., 208–209.

151. Ibid., 202.

152. Ibid., 202–203. Emphasis in original.

153. Halsell, Letter to Gunnar Myrdal, August 7, 1971.

154. Myrdal, Letter to Grace Halsell, October 26, 1971.

155. Ibid.

156. Myrdal, *An American Dilemma*, lxxx. Emphasis in original.

157. Ibid., 57.

158. Halsell, *Soul Sister*, 205.

Chapter Four

1. For more on Griffin's film *Black Like Me*, see chapter 2.

2. Solomon, "Skin Deep," C1.

3. Ibid.

4. Ibid.

5. Ibid.

6. Ibid.

7. Ibid.

8. Ibid.

9. Ibid.

10. Ibid.

11. Ibid.

12. Ibid.

13. Ibid.

14. Egalitarianjay02, "Race on the Oprah Show," online video clip.

15. Ibid.

16. Quoted in Trautman, *The Underdog in American Politics*, 176.

17. Strachan, "The Definitive History," online video clip.

18. Murray and Ouellette, *Reality TV*, 3.

19. Orbe, "Representations of Race in Reality TV," 345.

20. Edwards, *The Triumph of Reality TV*, 87.

21. Cutler, "Audio commentary, episode 6," *Black.White.*, DVD.

22. Ibid.

23. "Episode 1," *Black.White.*, DVD.

24. Ibid.

25. Ibid.

26. Cutler, "Audio commentary, episode 4," *Black.White.*, DVD.

27. Interestingly, after succumbing to months in the makeup chair and realizing the importance of the visuality of race, Brian, the crew's other test subject, started a postproduction nonprofit organization for African Americans suffering from vitiligo.

28. Carmen Wurgel, "Audio commentary, episode 2," *Black.White.*, DVD.

29. Ibid.

30. Ibid.

31. Sipe and VanderLaan, "Audio commentary, episode 4," *Black.White.*, DVD.

32. Renee Sparks, "Audio commentary, episode 2," *Black.White.*, DVD.

33. Ibid.

34. Bruno Wurgel, "Audio commentary, episode 1," *Black.White.*, DVD.

35. Griffin, *Black Like Me*, 15.

36. Bruno Wurgel, "Audio commentary, episode 1," *Black.White.* DVD.

37. For more on Cosby's conservatism, see Dyson, *Is Cosby Right?*

38. "Episode 1," *Black.White.*, DVD.

39. Ibid.

40. McAllister, *Whiting Up*, 1.

41. Ibid., 11.

42. Ibid., 264.

43. *Saturday Night Live*, "White Like Me," online video clip.

44. Murphy's dystopian imagining of rampant white and class privilege does not include the realities of either gender or sexuality.

45. McAllister, *Whiting Up*, 201.

46. Haggins, *Laughing Mad*, 75.

47. Ibid.

48. Ibid., 77.

49. "Episode 1," *Black.White.*, DVD.

50. McAllister, *Whiting Up*, 263.

51. "Episode 1," *Black.White.*, DVD.

52. Ibid.

53. Ibid.

54. Carbado and Gulati, *Acting White*, 1.

55. For more on the salvific wish and racial uplift, see Jenkins, *Private Lives, Proper Relations*; and Gaines, *Uplifting the Race*.

56. McAllister, *Whiting Up*, 239.

57. "Episode 1," *Black.White.*, DVD.

58. "Episode 3," *Black.White.*, DVD.

59. Ibid.

60. Ibid.

61. Ibid.

62. For more on *Barbershop* and its controversies, see Edwards, *Charisma and the Fictions of Black Leadership.*

63. Ice Cube, "Race Card," *Black.White.*, DVD.

64. "Episode 4," *Black.White.*, DVD.

65. That the film *Friday* outs Nick's blackness subtly reveals how much product placement and scripting are in this supposedly unscripted "racial experiment." *Friday* (1995) is the first film in a trilogy that also includes *Friday after Next* and *Next Friday.* All three films star the co-producer of *Black.White.*, Ice Cube.

66. "Episode 4," *Black.White.*, DVD.

67. Ibid.

68. "Episode 6," *Black.White.*, DVD.

69. "Episode 3," *Black.White.*, DVD.

70. "Episode 4," *Black.White.*, DVD.

71. "Episode 1," *Black.White.*, DVD.

72. Ibid.

73. Ibid.

74. Ibid.

75. Ibid.

76. Ibid.

77. Ibid.

78. Ibid.

79. Ibid.

80. Ibid.

81. Ibid.

82. Ibid.

83. Ibid. His emphasis.

84. Ibid.

85. Ibid.

86. Jackson, *Racial Paranoia*, 3.

87. Ibid.

88. Sue, *Microaggressions in Everyday Life*, 5.

89. "Episode 3," *Black.White.*, DVD.

90. Ibid.

91. Ibid. Her emphasis.

92. Ibid.

93. Ibid.

94. Ibid. Her emphasis.

95. Ibid.

96. "Episode 2," *Black.White.*, DVD.

97. Patterson, "Color Commentary."

98. "Episode 4," *Black.White.*, DVD.

99. Ibid.

100. "Episode 4," *Black.White.*, DVD.

101. Ibid.

102. Ibid. Her emphasis.

103. Ibid.

104. Ibid.

105. Ibid. Her emphasis.

106. Ibid. Her emphasis.

107. Ibid. Her emphasis.

108. "Episode 5," *Black.White.*, DVD.

109. Holland, *The Erotic Life of Racism*, 19. Emphasis in original.

110. Ibid., 95. Emphasis in original.

111. "Episode 6," *Black.White.*, DVD.

112. Ibid.

Epilogue

1. KXLY, "KXLY Exclusive," online video clip.

2. Samuels, "Rachel Dolezal's True Lies."

3. KXLY, "Raw Interview with Rachel Dolezal," online video clip.

4. Pelisek, "The Man Rachel Dolezal Claims Is Her Father Defends Her."

5. Humphrey, "How the *Coeur d'Alene Press* Broke the Dolezal Story," online video clip.

6. Dolan, "Dolezal Resigns from HREI."

7. Sunderland, "In Rachel's Dolezal's Skin."

8. Ibid.

9. Dolan and Selle, "Black Like Me?"

10. *The Smoking Gun*, "NAACP Impostor Sued School over Race Claims."

11. Harris-Perry, "Exclusive Full Interview," online video clip; and Sunderland, "In Rachel Dolezal's Skin."

12. Dolezal, "Spokane NAACP."

13. Kim, "Rachel Dolezal Breaks Her Silence on *Today*," online video clip.

14. Ibid.

15. Barstow, "Tea Party Lights Fuse," A1.

16. Kim, "Rachel Dolezal Breaks Her Silence on *Today*," online video clip.

17. Ronson, *So You've Been Publicly Shamed*, 35.

18. Ibid., 78–79.

19. Miller, "Rihanna Praises Rachel Dolezal."

20. Comedy Central, "*The Nightly Show*—Rachel Dolezal Race Controversy," online video clip.

21. Demby, "Who Gets to Be Black?" Emphasis in original.

22. Walker, "#AskRachel."

23. Hunt, "Tracee Ellis Ross."

24. Harris-Perry, "Exclusive Full Interview," online video clip.

25. Moncy, "A Life to Be Heard."

26. Ibid.

27. Campbell, "Rachel Dolezal," online video clip.

28. Sunderland, "In Rachel Dolezal's Skin."

29. Harris-Perry, "Exclusive Full Interview," online video clip.

30. Comedy Central, "*The Nightly Show*—Rachel Dolezal Race Controversy," online video clip.

31. Mercer, "Black Hair/Style Politics," 101. Emphasis in original.

32. Kim, "Rachel Dolezal Breaks Her Silence on *Today*," online video clip.

33. Harris-Perry, "Exclusive Full Interview," online video clip.

34. Ibid.

35. Mercer, "Black Hair/Style Politics," 111.

36. Harris-Perry, "Exclusive Full Interview," online video clip.

37. Williams, "Rachel Dolezal Scandal," online video clip.

38. Brown, "Rachel Dolezal Nailed the Hair," http://jezebel.com/rachel-dolezal-definitely-nailed-the-hair-ill-give-her-1710899988.

39. Ibid.

40. Kim, "Rachel Dolezal Breaks Her Silence on *Today*," online video clip.

41. Harris-Perry, "Exclusive Full Interview," online video clip.

42. Sunderland, "In Rachel's Dolezal's Skin."

43. *The Real Daytime*, "Race vs. State of Mind," online video clip.

44. Piper, *Out of Order, Out of Sight*, 303.

45. Ibid.

46. NBC News, "Rachel Dolezal," online video clip.

47. Samuels, "Rachel Dolezal's True Lies."

48. Ibid.

49. *The Real Daytime*, "Race vs. State of Mind," online video clip.

50. Samuels, "Rachel Dolezal's True Lies."

51. See Tate, *Everything but the Burden*.

52. Piper, *Out of Order, Out of Sight*, 279.

53. Bissinger, "Caitlyn Jenner: The Full Story."

54. Awkward, *Negotiating Difference*, 181.

55. hooks, "Eating the Other," 367.

56. Jamison, *The Empathy Exams*, 5.

Bibliography

Manuscript and Archival Collections

New York, NY
   Columbia University
      Rare Book and Manuscript Library
      John Howard Griffin Papers
Fort Worth, TX
   Texas Christian University
      Mary Couts Burnett Library
      Grace Halsell Papers

Books, Articles, and Dissertations

Angelou, Maya. *I Know Why the Caged Bird Sings*. New York: Ballantine, 1969.

Awkward, Michael. *Negotiating Difference: Race: Gender, and the Politics of Positionality*. Chicago: University of Chicago Press, 1995.

Baker, Houston, and Dana Nelson, eds. "Violence, the Body, and 'The South.'" *American Literature* 73 (2001): 231–244.

Baldwin, James. *No Name in the Street*. New York: Dial, 1972.

———. *Notes of a Native Son*. Boston: Beacon, 1955.

Baldwin, Kate. "Black Like Who? Cross-Testing the 'Real' Lines of John Howard Griffin's *Black Like Me*." *Cultural Critique* 40 (Autumn 1998): 103–143.

Bambara, Toni Cade, ed. *The Black Woman: An Anthology*. New York: Washington Square, 1970.

Barstow, David. "Tea Party Lights Fuse for Rebellion on Right." *New York Times*, February 15, 2010, A1.

Berlant, Lauren, ed. *Compassion: The Culture and Politics of an Emotion*. New York: Routledge, 2004.

Berlant, Lauren. "Poor Eliza." In *No More Separate Spheres!*, edited by Cathy N. Davidson and Jessamyn Hatcher, 291–323. Durham, NC: Duke University Press, 2002.

Berry, Stephen A. *The Jim Crow Routine: Everyday Performances of Race, Civil Rights, and Segregation in Mississippi*. Chapel Hill: University of North Carolina Press, 2015.

Bissinger, Buzz. "Caitlyn Jenner: The Full Story." *Vanity Fair*, June 25, 2015. http://www.vanityfair.com/hollywood/2015/06/caitlyn-jenner-bruce-cover-annie-leibovitz.

Bonazzi, Robert. *An Excerpt from "Reluctant Activist: The Authorized Biography of John Howard Griffin."* Myakka, FL: Myakka Motion Pictures, 2012.

———. *Man in the Mirror: John Howard Griffin and the Story of "Black Like Me."* New York: Orbis, 1997.

Browder, Laura. *Slippery Characters: Ethnic Impersonators and American Identities.* Chapel Hill: University of North Carolina Press, 2000.

Brown, Alfred F. "Letter to the Editor." *Ebony*, March 1970, 20–21.

Brown, Kara. "Rachel Dolezal Nailed the Hair, I'll Give Her That." *Jezebel*, June 12, 2015. http://jezebel.com/rachel-dolezal-definitely-nailed-the-hair-ill-give-her-1710899988.

Brown, William Wells. *Clotel: Or, The President's Daughter.* New York: Penguin, 1853.

Broyard, Bliss. *One Drop: My Father's Hidden Life—A Story of Race and Family Secrets.* New York: Little, Brown, 2007.

Carbado, Devon W., and Mitu Gulati. *Acting White? Rethinking Race in "Post-Racial" America.* New York: Oxford University Press, 2013.

Chafe, William H. "Race in America: The Ultimate Test of Liberalism." In *The Achievement of American Liberalism: The New Deal and Its Legacies*, edited by William H. Chafe. New York: Columbia University Press, 2003.

Chesnutt, Charles. *The Conjure Stories.* New York: W. W. Norton, 2011.

Chopin, Kate. "Desiree's Baby." In *Kate Chopin: Complete Novels and Stories*, edited by Sandra Gilbert. New York: Library of America, 2002.

Cobb, James C. *The Most Southern Place on Earth: The Mississippi Delta and the Roots of Regional Identity.* New York: Oxford University Press, 1992.

Cockrell, Dale. *Demons of Disorder: Early Blackface Minstrels and Their World.* Cambridge: Cambridge University Press, 1997.

Cox, Karen L. *Dreaming of Dixie: How the South Was Created in American Popular Culture.* Chapel Hill: University of North Carolina Press, 2011.

Craft, William, and Ellen Craft. *Running a Thousand Miles to Freedom: The Escape of William and Ellen Craft from Slavery.* Athens: University of Georgia Press, 1860.

Crowther, Bosley. "James Whitmore Stars in Book's Adaptation." *New York Times*, May 21, 1964, 42.

Davis, Angela. *Women, Race and Class.* New York: Random House, 1981.

Davis, F. James. *Who Is Black? One Nation's Definition.* University Park: Pennsylvania State University Press, 1991.

Demby, Gene. "Who Gets to Be Black? Honor the Struggle, but Don't Forget the Jokes." *The Code Switch*, June 17, 2015. http://www.npr.org/sections/codeswitch/2015/06/17/414972407/if-you-dont-get-to-be-black-without-the-struggle-lets-not-forget-the-jokes.

Derricotte, Toi. *The Black Notebooks.* New York: W. W. Norton, 1997.

Dolan, Maureen. "Dolezal Resigns from HREI." *Coeur d'Alene Press*, July 27, 2010. http://www.cdapress.com/news/local_news/article_5d0836f1-07f5-5520-88e7-7ef50f42e22f.html.

Dolan, Maureen, and Jeff Selle. "Black Like Me? Civil Rights Activist's Ethnicity Questioned." *Coeur d'Alene Press*, June 11, 2015. http://m.cdapress.com/news/local_news/article_385adfeb-76f3-5050-98b4-d4bf021c423f.html?mode=jqm.

Dolezal, Rachel. "Spokane NAACP." Facebook. June 15, 2015. https://www.facebook.com/spokane.naacp/posts/1623781377868883.

Dubner, Stephen J., and Steven D. Levitt. *Freakonomics: A Rogue Economist Explores the Hidden Side of Everything*. New York: William Morrow Paperbacks, 2009.

———. "Hoodwinked?" *New York Times* magazine, January 8, 2006, 26.

Dunbar, Paul Laurence. *Selected Poems*. New York: Dover, 1997.

Dyson, Michael Eric. *Is Cosby Right? Or Has the Black Middle Class Lost Its Mind?* New York: Basic *Civitas* Books, 2005.

Edwards, Erica R. *Charisma and the Fictions of Black Leadership*. Minneapolis: University of Minnesota Press, 2012.

Edwards, Leigh. *The Triumph of Reality TV: The Revolution in American Television*. Santa Barbara, CA: Praeger, 2013.

Emmett, Dan. "I Wish I Was in Dixie's Land." New York: Firth, Pond & Co., 1859.

Evers, Medgar. "Why I Live in Mississippi." *Ebony*, November 1958, 66.

E.V.G. "Letter to the Editor." *Sepia*, October 1960, 6.

Fabre, Michael. *The Unfinished Quest of Richard Wright*. New York: William Morrow, 1973.

Favor, J. Martin. *Authentic Blackness: The Folk in the New Negro Renaissance*. Durham, NC: Duke University Press, 1999.

Gaines, Kevin. *Uplifting the Race: Black Leadership, Politics and Culture during the Twentieth Century*. Chapel Hill: University of North Carolina Press, 1996.

Garcia, Claire Oberon, Vershawn Ashanti Young, and Charise Pimentel, eds. *From "Uncle Tom's Cabin" to "The Help": Critical Perspectives on White-Authored Narratives of Black Life*. New York: Palgrave Macmillan, 2014.

George, Nelson. *Post-Soul Nation: The Explosive, Contradictory, Triumphant and Tragic 1980s as Experienced by African Americans (Previously Known as Blacks and before That Negroes)*. New York: Penguin, 2004.

Giddings, Paula. *When and Where I Enter: The Impact of Black Women on Race and Sex in America*. Toronto: Bantam, 1984.

Griffin, John Howard. *Available Light: Exile in Mexico*. San Antonio, TX: Wings, 2008.

———. *Black Like Me*. New York: Signet, 1961.

———. *The Church and the Black Man*. Dayton, OH: Pflaum Press, 1969.

———. "Journey into Shame." *Sepia*, April 1960, 12–18.

———. "Journey into Shame." *Sepia*, September 1960, 28–34.

———. *Prison of Culture: Beyond "Black Like Me."* San Antonio, TX: Wings, 2011.

———. *Scattered Shadows: A Memoir of Blindness and Vision*. New York: Orbis, 2004.

———. *A Time to Be Human*. New York: Macmillan, 1977.

———. "White Man Who Turned Negro Is Praised and Damned." *Sepia*, October 1960, 11–18.

Gubar, Susan. *Racechanges: White Skin, Black Face in American Culture*. New York: Oxford University Press, 1997.

Haggins, Bambi. *Laughing Mad: The Black Comic Persona in Post-Soul America*. New Brunswick, NJ: Rutgers University Press, 2007.

Halberstam, Judith. *The Queer Art of Failure*. Durham, NC: Duke University Press, 2011.

Halsell, Grace. *Bessie Yellowhair*. New York: William Morrow, 1973.

———. *Black/White Sex*. New York: William Morrow, 1972.

———. "I Lived Six Months as a Black Woman." *Ebony*, December 1969, 124–130.

———. *The Illegals*. New York: Stein and Day, 1978.

———. *In Their Shoes*. Fort Worth: Texas Christian University Press, 1996.

———. *Soul Sister*. Washington, DC: Crossroads International, 1999.

Halsell, H. H. *Cowboys and Cattleland*. Nashville, TN: Parthenon, 1938.

Harburg, Ernie, and Harold Meyerson. *Who Put the Rainbow in "The Wizard of Oz"?: Yip Harburg, Lyricist*. Ann Arbor: University of Michigan Press, 1993.

Harburg, E. Y., and Fred Saidy. *Finian's Rainbow: A Musical Satire*. New York: Random House, 1946.

Harper, Frances E. W. *Iola Leroy, Or Shadows Uplifted*. New York: Dover, 2010.

Harris, Trudier. *The Scary Mason-Dixon Line: African American Writers and the South*. Baton Rouge: Louisiana State University Press, 2009.

Hartman, Saidiya V. *Lose Your Mother: A Journey along the Atlantic Slave Route*. New York: Farrar, Straus and Giroux, 2007.

———. *Scenes of Subjection: Terror, Slavery, and Self-Making in Nineteenth-Century America*. New York: Oxford University Press, 1997.

Heffernan, Kevin. *Ghouls, Gimmicks, and Gold: Horror Films and the American Movie Business, 1953–1968*. Durham, NC: Duke University Press, 2004.

Henderson, Mae G., and E. Patrick Johnson, eds. *Black Queer Studies: A Critical Anthology*. Durham, NC: Duke University Press, 2005.

Hobbs, Allyson. *A Chosen Exile: A History of Racial Passing in American Life*. Cambridge, MA: Harvard University Press, 2014.

Hobson, Fred. *But Now I See: The White Southern Racial Conversion Narrative*. Baton Rouge: Louisiana State University Press, 1999.

Hobson, Laura Z. *The Gentleman's Agreement*. New York: Simon & Schuster, 1947.

Holland, Sharon Patricia. *The Erotic Life of Racism*. Durham, NC: Duke University Press, 2012.

Holloway, Jonathan Scott. *Jim Crow Wisdom: Memory and Identity in Black America since 1940*. Chapel Hill: University of North Carolina Press, 2013.

hooks, bell. *Black Looks: Race and Representation*. Boston: South End, 1992.

Horton, Carol A. *Race and the Making of American Liberalism*. Oxford: Oxford University Press, 2005.

Hudson, Angela Pulley. *Real Native Genius: How an Ex-Slave and a White Mormon Became Famous Indians*. Chapel Hill: University of North Carolina Press, 2015.

Hughes, Langston. "Who's Passing for Who?" In *The Collected Works of Langston Hughes: The Short Stories*, edited by Baxter R. Miller, 163–166. Columbia: University of Missouri Press.

Hunt, Stacey Wilson. "Tracee Ellis Ross: Rachel Dolezal 'Isn't Funny Anymore' after Charleston." *The Hollywood Reporter*, June 25, 2015. http://www.hollywoodreporter.com/news/tracee-ellis-ross-rachel-dolezal-805129.

Hurst, Fannie. *Imitation of Life*. Durham, NC: Duke University Press, 2004.

Isherwood, Charles. "A Pot of Sunny Gold in Those Green Hills." *New York Times*, October 30, 2009, C1.

Jackson, John L., Jr. *Racial Paranoia: The Unintended Consequences of Political Correctness*. New York: Basic Civitas Books, 2008.

————. *Real Black: Adventures in Racial Sincerity*. Chicago: University of Chicago Press, 2005.

Jackson, Walter A. *Gunnar Myrdal and America's Conscience: Social Engineering and Racial Liberalism, 1938–1987*. Chapel Hill: University of North Carolina Press, 1994.

Jacobs, Harriet. *Incidents in the Life of a Slave Girl*. New York: Harcourt Brace Jovanovich, 1973.

Jacobson, Matthew Frye. *Whiteness of a Different Color: European Immigrants and the Alchemy of Race*. Cambridge, MA: Harvard University Press, 1998.

Jamison, Leslie. *The Empathy Exams*. Minneapolis: Graywolf, 2014.

Jenkins, Candice M. *Private Lives, Proper Relations: Regulating Black Intimacy*. Minneapolis: University of Minnesota Press, 2007.

Johnson, E. Patrick. *Appropriating Blackness: Performance and the Politics of Authenticity*. Durham, NC: Duke University Press, 2003.

Johnson, James Weldon. *Autobiography of an Ex-Colored Man and Other Writings*. New York: Barnes and Noble Classics, 2007.

Kennedy, John F. "Radio and Television Report to the American People on Civil Rights," June 11, 1963. http://www.presidency.ucsb.edu/ws/?pid=9271.

Kennedy, Randall. "Racial Passing." *Ohio State Law Journal* 62 (2001), 1145–1193.

Kennedy, Stetson. *The Klan Unmasked*. Tuscaloosa: University of Alabama Press, 2011.

————. "Reporter Posing as Negro Branded as an 'Uncle Tom.'" *Atlanta Daily World*, August 17, 1948, 1.

————. *Southern Exposure*. Tuscaloosa: University of Alabama Press, 1991.

Kroeger, Brooke. *Passing: When People Can't Be Who They Are*. New York: Public Affairs, 2003.

Larsen, Nella. *Passing*. New York: Modern Library, 2000.

Lee, Harper. *Go Set a Watchman*. New York: Random House, 2015.

————. *To Kill a Mockingbird*. New York: Warner Books Inc., 1960.

Lewis, David. *W. E. B. Du Bois 1919–1963: The Fight for Equality and the American Century*. New York: Henry Holt, 2001.

Lewis, Eugene. "Letter to the Editor." *Ebony*, February 1970, 10.

Lewis, Sinclair. *Kingsblood Royal*. New York: Random House, 1947.

Lhamon, W. T., Jr. *Raising Cain: Blackface Performance from Jim Crow to Hip Hop*. Cambridge, MA: Harvard University Press, 1998.

Lipsitz, George. *The Possessive Investment in Whiteness: How White People Profit from Identity Politics*. Philadelphia: Temple University Press, 1998.

Lott, Eric. *Love and Theft: Blackface Minstrelsy and the American Working Class*. New York: Oxford University Press, 1995.

MacPherson, Tara. *Reconstructing Dixie: Race, Gender, and Nostalgia in the Imagined South*. Durham, NC: Duke University Press, 2003.

Mahar, William J. *Behind the Burnt Cork Mask: Early Blackface Minstrelsy and Antebellum American Popular Culture*. Urbana: University of Illinois Press, 1999.

Mailer, Norman. "The White Negro: Superficial Reflections on the White Negro." In *Advertisements for Myself*. Cambridge, MA: Harvard University Press, 1992, 337–358.

Martin, Charles D. *The White African American Body: A Cultural and Literary Exploration*. New Brunswick, NJ: Rutgers University Press, 2002.

McAllister, Marvin. *Whiting Up: Whiteface Minstrels and Stage Europeans in African American Performance*. Chapel Hill: University of North Carolina Press, 2011.

McGuire, Danielle L. *At the Dark End of the Street: Black Women, Rape, and Resistance—A New History of the Civil Rights Movement from Rosa Parks to the Rise of Black Power*. New York: Vintage, 2010.

McLaurin, Melton A. *Separate Pasts: Growing Up White in the Segregated South*. Athens: University of Georgia Press, 1988.

Mercer, Kobena. "Black Hair/Style Politics." In *Welcome to the Jungle: New Positions in Black Cultural Studies*. New York: Routledge, 1994, 97–128.

Miles, Tya. *Tales from the Haunted South: Dark Tourism and Memories of Slavery from the Civil War Era*. Chapel Hill: University of North Carolina Press, 2015.

Miller, Julie. "Rihanna Praises Rachel Dolezal: 'I Think She Was a Bit of a Hero.'" *Vanity Fair*, October 6, 2015. http://www.vanityfair.com/hollywood/2015/10/rihanna-rachel-dolezal.

Moncy, Shawntelle. "A Life to Be Heard." *Easterner Online*, February 15, 2015. http://easterneronline.com/35006/eagle-life/a-life-to-be-heard/.

Morrison, Jane Fort. "Letter to the Editor." *Ebony*, February 1970, 10.

Morrison, Toni. *The Bluest Eye*. New York: Plume, 1970.

———. *Playing in the Dark: Whiteness and the Literary Imagination*. New York: Vintage, 1992.

Moynihan, Daniel Patrick. "The Negro Family: The Case for National Action." Washington, DC: Office of Policy Planning and Research, United States Department of Labor, 1965. http://www.dol.gov/oasam/programs/history/webid-meynihan.htm.

Murray, Susan, and Laurie Ouellette, eds. *Reality TV: Remaking Television Culture*. New York: New York University Press, 2004.

Myrdal, Gunnar. *An American Dilemma: The Negro Problem and Modern Democracy*. 2 vols. New Brunswick, NJ: Transaction, 1995.

"NAACP Impostor Sued School over Race Claims." *The Smoking Gun*, June 15, 2015. http://www.thesmokinggun.com/documents/bizarre/rachel-dolezal-discrimination-lawsuit-786451.

Nashrulla, Tasneem. "Rachel Dolezal Posted a Tribute to the Charleston Church Shooting Victims." *BuzzFeed News*, June 22, 2015. http://www.buzzfeed.com/tasneemnashrulla/rachel-dolezal-posted-a-tribute-to-the-charleston-church-sho#.qw7W2E26Z9.

Neal, Mark Anthony. *New Black Man*. New York: Routledge, 2006.

Nemiroff, Robert. *To Be Young, Gifted and Black: Lorraine Hansberry in Her Own Words*. Englewood Cliffs, NJ: Prentice-Hall, 1969.

Nerad, Julie Cary, ed. *Passing Interest: Racial Passing in US Novels, Memoirs, Television, and Film 1990–2010*. Albany: State University of New York Press, 2014.

"No Help to Our Cause." *Atlanta Daily World*, August 31, 1948, 1.

Orbe, Mark P. "Representations of Race in Reality TV: Watch and Discuss." *Critical Studies in Media Communication* 25 (2008): 345–352.

Patterson, Troy. "Color Commentary: FX's Creepy New Race-Swap Show." *Slate*, March 8, 2006. http://www.slate.com/articles/arts/television/2006/03/color _commentary.html.

Pelisek, Christine. "The Man Rachel Dolezal Claims Is Her Father Defends Her." *People Magazine*, June 17, 2015. http://www.people.com/article/man-identified -by-dolezal-as-father-defends-her-albert-wilkerson.

Peper, William. "'Black Like Me' Hits Hard." *New York World-Telegram & Sun*, May 18, 1964, n.p.

Peterson, Russell. "I Was a Teenage Negro! Blackface as a Vehicle of White Liberalism in *Finian's Rainbow*." *American Studies* 47 (Fall–Winter 2006): 35–60.

Pierce-Baker, Charlotte. *Surviving the Silence: Black Women's Stories of Rape*. New York: W. W. Norton, 1998.

Piper, Adrian. *Out of Order, Out of Sight. Volume 2: Selected Writings in Art Criticism 1967–1992*. Cambridge, MA: MIT Press, 1996.

Pittenger, Mark. *Class Unknown: Undercover Investigations of American Work and Poverty from the Progressive Era to the Present*. New York: New York University Press, 2012.

"The Press: Meat Makes News." *Time*, April 30, 1945, 61.

Raiford, Leigh. "Come Let Us Build a World Together: SNCC and Photography of the Civil Rights Movement." *American Quarterly* 59 (December 2007): 1129–1157.

Richardson, Riché. *Black Masculinity and the U.S. South: From "Uncle Tom" to "Gangsta."* Athens: University of Georgia Press, 2007.

Roberts, Dorothy. *Killing the Black Body: Race, Reproduction, and the Meaning of Liberty*. New York: Pantheon, 1997.

Ronson, Jon. *So You've Been Publicly Shamed*. New York: Riverhead, 2015.

Roosevelt, Eleanor. "If I Were a Negro." *Negro Digest*, October 1943, 8–9.

———. "My Day." *The Eleanor Roosevelt Papers Project*, August 15, 1948.

Samuels, Allison. "Rachel Dolezal's True Lies." http://www.vanityfair.com/news /2015/07/rachel-dolezal-new-interview-pictures-exclusive.

Sandweiss, Martha A. *Passing Strange: A Gilded Age Tale of Love and Deception across the Color Line*. New York: Penguin, 2009.

Savage, Barbara Dianne. *Broadcasting Freedom: Radio, War, and the Politics of Race, 1938–1948*. Chapel Hill: University of North Carolina Press, 1999.

Schuyler, George. *Black No More: Being an Account of the Strange and Wonderful Workings of Science in the Land of the Free, A.D. 1933–1940*. Boston: Northeastern University Press, 1989.

Scott, Vernon. "'Black' Was Shot Undercover in Dixie." *Dallas Times Herald*, March 26, 1964, A–27.

Sedgwick, Eve. *Between Men: English Literature and Homosocial Desire*. New York: Columbia University Press, 1985.

Senna, Danzy. *Caucasia: A Novel*. New York: Riverhead, 1998.

Singh, Nikhil Pal. *Black Is a Country: Race and the Unfinished Struggle for Democracy*. Cambridge, MA: Harvard University Press, 2005.

Smith, Barbara. "A Press of Our Own: Kitchen Table: Women of Color Press." In *Ain't Gonna Let Nobody Turn Me Around: Forty Years of Movement Building with*

Barbara Smith, edited by Virginia Eubanks and Alethia Jones, 153–156. Albany: State University of New York Press, 2014.

Smith, Gilbert. "Letter to the Editor." *Sepia*, October 1960, 6.

Smith, Lillian. *Killers of the Dream*. New York: W. W. Norton & Co., 1994.

Solomon, Joshua. "Skin Deep; Reliving 'Black Like Me': My Own Journey into the Heart of Race-Conscious America." *Washington Post*, October 30, 1994, C1.

"Soul on Ink: Farewell to the Fort Worth Publishing House That Gave Us *Sepia, Jive,* and *Bronze Thrills.*" *Texas Monthly*, October 1983, 114–118.

Sprigle, Ray. *In the Land of Jim Crow*. New York: Simon and Schuster, 1949.

——. "I Was a Negro in the South for 30 Days." *Pittsburgh Post-Gazette*, August 9–September 1, 1948. (Articles ran on page 1 or 1 and 2 each day.)

Steigerwald, Bill. "Chasing Old Ghosts through the New South." *Pittsburgh Post-Gazette*, June 8, 2009. http://townhall.com/columnists/billsteigerwald/2009 /06/08/chasing_old_ghosts_through_the_new_south/page/full.

——. "Sprigle's Secret Journey." http://old.post-gazette.com/sprigle/Sprigle introduction.asp.

Stewart, Perry. "James Whitmore Brings Humor of Will Rogers to Will Rogers." *Fort Worth Star-Telegram*, n.d.

Stowe, Harriet Beecher. *Uncle Tom's Cabin*. New York: Barnes and Noble Classics, 2004.

Strachan, Maxwell. "The Definitive History of 'George Bush Doesn't Care About Black People.'" *Huffington Post*, August 28, 2015. http://www.huffingtonpost.com /entry/kanye-west-george-bush-black-people_us_55d67c12e4b020c386de2f5e.

Strausbaugh, John. *Black Like You: Blackface, Whiteface, Insult and Imitation in American Popular Culture*. New York: Jeremy P. Tarcher/Penguin, 2006.

Sue, Derald Wing. *Microaggressions in Everyday Life: Race, Gender, and Sexual Orientation*. Hoboken, NJ: John Wiley and Sons, 2010.

Sunderland, Mitchell. "In Rachel Dolezal's Skin." *Broadly*, December 7, 2015. https:// broadly.vice.com/en_us/article/rachel-dolezal-profile-interview.

Tate, Greg, ed. *Everything but the Burden: What White People Are Taking from Black Culture*. New York: Broadway Books, 2003.

Taylor, Ula. "The Historical Evolution of Black Feminist Theory and Praxis." *Journal of Black Studies* (November 1998): 234–253.

Thurston, Baratunde. *How to Be Black*. New York, HarperCollins, 2012.

Torres, Sasha, ed. *Living Color: Race and Television in the United States*. Durham, NC: Duke University Press, 1998.

"To Suffer as a Black." *Chicago Defender*, December 27, 1969, 22.

Trapp, William. "Letter to the Editor." *Sepia*, October 1960, 6.

Trautman, Karl G. *The Underdog in American Politics: The Democratic Party and Liberal Values*. New York: Palgrave MacMillan, 2010.

Twain, Mark. *Pudd'nhead Wilson and Those Extraordinary Twins*. New York: Barnes and Noble Classics, 2005.

"$273,000 Budget on Reade-Sterling Black Like Me." *Variety*, July 17, 1963, 3.

Umoja, Akinyele Omowale. *We Will Shoot Back: Armed Resistance in the Mississippi Freedom Movement*. New York: New York University Press, 2013.

Wald, Gayle. *Crossing the Line: Racial Passing in Twentieth-Century U.S. Literature and Culture*. Durham, NC: Duke University Press, 2000.

Walker, Alice. *The Third Life of Grange Copeland*. New York: Harcourt, 1970.

Walker, Torraine. "#AskRachel: How a Twitter Hashtag Became Black America's Family Reunion." *The Huffington Post*, June 15, 2015. http://www.huffingtonpost.com/torraine-walker/askrachel-twitter-hashtag_b_7585620.html.

Wallace, Maurice O. *Constructing the Black Masculine: Identity and Ideality in African American Men's Literature and Culture, 1775–1995*. Durham, NC: Duke University Press, 2002.

Washington, Booker T. *Up from Slavery*. Oxford: Oxford University Press, 1995.

Weigman, Robyn. *American Anatomies: Theorizing Race and Gender*. Durham, NC: Duke University Press, 1995.

White, Walter F. "I Investigate Lynchings." *American Mercury* 61 (January 1, 1929).

Wright, Richard. *Black Boy (American Hunger): A Record of Childhood and Youth*. New York: HarperCollins, 1945.

Film and Television

Black Like Me. Directed by Carl Lerner. Performers Al Freeman Jr., James Whitmore, and Richard Ward. 1964. Video Service Corp., 2012. DVD.

Black.White. Directed by R. J. Cutler. Performers Rose Bloomfield, Bruno Marcotulli, and Brian Sparks. 2006. Beverly Hills, CA: Twentieth Century Fox Home Entertainment, 2006. DVD.

Finian's Rainbow. Directed by Francis Ford Coppola. Performers Fred Astaire, Petula Clark, and Keenan Wynn. 1968. Burbank, CA: Warner Home Video, 2005. DVD.

48 Hours. Directed by Walter Hill. Performers Eddie Murphy, Nick Nolte, and Annette O'Toole. 1982.

Gentleman's Agreement. Directed by Elia Kazan. Performers Gregory Peck, Dorothy McGuire, and John Garfield. 1947. Los Angeles, CA: Twentieth Century Fox, 2013. DVD.

Heart Condition. Directed by James D. Parriott. Performers Bob Hoskins, Denzel Washington, and Chloe Webb. 1990. www.youtube.com/watch?v=e_4owIxvg2You.

Soul Man. Directed by Steve Miner. Performers Rae Dawn Chong, C. Thomas Howell, and Ayre Gross. 1986. Troy, MI: Anchor Bay Entertainment, 2002. DVD.

Watermelon Man. Directed by Melvin Van Peebles. Performers Godfrey Cambridge, Estelle Parsons, and Howard Cain. 1970. Culver City, CA: Sony Home Entertainment, 2004. DVD.

White Man's Burden. Directed by Desmond Nakano. Performers Harry Belafonte, John Travolta, and Kelly Lynch. 1995. August 11, 2014. www.youtube.com/watch?v=41vG52OfykI.

Online Videos

Campbell, Lauren. "Rachel Dolezal (2014) Talking about Her Experience as a 'Black Woman.'" Online video clip. YouTube. June 12, 2015. https://www.youtube.com/watch?v=6zd-8jF9PzA/.

Comedy Central. "*The Nightly Show*—Rachel Dolezal Race Controversy—Convert or Incognegro." Online video clip. YouTube. June 16, 2015. https://www.youtube.com/watch?v=ymc8ue8O_uA.

Egalitarianjay02. "Race on the Oprah Show: A Twenty-Five Year Look Back." Online video clip. YouTube. July 25, 2012. https://www.youtube.com/watch?v=C1IRnf3_YmY.

Harris-Perry, Melissa. "Exclusive Full Interview: Rachel Dolezal Breaks Her Silence." Online video clip. MSNBC. June 17, 2015. http://www.msnbc.com/melissa-harris-perry/watch/rachel-dolezal-breaks-her-silence-465691715976.

Humphrey, Jeff. "How the *Coeur d'Alene Press* Broke the Dolezal Story." Online video clip. KXLY. June 15, 2015. http://www.kxly.com/news/north-idaho-news/how-the-coeur-dalene-press-broke-the-dolezal-story/33598298.

Kim, Eun Kyung. "Rachel Dolezal Breaks Her Silence on *Today*: 'I Identify as Black.'" Online video clip. *Today*, June 16, 2015. http://www.today.com/news/rachel-dolezal-speaks-today-show-matt-lauer-after-naacp-resignation-t26371.

KXLY. "KXLY Exclusive: Rachel Dolezal Responds to Race Allegations." Online video clip. YouTube. June 11, 2015. https://www.youtube.com/watch?v=_7Gb9kK8HGk.

———. "Raw Interview with Rachel Dolezal." Online video clip. YouTube. June 11, 2015. https://www.youtube.com/watch?v=oKRj_h7vmMM.

NBC News. "Rachel Dolezal: 'I Definitely Am Not White.'" Online video clip. YouTube. June 17, 2015. https://www.youtube.com/watch?v=3B24Bbsf3U4.

The Nightly Show. Online video clip. Facebook. June 15, 2015. https://www.facebook.com/thenightlyshow/videos/396102680594373/.

The Real Daytime. "Race vs. State of Mind: Rachel Dolezal's Thoughts on Whiteness." Online video clip. YouTube. November 2, 2015. https://www.youtube.com/watch?v=54QrcxCK01o.

Saturday Night Live. "White Like Me." Online video clip. NBC.com. Original airdate December 15, 1984. http://www.nbc.com/saturday-night-live/video/white-like-me/n9308.

Williams, Wendy. "Rachel Dolezal Scandal." Online video clip. YouTube. June 15, 2015. https://www.youtube.com/watch?v=mQZ9PvbmMfs.

Index

Note: Page numbers in italics indicate illustrations.

Halsell's first impressions of, 92–93; Halsell's urban wasteland construct of, 92–93; medical care in, 96–97; slumming fantasy of, 91–92

Harper, Frances, 18, 115

Harris, Trudier, 24

Harris-Perry, Melissa, 162, 166, 167

Hartman, Saidiya, 24

Heart Condition (1990 film), 123

Heffernan, Kevin, 71

Hep (magazine), 59

Hill, Marjorie, 45

Hill, P. W., 45–46

Hip-hop: *Black.White.* and, 145–47, 155; new-millennium revolution of, 126; stereotyping of, 137, 145

Hobbs, Allyson, 17–19

Hobson, Laura Z., 11, 173n36, 177n127

Holland, Sharon Patricia, 156

Holloway, Jonathan Scott, 29, 38–39

Hollywood Reporter, 164

Homoeroticism: in *Black Like Me,* 81. *See also* Queerness

Homophobia, Halsell's, 100–103

hooks, bell, 8, 50, 171

Horton, Carol A., 85

Hoskins, Bob, 123

Howard University, Dolezal and, 161, 162, 165

Howell, C. Thomas, 122–23

Hubris, of white ally, 35–39

Huff, Will, 133

Hughes, Langston, 18

Humphrey, Jeff, 158–59

Hurricane Katrina, 127–28, 150

Ice Cube, 145

"If I Were a Negro" (*Negro Digest*), 38–39

I Know Why the Caged Bird Sings (Angelou), 115

The Illegals (Halsell), 120

Incidents in the Life of a Slave Girl (Jacobs), 114–15

Interim period, of racial impersonation (1969–2006), 121–26

Interracial marriage/sex, 75–76, 118–20

In Their Shoes (Halsell), 103

In the land of Jim Crow (Sprigle), 14, 26–27, 29, 31, 36, 39, 81

Intimacy, failures in *Black.White.,* 155–58

Iola Leroy (Harper), 18

"I Was a Negro in the South for 30 Days" (Sprigle), 12, 14–50; black testimony *vs.* Sprigle's perceptions in, 45–46; book-length memoir from, 14; criticism of, 31, 48; Dixie terror in, 22–25; Dobbs' tutorial for, 28–30; empathy attempt in, 42–44; fiftieth-anniversary reprint of, 26; first column, 14; geography of blackness in, 19–26; good niggerhood in, 26–35, 81; lynching account in, 30, 34–35, 42; North's forgiving depiction in, 14, 25–26; "passing in reverse" in, 17; pattern/affect of blackness in, 21; pitch for story, 14; segregated rail travel in, 16–17, 20–21; sentimentality in, 39–45; sharecroppers' stories in, 32–34; South as alien land in, 20, 21–22; South as nostalgic, pastoral fantasy in, 19–20; South as "pastoral in blood" in, 22; Sprigle's appropriation of Eliza in, 39–41; Sprigle's fear and anxiety during, 29–30; Sprigle's hubris over, 35–39, 42, 47–49; Sprigle's motivation for, 18–19, 45; Sprigle's pacifying recommendations in, 46–48; Sprigle's physical alteration for, 15–17; Sprigle's racial faux pas in, 29–30; Sprigle's return to whiteness, 49–50, 61; Sprigle's traveling companion in (Dobbs), 26–30, 39; Sprigle's writing style in, 30–31; stereotypes in, 23

"I Was a Teenage Negro!: Blackface as a Vehicle of White Liberalism in *Finian's Rainbow*" (Peterson), 3

"I Wish I Was in Dixie's Land" (anthem), 22

Wright, Richard, 6, 10, 24–25, 41

Wurgel, Bruno: blackness tutorial for, 142; confrontation with new blackness, 136–37, 138; family relationships of, 130; good nigger-hood of, 149; racial myopia of, 146–50, 152

Wurgel, Carmen: blackness tutorial for, 142; changes experienced by, 151–57; family relationships of, 130; hypervisibility as black woman, 152; reaction to family's new blackness, 138; transformation and beauty ideals of, *135*, 135–36

Wurgel, Rose. *See* Bloomfield, Rose

Wurgel family, 121–57. *See also Black. White.; individual family members*

Wynn, Keenan, 3, 5

"Young, gifted and black," 83–84

Zetar, 90